The pure points™ cookbook

SUE ASHWORTH

SIMON & SCHUSTER
A VIACOM COMPANY

For enquiries regarding joining Weight Watchers please call 08457 123000
For enquiries regarding this book please call 01223 448770

First published in Great Britain by Simon & Schuster UK Ltd, 2000
A Viacom Company.

Copyright © 2001, Weight Watchers International, Inc.

First published 2000
Reprinted 2003

Simon & Schuster UK Ltd
Africa House
64–78 Kingsway
London
WC2B 6AH

The author would like to thank Sian Davis for her help with recipe development.

Photography: Steve Lee
Styling: Marian Price
Food preparation: Wendy Lee

Design: Jane Humphrey
Typesetting: Stylize Digital Artwork

A CIP catalogue for this book is available from the British Library

ISBN 0 74324 843 0

Pictured on the front cover, left to right: *Speedy Tomato Soup;*
Easy Chicken Tikka; Pineapple Meringue with Strawberry Sauce;
Spaghetti Bolognese; Baked Lemon Sponge with Lemon Sauce
Pictured on the back cover, left to right: *Pasta and Sweet Pepper Salad;*
Saturday Sundaes; Vegetable Noodles with Ginger and Soy;
Banana Squares; Provençal Fish Stew

Recipe notes:
Egg size is medium, unless otherwise stated.
Fruit and vegetables are medium-sized, unless otherwise stated.

Printed and bound in Singapore

contents

Welcome to the new Weight Watchers Programme Cookbook. If you're trying to lose weight or just maintain your new-found figure, this is the cookbook for you.

The Weight Watchers organisation has an amazing record for helping people lose weight by offering support where it's needed. Group Meetings held by Weight Watchers Leaders offer encouragement to slimmers, giving its Members a positive approach towards the benefits of achieving and maintaining a slimmer shape. It's no wonder Weight Watchers has a world-wide reputation for success.

A new philosophy of food

Based on the sound principles of steady weight loss, the Weight Watchers Programme doesn't offer crash, cranky diets. No way! The Weight Watchers philosophy is based on common sense and good nutrition in order to give your body all it needs to get slim, fit and healthy. Weight Watchers doesn't believe in banning foods either – often that's the quickest way to failure – for no-one likes to be deprived of their favourite foods. Instead, Weight Watchers is based on a Programme in which you add up Points to reach your daily total. By following Weight Watchers Pure Points, you are on your way to finding the new you.

Often when you embark on a weight loss programme, you take a renewed interest in food, looking more closely at labels, scanning ingredients and reading recipes. That's where this new Programme cookbook comes in handy. Because it's written with you in mind, all the recipes have the Points worked out per portion, so that you can fit them into your daily plan. All the recipes are tasty and good for you, full of fresh, healthy flavours so they are also suitable for the whole family, and not just for those who are dieting.

There's an enormous variety of recipes to choose from among these pages. You may be looking for the low Point equivalent of your favourite family meal and you should find it! We have given you recipes for Bangers and Mash (page 117), Fish 'n' Chips (page 62), Chilli con Carne (page 105), Lasagne (page 102) and Macaroni Cheese (page 143), not to mention trifle (page 184), Easy Cheesy Scones (page 191), Bread and Butter Pudding with Raspberries (page 166) and Chocolate Sponge Cake (page 195). On the other hand, you may be after something totally different and so why not try Chilli Bean Cakes with Pineapple Chutney (page 132), Roasted Vegetable Salad with Feta and Toasted Almonds (page 46) or Moroccan Spiced Chicken (page 89).

Good ingredients mean good flavour

Whether you're quite new to cooking or you're a real expert, you'll enjoy the recipes in this book. We have tried to keep the instructions simple and straightforward, avoiding anything too tricky or over-complicated. After all, our busy lifestyles mean that while many of us love to cook, there isn't always the time to do it. That doesn't mean that we have compromised on flavour. Far from it! We know that a recipe has to taste good if you're going to make it.

Flavour is everything in these recipes, and that's why it is important to spend a few minutes discussing ingredients. On the whole, the recipes rely on reducing the fat to cut calories and keep the Points low. You might think that by losing the fat,

you'd be losing the flavour, but that is certainly not the case. However, it is important to choose some ingredients that really add good tastes to your food, and that's why we feel quite strongly about using certain ingredients.

Take oil, for example. You may only be using a small amount, so why not use one that tastes good? The initial expense will be more, yet it will last much longer because you're using less. In dressings, a fruity olive oil can give so much to the finished flavour of your salad. In stir-fries, look out for stir-fry oil which is infused with the flavour of ginger, garlic and spices and gives your recipes a good kick-start, far better than if you were to use a bland vegetable oil.

The same goes for sugars too. If you haven't tried them, choose unrefined cane sugars from Mauritius. A light muscovado sugar has a wonderful flavour and you can make a light, easy pudding simply by topping fresh fruit with low-fat plain yogurt or fromage frais and finishing it off with a teaspoon of light muscovado sugar, which melts into a delicious toffee-like sauce. Use the light or dark muscovado sugars in our recipes for Pears in Mulled Wine (page 159), Orchard Fruit Crumbles (page 159) and Chocolate Bread Pudding with Luscious Chocolate Sauce (page 158).

Fresh herbs are used in abundance throughout the recipes; they add fabulous flavours and a real finishing touch to all kinds of foods. If you can, choose and use fresh herbs, though dried ones will do and are perfectly acceptable in pasta sauces, stews and casseroles where their flavours have time to develop. Do make sure that you review your herb and spice rack from time to time. Dried herbs that are more than a few months old will have a similar effect to adding sawdust to your recipe!

Pots of growing herbs in the most popular varieties are widely available now as well as little packets of fresh herbs, though they can be quite pricey. It's well worth considering cultivating your own herbs. It's not recommended to re-pot supermarket "growing herbs" – better to buy them from garden centres or grow them from seed. Even a window box on a sunny kitchen window sill will produce a small selection of fresh herbs throughout the summer and with a bigger plot, you'll have plenty to snip away at. Herbs look great in tubs and hanging baskets too.

Storecupboard tips

If you can, keep your store-cupboard well-stocked with a selection of essential ingredients (not biscuits and cakes!). Good quality stock cubes, a couple of different vinegars and mustards, horseradish sauce, tomato purée, sun-dried tomato paste, canned tomatoes, beans and vegetables, fish in brine, soy and chilli sauces, a range of rice and pasta and a good selection of spices. Small jars of prepared ingredients to keep in the fridge when opened are handy too – garlic, ginger, lemon grass, coriander and curry pastes, for instance.

Some recipes take short-cuts by using pre-prepared sauces, especially some of the pasta dishes. It makes good sense to use products which taste good, yet save you some time. You'll be pleased to know that only ingredients that are widely available have been chosen, so you shouldn't have any difficulty in tracking them down.

Talking of foods that are easily available, there is now an unbelievable choice of food on sale in our shops and supermarkets, often quite bewildering. Sometimes you may look at a recipe and think 'I don't know where to buy that'. Yet if you've never seen or heard of an ingredient before, it doesn't mean that it isn't there! Thai red and green curry pastes are a case in point. You'll find them with the Oriental ingredients, or with the herbs and spices and all you have to do is look. (If they're not there, grab the manager, and ask him why not).

The organic option

If you're keen on eating organically-produced food, there is nothing to stop you from choosing organic ingredients, where available. You may have to pay a premium for this and that's entirely up to you. There's no doubt that demand for organic foods is increasing, making it more widely available and eventually this will lead to lower prices.

Juicing

Drinking plenty of fresh juice from fruits and vegetables is great for boosting your intake of vitamins – in a very pleasant and natural way. Using a juice extractor can help you to increase your consumption of vitamins – but it's not necessarily cheaper than buying ready-made juices.

Remember that juice extractors are not the same as food processors, liquidisers or blenders – although some food processors do come with attachments for extracting juice. With a food processor or blender, the juice and pulp is blended together, whereas a juice extractor separates the two, producing a smooth liquid and separate pulp.

Make up your own ideas for juice recipes – depending on whether you prefer savoury or sweet. Try carrot and tomato; watercress and celery; or tomato, red pepper and cucumber with a dash of Tabasco pepper sauce or Worcestershire sauce to pep them up. All these vegetable versions have no Points. For sweeter fruit flavours, try a tropical trio of papaya, mango and kiwi fruit; a duo of raspberries and nectarine; or Cantaloupe melon with a hint of fresh root ginger.

Enjoying food and enjoying life

The main aim of this cookbook is to help you to enjoy your food, without guilt, and without feeling as if you're missing out. If you didn't love food, you probably wouldn't be in need of Weight Watchers but we think it should be enjoyed in the context of a healthy, well-balanced lifestyle, where fitness and well-being play a vital role. Think about yourself, think about your body and think about what you subject it to. Fatty, heavy foods will make you feel the same. Lighter, natural foods will benefit your body, making you feel better from the inside out. In the long term, it's the best solution for optimum health and fitness. Remember, there's only one you, and you only have one life to live, so you might as well make the most of it!

1 soups

Soups are wonderful! That's why we've devoted a whole chapter to them. They're quick to make, they're full of nutritious vegetables and they're very, very tasty. They can also be very filling and use up only a few Points.

Cauliflower and stilton soup

3½	Points per serving
13½	Total Points per recipe

15 g (½ oz) polyunsaturated margarine

1 large onion, chopped

2 garlic cloves, crushed

½ small cauliflower, broken into florets

2 vegetable stock cubes, dissolved in
     850 ml (1½ pints) boiling water

300 ml (½ pint) skimmed milk

200 g (7 oz) low-fat soft cheese

2 tablespoons chopped fresh chives

50 g (1¾ oz) blue Stilton cheese, crumbled

salt and freshly ground black pepper

Ⓥ *if using vegetarian Stilton Serves 4. (200 Calories per serving) Preparation time 10 minutes. Cooking time 35 minutes. Freezing recommended. Low-fat soft cheese gives a delightfully creamy texture to this unusual soup.*

1   Melt the margarine in a large saucepan and sauté the onion and garlic for about 5 minutes, until softened.

2   Add the cauliflower and vegetable stock to the saucepan and bring up to the boil. Cover and cook over a very low heat for about 20 minutes, until the cauliflower is tender.

3   Transfer to a liquidiser or food processor, add the milk, and blend for about 15 seconds. Reserve 2 tablespoons of low-fat soft cheese, then add the remainder to the soup with half the chives. Blend for a few more seconds until smooth. Return to the saucepan, add the blue cheese, then reheat gently. Season to taste with salt and pepper.

4   Ladle the soup into warmed bowls and spoon half a tablespoon of soft cheese on top of each portion. Sprinkle with the remaining chives and a little extra ground black pepper and serve at once.

Variation: Use grated Cheddar cheese if you're not keen on blue cheese – a mature one will give the best flavour. The Points per serving will be the same.

Summer vegetable soup

1	Point per serving
3½	Total Points per recipe

2 vegetable stock cubes, dissolved in 1 litre
     (1¾ pints) hot water

1 bunch spring onions, trimmed and
     finely chopped

1 garlic clove, crushed

3 celery sticks, finely sliced

1 large courgette, chopped

125 g (4½ oz) fine green beans, trimmed
     and sliced

1 tablespoon green pesto sauce

about 12 basil leaves, torn into shreds

25 g (1 oz) tiny pasta shapes

50 g (1¾ oz) crisp lettuce or Chinese leaves,
     finely shredded

salt and freshly ground black pepper

Ⓥ *Serves 4. (70 Calories per serving) Preparation time 10 minutes. Cooking time 20 minutes. Freezing not recommended. I love making this delicious soup – it's one of the nicest ways to eat your greens. Better still, a very generous portion has very few Points.*

1   Pour the stock into a large saucepan and bring up to the boil.

2   Add the spring onions, garlic, celery, courgette and green beans. Return to the boil, then reduce the heat. Cover and simmer for 10 minutes.

3   Add the pesto sauce, basil leaves and pasta shapes and cook until they are just tender, about 6–8 minutes. Add the shredded lettuce or Chinese leaves and cook for another 2 minutes. Season to taste.

4   Ladle the soup into warmed bowls and serve immediately.

Cook's note: Avoid overcooking the soup; the vegetables should retain their fresh flavours and colours.

Variation: Use well-washed spinach leaves instead of lettuce or Chinese leaves.

Red pepper and soft cheese soup

1½	Points per serving
7	Total Points per recipe

1 tablespoon polyunsaturated margarine

1 large onion, chopped

2 red peppers, de-seeded and chopped

2 celery sticks, sliced

1 carrot, chopped

1 tablespoon paprika

2 vegetable stock cubes, dissolved in 1 litre
    (1¾ pints) boiling water

200 g (7 oz) packet of low-fat soft cheese
    with garlic and herbs

salt and freshly ground black pepper

chopped fresh coriander or parsley,
    to garnish

Ⓥ Serves 4. (150 Calories per serving) Preparation time 10 minutes. Cooking time 35 minutes. Freezing recommended. This recipe is so easy! You'll be delighted with the way red peppers make such a delicious soup when combined with the creamy taste and texture of low-fat soft cheese.

1 Melt the margarine in a large saucepan. Reserve a little chopped onion and red pepper and add the remainder to the saucepan with the celery and carrot. Sauté gently for about 5 minutes, until softened. Add the paprika and cook gently, stirring constantly, for about one more minute.

2 Add the vegetable stock to the saucepan. Bring up to the boil, then reduce the heat. Cover and cook over a very low heat for about 20 minutes.

3 Transfer the soup to a liquidiser or food processor. Add the soft cheese and blend for about 15 seconds, until smooth. Return to the saucepan and reheat gently. Season to taste with salt and pepper.

4 Ladle the soup into warmed bowls and serve, scattered with the reserved onion and red pepper and sprinkled with chopped fresh coriander or parsley.

Zero point soup

0	Points per serving
0	Total Points per recipe

2 vegetable stock cubes, dissolved in 1 litre
    (1¾ pints) hot water

1 bunch of spring onions, trimmed and
    finely sliced

1 carrot, cut into fine strips

1 teaspoon Thai seven-spice seasoning

1 leek, finely shredded

1 small courgette, finely shredded

1 small red or yellow pepper, de-seeded and
    finely shredded

50 g (1¾ oz) Savoy or white cabbage,
    shredded

a pinch of dried red chilli flakes (optional)

salt and freshly ground black pepper

To garnish

1 tablespoon chopped fresh coriander or
    parsley

2 teaspoons sesame seeds

Ⓥ Serves 4. (65 Calories per serving) Preparation time 10 minutes. Cooking time 15 minutes. Freezing not recommended. What could be better than great-tasting food with no Points? You can enjoy this any time you want something extra to fill up with.

1 Pour the stock into a large saucepan and add the spring onions and carrot. Bring up to the boil, then cover and reduce the heat. Simmer for 5 minutes.

2 Add the Thai seven-spice seasoning, leek, courgette, pepper and cabbage. Add the red chilli flakes, if using, and cook for 5 more minutes.

3 Season the soup, then ladle into warmed bowls and serve, garnished with chopped fresh coriander or parsley and sesame seeds.

Variation 1: For an even quicker version of this light and delicious soup, use 450 g (1 lb) of ready-prepared stir-fry vegetables, adding them to the stock with the seven-spice seasoning.

Variation 2: If you can't find Thai seven-spice seasoning, use Chinese five-spice powder instead.

Minestrone soup

1½	Points per serving
6	Total Points per recipe

1 tablespoon olive oil

1 onion, chopped

1 carrot, chopped

125 g (4½ oz) green beans, sliced

1 courgette, chopped

2 vegetable stock cubes, dissolved in
　　300 ml (½ pint) boiling water

600 ml (1 pint) tomato juice

2 teaspoons mixed dried Italian herbs

40 g (1½ oz) tiny pasta shapes

50 g (1¾ oz) canned red kidney beans,
　　rinsed and drained

2 tomatoes, chopped

50 g (1¾ oz) cabbage, finely shredded

salt and freshly ground black pepper

 Serves 4. (155 Calories per serving) Preparation time 10 minutes. Cooking time 35 minutes. Freezing recommended. This is ideal for a meal when you want a warming pot of nutritious soup.

1　Heat the olive oil in a large saucepan. Add the onion, carrot, green beans and courgette and sauté gently for about 5 minutes, until softened.

2　Add the vegetable stock, tomato juice and dried herbs to the saucepan. Bring up to the boil, then reduce the heat. Cover and cook over a very low heat for about 15 minutes.

3　Add the pasta shapes, red kidney beans and tomatoes and cook for 5 more minutes, or until the pasta is tender. Add most of the cabbage and cook for another 2–3 minutes. Season to taste with salt and pepper.

4　Ladle the soup into warmed bowls and garnish with the reserved cabbage.

Variation: Instead of using red kidney beans, try canned borlotti beans or cannellini beans for a change.

menu plan

Italian Supper

If you love all things Italian, try this memorable Minestrone, followed by a simply fabulous dessert.

✳

Minestrone Soup
page 10, (1 serving) 1½ Points

✳

Warm Peaches with Amaretti and Ricotta
page 157, (1 serving) 3 Points

✳

Total Points: 4½ Points

Chilli prawn soup

1½	Points per serving
6½	Total Points per recipe

1 tablespoon stir-fry or vegetable oil

1 bunch spring onions, finely sliced or
    1 large onion

1 red pepper, de-seeded and finely sliced

1 yellow pepper, de-seeded and finely sliced

2 chicken stock cubes, dissolved in 1 litre
    (1¾ pints) hot water

2–3 teaspoons chilli sauce

1 teaspoon Chinese five-spice powder

50 g (1¾ oz) thread egg noodles

100 g (3½ oz) prawns, defrosted if frozen

salt and freshly ground black pepper

Serves 4. (145 Calories per serving) Preparation time 10 minutes. Cooking time 15 minutes. Freezing not recommended. Enjoy a delicious bowl of this spicy soup for supper with some bread, remembering to add the extra Points.

1 Heat the stir-fry oil in a large saucepan and add the spring onions and peppers. Stir-fry for 2–3 minutes.

2 Add the stock, chilli sauce, Chinese five-spice powder and noodles. Bring up to the boil, then simmer for 5 minutes, until the noodles are tender.

3 Add the prawns, cook for 2 minutes, then season with salt and pepper. Ladle into warmed bowls and serve at once.

Cook's note: Stir-fry oil is flavoured with garlic, ginger and spices and gives an excellent flavour to this soup but if you don't have any you could simply use vegetable oil instead.

Variation 1: Add marinated tofu instead of prawns and use vegetable stock cubes instead of chicken for a vegetarian version. The Points per serving will be the same.

Variation 2: Try using 50 g (1¾ oz) rice or small pasta shapes instead of noodles. The Points per serving will be the same.

Harvest vegetable soup

1½	Points per serving
6	Total Points per recipe

15 g (½ oz) polyunsaturated margarine

1 onion, chopped finely

1 carrot, chopped

175 g (6 oz) swede, diced

1 vegetable stock cube dissolved in 600 ml
    (1 pint) hot water

75 g (2¾ oz) fine green beans, trimmed
    and chopped

1 tablespoon cornflour

300 ml (½ pint) skimmed milk

75 g (2¾ oz) canned or frozen sweetcorn

125 g (4½ oz) low-fat plain fromage frais

salt and freshly ground black pepper

chopped fresh parsley, to garnish

Ⓥ *Serves 4. (135 Calories per serving) Preparation time 10 minutes. Cooking time 25 minutes. Freezing recommended. This chunky, creamy soup is very satisfying as a meal, and just the thing to lift your spirits on a chilly autumn or winter day.*

1 Melt the margarine in a large saucepan and sauté the onion gently until softened, about 3–4 minutes.

2 Add the carrot, swede and vegetable stock. Bring up to the boil, then reduce the heat. Cover and simmer for about 15 minutes until the vegetables are tender. Add the green beans.

3 Blend the cornflour with 2–3 tablespoons of the milk. Add the remaining milk to the saucepan with the sweetcorn and fromage frais, then stir in the blended cornflour. Heat gently, stirring constantly, until almost boiling, then cook gently for another 2–3 minutes.

4 Season the soup with salt and pepper, then ladle into warmed soup bowls and serve, garnished with parsley.

Variation: Use frozen peas instead of sweetcorn.

Spanish bean soup

3½	Points per serving
14½	Total Points per recipe

1 tablespoon chilli oil or vegetable oil

1 onion, chopped

1 red or green pepper, de-seeded and chopped

125 g (4½ oz) mushrooms, wiped and sliced

1 tablespoon paprika

447g can of mixed beans in spicy sauce

1 litre (1¾ pints) tomato juice

1 vegetable stock cube, dissolved in 100 ml
    (3½ fl oz) boiling water

50 g (1¾ oz) Spanish-style chorizo or
    cooked continental sausage, sliced

salt and freshly ground black pepper

chopped fresh coriander or parsley, to garnish

Serves 4. (240 Calories per serving) Preparation time 10 minutes. Cooking time 15 minutes. Freezing recommended. This spicy, filling soup is so quick to make. Simply open a can of beans in spicy sauce, add a few vegetables and some sliced cooked sausage, then simmer to make a scrumptious meal-in-a-bowl.

1 Heat the chilli oil or vegetable oil in a large saucepan and sauté the onion and pepper for 3–4 minutes, until softened. Add the mushrooms and paprika and cook, stirring, for 2 more minutes.

2 Tip in the can of beans, then add the tomato juice, vegetable stock and sliced sausage. Bring up to the boil, then reduce the heat and simmer gently, stirring occasionally, for 5 minutes.

3 Season with salt and pepper and serve in warmed bowls, sprinkled with chopped fresh coriander or parsley.

Variation: For a vegetarian version, chop 125 g (4½ oz) cooked vegetarian sausage and add with the beans as above. The Points per serving will be 4.

Seafood soup

3	Points per serving
12	Total Points per recipe

600 ml (1 pint) skimmed milk

250 g (9 oz) smoked haddock fillet

1 vegetable stock cube dissolved in 450 ml
    (16 fl oz) hot water

1 onion, finely chopped

175 g (6 oz) potato, diced

75 g (2¾ oz) frozen peas

75 g (2¾ oz) canned or frozen sweetcorn

2 tablespoons cornflour, blended with a
    little water

100 g (3½ oz) prawns, defrosted if frozen

2 tablespoons chopped fresh parsley

salt and freshly ground black pepper

Serves 4. (235 Calories per serving) Preparation time 15 minutes. Cooking time 30 minutes. Freezing recommended. If you love seafood, you'll love this delicous combination of seafood and vegetables.

1 Put the milk and fish fillet into a large saucepan. Bring up to simmering point, then cook gently for 6–8 minutes. Strain the milk and reserve. Skin and flake the fish, discarding any bones and set aside.

2 Put the vegetable stock, onion and potato into the saucepan. Bring up to the boil, then reduce the heat and cook for 10 minutes, or until the potato is tender.

3 Add the strained milk, peas, sweetcorn and blended cornflour. Bring up to the boil, stirring, until thickened.

4 Add the prawns, the flaked smoked fish and parsley to the saucepan. Cook gently for 2-3 minutes until thoroughly heated. Season to taste, then serve.

Variation 1: If you love mussels, you could add 250 g (9 oz) to this soup with the prawns. Make sure that they have been well-scrubbed, and they are not damaged. Discard any that fail to open once cooked. This will not add any Points.

Variation 2: If you would like to use a smoked cod fillet, the Points per serving will remain the same.

Light Lunch for One

Satisfy your appetite with
this two-course meal for one.
Any leftover soup and salad
will keep for 2 or 3 days in
the refrigerator.

✳

Super Speedy Tomato Soup
page 15, (1 serving) 1 Point

✳

Sweetcorn and Bean Salad
page 55, (1 serving) 3 Points

✳

Total Points: 4 Points

Super speedy tomato soup

1	Point per serving
1½	Total Points per recipe

600 ml (1 pint) tomato juice

½ vegetable stock cube, dissolved in
    4 tablespoons hot water

1 teaspoon garlic purée

1 teaspoon Tabasco sauce

1 tablespoon chopped fresh chives,
    basil or coriander

salt and freshly ground black pepper

2 tablespoons low-fat plain yogurt, to garnish

Serves 2. (60 Calories per serving) Preparation and cooking time 10 minutes. Freezing recommended. This is the quickest home-made soup ever! It makes a very tasty light meal, snack or starter.

1　Put the tomato juice and stock into a saucepan and add the garlic purée and Tabasco sauce. Bring up to the boil, reduce the heat, then add most of the chopped chives, basil or coriander, reserving some for garnish.

2　Season the soup with salt and pepper, adding a few more drops of Tabasco sauce, if you like your food to be spicy.

3　Serve the soup, topping each portion with a tablespoon of yogurt, chopped fresh herbs and a little extra ground black pepper.

Variation: Instead of tomato juice, use V8 vegetable juice.

Cock-a-leekie soup

1½	Points per serving
6½	Total Points per recipe

1 medium chicken leg quarter, skinned

1 chicken stock cube

50 g (1¾ oz) pearl barley

1 bay leaf

2 onions, sliced

2 leeks, sliced

1 carrot, chopped

2 tablespoons chopped fresh parsley

salt and freshly ground black pepper

Serves 4. (155 Calories per serving) Preparation time 10 minutes. Cooking time 1 hour. Freezing recommended. Simmering a chicken quarter with the vegetables gives this soup a great flavour. It's inexpensive and very nourishing too.

1　Put the chicken portion into a large saucepan and add 1.2 litres (2 pints) of cold water and the stock cube. Add the pearl barley and bay leaf, and bring up to the boil. Reduce the heat and simmer gently, partially covered, for 30 minutes.

2　Add the onions, leeks and carrot to the saucepan and continue to cook for about 20 minutes until the vegetables are tender and the pearl barley is cooked.

3　Lift the chicken portion from the saucepan, cool slightly, then remove all the meat from the bones. Chop the meat and return to the saucepan with the parsley.

4　Remove the bay leaf, reheat the soup and season to taste. Ladle into warmed bowls.

Garden vegetable soup

3	Points per serving
12	Total Points per recipe

15 g (½ oz) polyunsaturated margarine

1 onion, finely chopped

350 g (12 oz) spinach or watercress

125 g (4½ oz) fresh or frozen peas

1 tablespoon chopped fresh mint

1 vegetable stock cube dissolved in 450 ml
    (16 fl oz pint) hot water

200 g (7 oz) low-fat soft cheese

2 tablespoons cornflour

450 ml (16 fl oz) skimmed milk

salt and freshly ground black pepper

mint sprigs, to garnish

Serves 4. (215 Calories per serving) Preparation time 10 minutes. Cooking time 25 minutes. Freezing recommended. The perfect bowl of soup in Springtime.

1　Melt the margarine in a large saucepan and sauté the onion until softened. Add the spinach or watercress and cook until wilted, about 3–4 minutes.

2　Add most of the peas, reserving some for later, along with the chopped mint and stock. Bring up to the boil, then reduce the heat and simmer for 10 minutes.

3　Transfer to a liquidiser or food processor. Add most of the soft cheese, reserving some for garnishing, and blend until smooth. Return to the saucepan.

4　Blend the cornflour with 2–3 tablespoons of the milk, then add to the saucepan with the remaining milk and reserved peas. Bring to the boil, stirring until thickened, then cook gently for 2 minutes.

5　Season to taste, then serve, topped with the reserved soft cheese and mint sprigs.

Creamy watercress soup

3	Points per serving
12½	Total Points per recipe

V Serves 4. (210 Calories per serving) Preparation time 10 minutes. Cooking time 30 minutes. Freezing recommended.

25 g (1 oz) polyunsaturated margarine

1 large onion, chopped

2 bunches of watercress

a generous handful of parsley

2 vegetable stock cubes, dissolved in
    600 ml (1 pint) hot water

200 g (7 oz) low-fat soft cheese

2 tablespoons cornflour

425 ml (¾ pint) skimmed milk

salt and freshly ground black pepper

4 tablespoons low-fat plain yogurt, to
    garnish

1 Melt the margarine in a large saucepan and fry the onion gently over a low heat for about 3 minutes, until softened, but not browned.

2 Reserve a few watercress sprigs for garnish, then add the remainder to the saucepan with all the parsley – including the stems (they will add to the finished flavour of the soup). You don't have to chop the watercress or parsley as it will be blended later.

3 Pour the stock into the saucepan and bring up to the boil, then cover and reduce the heat to low. Simmer gently for 15–20 minutes.

4 Transfer the soup to a liquidiser or food processor. Add the low-fat soft cheese and blend until smooth. Return the soup to the saucepan.

5 Blend the cornflour with 3–4 tablespoons of the milk. Add to the soup with the remaining milk and bring up to the boil, stirring, until the soup thickens. Simmer gently for about 2 minutes.

6 Season the soup with salt and pepper, ladle into warmed bowls and garnish each portion with a spoonful of yogurt and the remaining sprigs of watercress.

Cook's note: This soup is delicious served chilled in the summer months. If you plan to do this, make it the day before, then refrigerate it overnight. And do point out to your guests that the soup is chilled, otherwise they'll be surprised when they taste it.

Variation: You could use baby spinach leaves or rocket instead of watercress for a change – just make sure you wash the leaves thoroughly first. You'll need about 350 g (12 oz).

Yellow split pea soup

3	Points per serving
12	Total Points per recipe

V Serves 4. (275 Calories per serving) Preparation time 10 minutes + soaking. Cooking time 1–1½ hours. Freezing recommended.

225 g (8 oz) dried yellow split peas

25 g (1 oz) polyunsaturated margarine

1 large onion, chopped

2 carrots, finely chopped

2 ham or vegetable stock cubes, dissolved
    in 1 litre (1¾ pints) hot water

1 teaspoon dried thyme

salt and freshly ground black pepper

1 tablespoon chopped fresh parsley,
    to garnish

1 Put the split peas into a bowl and cover with boiling water. Add ½ teaspoon of salt, then leave to soak for about 12 hours, or overnight. Rinse and drain well.

2 Melt the margarine in a large saucepan and add the onion. Sauté for about 5 minutes over a medium heat, until lightly browned. Add the carrots to the saucepan and stir well.

3 Pour the stock into the saucepan and add the dried thyme. Bring up to the boil, then reduce the heat, cover and simmer until the split peas are tender, about 1–1½ hours.

4 Taste the soup to check the seasoning, adding salt and pepper according to taste. Serve in warmed soup bowls, garnished with chopped fresh parsley.

Variation: For a quicker cooking time with less preparation, use red lentils instead of split peas. They don't need to be pre-soaked, and they only take about 45 minutes to cook.

Coconut milk soup with ginger and Coriander

4½	Pcints per serving
18	Total Points per recipe

1 tablespoon stir-fry oil or sesame oil

6 shallots, finely chopped

2 teaspoons finely grated root ginger

3 tablespoons chopped fresh coriander

300 ml sachet of Bart Spices 88% fat-free
   coconut milk

1 tablespoon Thai red curry paste

2 vegetable or chicken stock cubes, dissolved
   in 425 ml (¾ pint) hot water

1 tablespoon cornflour

250 ml (9 fl oz) skimmed milk

salt and freshly ground black pepper

coriander sprigs, to garnish

Ⓥ if using vegetable stock cube Serves 4 (150 Calories per serving) Preparation time 10 minutes. Cooking time 30 minutes. Freezing recommended. If you love subtle and spicy flavours, you will adore this soup and it's so simple to make.

1 Heat the stir-fry oil or sesame oil in a large saucepan and sauté the shallots and ginger for 2-3 minutes, until softened.

2 Add the coriander, coconut milk, red curry paste and stock. Bring up to the boil, then reduce the heat and simmer for 15–20 minutes.

3 Blend the cornflour with 2–3 tablespoons of the milk. Add to the saucepan with the remaining milk. Bring up to the boil, stirring constantly, then reduce the heat and cook gently for 2–3 minutes. Season to taste.

4 Ladle into warm serving bowls and garnish with fresh coriander.

Cook's note 1: Stir-fry oil has been flavoured with ginger, garlic and spices giving added depth of flavour to the soup.

Cook's note 2: You can buy chopped "fresh" ginger and coriander in jars, saving preparation time. Look for them in the spices section of your supermarket; you might also find them with the Oriental foods.

Variation: Use 1 large onion instead of the shallots, if you prefer.

Cream of celery and almond soup

3	Points per serving
13	Total Points per recipe

2 rashers of streaky bacon, chopped

6 celery sticks, trimmed and chopped

1 onion, chopped

1 teaspoon finely chopped fresh root
   ginger (optional)

2 vegetable stock cubes, dissolved in
   600 ml (1 pint) hot water

2 tablespoons cornflour

300 ml (½ pint) skimmed milk

25 g (1 oz) ground almonds

salt and freshly ground black pepper

To serve

4 tablespoons half-fat crème fraîche

15 g (½ oz) toasted flaked almonds

celery leaves

Serves 4. (165 Calories per serving) Preparation time 10 minutes. Cooking time 35 minutes. Freezing recommended. A very flavoursome soup and ideal for a light meal.

1 Dry-fry the bacon in a large saucepan, cooking gently until crisp. Remove and drain on kitchen paper. Break into little bits for garnishing later.

2 Add the celery and onion to the saucepan which the bacon was cooked in and sauté for 5 minutes, without browning. Add the ginger, if using, and stock. Bring up to the boil, cover, reduce the heat and simmer for about 20 minutes.

3 Transfer the soup to a liquidiser or food processor and blend for 15–20 seconds, until smooth. Return to the saucepan.

4 Blend the cornflour with 4 tablespoons of the milk. Add to the soup with the remaining milk and ground almonds. Heat, stirring, until thickened, then cook gently for 2 minutes. Check the seasoning, adding salt and pepper to taste.

5 Serve the soup in warmed bowls, topped with the crème fraîche and garnished with the flaked almonds, crispy bacon bits and celery leaves.

Variation: Leave out the bacon if you're cooking this soup for vegetarians and sauté the celery and onion in 3 teaspoons of butter or margarine instead (Points remain the same).

Parsnip and lemon soup

2	Points per serving
7½	Total Points per recipe

15 g (½ oz) polyunsaturated margarine

1 onion, chopped

450 g (1 lb) parsnips, peeled and chopped

½ teaspoon ground cumin

2 vegetable stock cubes dissolved in 600 ml
    (1 pint) hot water

1 tablespoon chopped fresh parsley

300 ml (½ pint) skimmed milk

finely grated zest of 1 lemon

salt and freshly ground black pepper

To garnish

parsley sprigs

lemon zest

Serves 4. (130 Calories per serving) Preparation time 10 minutes. Cooking time 35 minutes. Freezing recommended. Parsnips and lemons are a delicious combination for soup.

1   Melt the margarine in a large saucepan and sauté the onion until softened, about 5 minutes. Add the parsnips and cook, stirring, for another 2–3 minutes.

2   Add the ground cumin, vegetable stock and chopped parsley. Bring to the boil, then reduce the heat and simmer gently for about 20 minutes, or until the parsnips are tender.

3   Transfer the mixture to a food processor or blender and liquidise until smooth. Return to the saucepan and add the milk and lemon zest. Reheat gently. Season to taste with salt and pepper.

4   Ladle the soup into warmed bowls, then garnish with parsley sprigs and lemon zest.

Variation 1: Try using fresh coriander in the recipe instead of parsley, for a change.

Variation 2: Orange zest also tastes delicious with parsnips, so try it instead of lemon zest.

Beef consommé

½	Point per serving
1	Total Points per recipe

2 × 295 g cans of condensed beef
    consommé

1 red pepper, de-seeded and sliced into
    fine strips

1 leek, shredded

100 g (3½ oz) mushrooms, sliced

salt and freshly ground black pepper

1 teaspoon sesame seeds

Serves 4. (50 Calories per serving) Preparation and cooking time 20 minutes. Freezing not recommended. Make more of condensed consommé by adding lots of very finely sliced vegetables to create a light, nourishing soup. It makes a very elegant starter for a special meal with very few Points.

1   Empty the cans of consommé into a large saucepan and add two cans of water. Heat gently, stirring.

2   Add the vegetables and simmer gently for about 10 minutes, so that the vegetables are cooked, yet still retain their bright colour.

3   Season the soup to taste, then ladle the vegetables into warmed soup plates, piling them into the middle. Pour the consommé around, sprinkle with the sesame seeds and serve at once.

Variation 1: You could transform this recipe into a vegetarian soup by using a clear vegetable broth instead of beef consommé. Two good quality vegetable stock cubes dissolved in 1 litre (1¾ pints) of hot water will do the trick. The Points per serving will be 0.

Variation 2: Vary the vegetables as you wish to make your own version of this quick and easy soup – just make sure they are finely shredded.

Fresh herb soup

2½	Points per serving
10½	Total Points per recipe

15 g (½ oz) polyunsaturated margarine

1 bunch spring onions, trimmed and
     chopped

225 g (8 oz) spinach, thoroughly washed

4 tablespoons mixed chopped fresh herbs
     (e.g. chives, parsley, marjoram, basil)

2 vegetable stock cubes, dissolved in
     300 ml (½ pint) water

1 tablespoon green pesto sauce

200 g (7 oz) low-fat soft cheese

1 tablespoon cornflour

425 ml (¾ pint) skimmed milk

salt and freshly ground black pepper

To serve

4 tablespoons low-fat plain yogurt

fresh herb sprigs, optional

Ⓥ *Serves 4. (200 Calories per serving) Preparation time 15 minutes. Cooking time 20 minutes. Freezing recommended. This soup is perfect for using up a glut of garden fresh herbs; it is one of my all-time favourites, so I hope you enjoy it too.*

1 Melt the margarine in a large saucepan and sauté the spring onions until softened, about 3–5 minutes. Add the spinach and cook, stirring occasionally, until it has wilted, about another 2 minutes.

2 Add the herbs and vegetable stock to the saucepan and bring to the boil, then add the pesto sauce. Reduce the heat, cover and simmer for 10 minutes.

3 Transfer the soup to a liquidiser or food processor and add the soft cheese. Blend for about 15–20 seconds until smooth, then return to the saucepan.

4 Blend the cornflour with 2–3 tablespoons of the milk, add to the soup with the remaining milk and bring up to the boil, stirring constantly until thickened and smooth.

5 Taste and season the soup, then serve in warmed bowls, topped with yogurt and garnished with sprigs of fresh herbs, if desired.

Variation 1: Choose a low-fat soft cheese flavoured with chives or garlic and herbs, if you like.

Variation 2: The soup is delicious when served chilled in summer. Ladle it into chilled bowls and add an ice cube to each portion.

Curried vegetable soup

1½	Points per serving
6	Total Points per recipe

15 g (½ oz) polyunsaturated margarine

1 onion, sliced

2 celery sticks, chopped

1 garlic clove, crushed

225 g (8 oz) mushrooms, sliced

2 vegetable stock cubes, dissolved in 1 litre
     (1¾ pints) hot water

1 carrot, chopped

1 medium parsnip, chopped

2 tablespoons medium curry paste

2 tablespoons chopped fresh mint or
     coriander

salt and freshly ground black pepper

4 tablespoons low-fat plain yogurt

Ⓥ *Serves 4. (105 Calories per serving) Preparation time 15 minutes. Cooking time 35 minutes. Freezing recommended.*

1 Melt the margarine in a large saucepan and sauté the onion, celery and garlic for about 3 minutes, until softened, but not browned. Add the mushrooms and cook for another 2–3 minutes.

2 Pour in the vegetable stock and bring up to the boil. Reduce the heat, add the carrot, parsnip and curry paste and cook for about 20 minutes, until the vegetables are tender.

3 Transfer about half the soup to a liquidiser or food processor and blend for about 15–20 seconds, until smooth. Return to the remaining soup in the saucepan and add 1 tablespoon of the mint or coriander. Reheat gently, then season to taste.

4 Ladle the soup into warmed bowls and top each portion with a tablespoon of yogurt. Garnish with the remaining mint or coriander, and serve at once.

Chestnut and mushroom soup

2	Points per serving
8½	Total Points per recipe

2 teaspoons vegetable oil

1 onion, finely chopped

1 carrot, chopped

350 g (12 oz) mushrooms, sliced

175 g (6 oz) peeled, roasted chestnuts or
   canned chestnuts

2 vegetable stock cubes, dissolved in 1 litre
   (1¾ pints) hot water

2 tablespoons chopped fresh parsley

100 g (3½ oz) low-fat plain fromage frais

1 tablespoon cornflour

2 tablespoons medium sherry

salt and freshly ground black pepper

parsley sprigs, to garnish

Ⓥ *Serves 4. (170 Calories per serving) Preparation time 10 minutes (if using canned chestnuts). Cooking time 35 minutes. Freezing recommended. This a lovely soup to make for a festive occasion. Use freshly roasted chestnuts when they are in season, otherwise use canned ones.*

1 Heat the vegetable oil in a large saucepan and sauté the onion, carrot and mushrooms until softened, about 5 minutes.

2 Add the chestnuts and vegetable stock to the saucepan and bring to the boil. Reduce the heat, cover and simmer for 20 minutes.

3 Transfer the soup to a liquidiser or food processor and add the parsley and most of the fromage frais. Blend for about 15–20 seconds until smooth, then return to the saucepan.

4 Blend the cornflour with 2–3 tablespoons of cold water, add to the soup with the sherry and bring up to the boil, stirring constantly until thickened and smooth.

5 Taste and season the soup, then serve in warmed bowls, garnished with the reserved fromage frais and parsley sprigs.

Cook's note: To roast chestnuts, pierce them with a sharp knife on the flat side, then roast them on a baking sheet in an oven preheated to Gas Mark 6/200°C/400°F for 15–20 minutes.

Chicken broth

1½	Points per serving
7	Total Points per recipe

2 teaspoons vegetable oil

1 medium skinless, boneless chicken breast,
   chopped into small pieces

2 chicken stock cubes, dissolved in 1 litre
   (1¾ pints) hot water

1 large onion, finely chopped

2 carrots, diced

1 turnip, diced

2 celery sticks, finely sliced

2 tablespoons chopped fresh parsley

50 g (1¾ oz) long grain rice

salt and freshly ground black pepper

Serves 4. (155 Calories per serving) Preparation time 10 minutes. Cooking time 40 minutes. Freezing recommended. What could be more delicious than a bowl of chicken soup? It's the ultimate comfort food.

1 Heat the vegetable oil in a large saucepan and add the chicken. Cook for 3–4 minutes, stirring, until sealed and browned.

2 Add all the remaining ingredients apart from the rice and bring up to the boil. Reduce the heat and simmer gently, partially covered, for 20 minutes.

3 Add the rice to the saucepan and cook for about 12–15 more minutes, or until the rice is tender.

4 Season the soup to taste, then ladle into warmed bowls and serve at once.

Irish leek and potato soup

1	Point per serving
4½	Total Points per recipe

15 g (½ oz) polyunsaturated margarine

1 onion, chopped

3 leeks, sliced

2 medium potatoes, cut into chunks

2 vegetable stock cubes, dissolved in 1 litre

    (1¾ pints) hot water

150 ml (¼ pint) skimmed milk

2 tablespoons chopped fresh parsley

salt and freshly ground black pepper

Ⓥ *Serves 4. (125 Calories per serving) Preparation time 10 minutes. Cooking time 35 minutes. Freezing recommended. Potatoes and leeks are one of the all-time great pairings of ingredients for soup.*

1 Melt the margarine in a large saucepan and sauté the onion and leeks for about 5 minutes, until softened, but not browned.

2 Add the potatoes and vegetable stock, bring up to the boil, then reduce the heat and simmer gently for about 20 minutes, or until the potatoes are tender.

3 Transfer about half of the soup to a liquidiser or food processor and blend for about 15–20 seconds until smooth. Return to the saucepan with the remaining soup. Add the milk.

4 Reheat the soup, add the parsley and season to taste with salt and pepper. Ladle into warmed soup bowls and serve at once.

Quick chicken and sweetcorn soup

2	Points per serving
7½	Total Points per recipe

326 g can of sweetcorn, drained

2 chicken stock cubes, dissolved in 1 litre

    (1¾ pints) of hot water

a pinch of dried chilli flakes (optional)

1 tablespoon cornflour

150 ml (¼ pint) skimmed milk

100 g (3½ oz) cooked chicken, chopped

1 tablespoon chopped fresh coriander

    or parsley

salt and freshly ground black pepper

coriander or parsley sprigs, to garnish

    (optional)

Serves 4. (170 Calories per serving) Preparation time 5 minutes. Cooking time 15 minutes. Freezing recommended. A friend once cooked this simply delicious soup for me. I was very impressed, so I thought I would create a similar recipe for Weight Watchers.

1 Tip the sweetcorn into a large saucepan and add the chicken stock and chilli flakes (if using). Bring up to the boil, then reduce the heat and simmer for 10 minutes.

2 Transfer the mixture to a liquidiser or food processor and blend for 15–20 seconds until smooth. Return the soup to the saucepan.

3 Blend the cornflour with 2–3 tablespoons of the milk, then stir into the saucepan with the remaining milk. Add the chicken and coriander or parsley. Reheat, then add salt and pepper, according to taste.

4 Ladle the soup into warmed bowls and serve at once. Garnish with coriander or parsley sprigs if desired.

Cook's note: You can buy prepared coriander or parsley in small jars, ready for immediate use. Keep refrigerated once opened, and use within six weeks.

2 chapter

starters and light meals

Because we believe that food should look as good as it tastes, you'll notice when you make these tasty recipes that they are alive with colours, textures and great flavours. Eating healthily is a pleasure for all the senses – and something that you'll enjoy for the rest of your life.

Oven-roasted tomato tartlets

1	Point per serving
10	Total Points per recipe

1 kg (2 lb 4 oz) plum tomatoes

1 teaspoon salt

8 sheets of filo pastry

2 tablespoons olive oil

2 tablespoons fresh basil leaves, torn
    (optional)

freshly ground black pepper

Ⓥ Makes 8. (120 Calories per serving) Preparation time 15 minutes. Cooking time 1¼ hours. Freezing recommended for the roasted tomatoes only. Slow roasting tomatoes brings out their wonderful rich flavour.

1 Preheat the oven to Gas Mark 2/150°C/300°F.

2 Slice the tomatoes in half horizontally and arrange cut-side up on a cooling rack. Lift the cooling rack over a baking sheet and then sprinkle the salt over the tomatoes.

3 Roast the tomatoes in the oven for 1 hour, until they are beginning to dry out a little.

4 After the tomatoes have cooked, increase the oven temperature to Gas Mark 5/190°C/375°F. Cut each sheet of filo pastry in half, brush with olive oil and sandwich two halves together. Press into 8 individual tartlet tins scrunching up the edges with your fingers so the pastry fits into the tins. Brush the insides of the tartlet cases with any remaining olive oil and place a crumpled piece of foil into each one. Bake for 15 minutes, until the pastry is crisp and golden.

5 Carefully remove the pastry cases from the tins and fill with the roasted tomato halves.

6 Scatter each tartlet with a little torn basil, if using, and a generous grinding of black pepper.

Cook's note: It's better to tear fresh basil rather than chop it, since this prevents it from bruising.

Eggs benedict

4½	Points per serving
9	Total Points per recipe

1 teaspoon malt vinegar

2 eggs

1 English muffin, halved

2 teaspoons low-fat spread

25 g (1 oz) wafer-thin ham

1 tomato, sliced

2 tablespoons half-fat crème fraîche

2 tablespoons Weight Watchers from Heinz
    90% fat-free mayonnaise

a pinch of paprika

Serves 2. (275 Calories per serving) Preparation and cooking time 20 minutes. Freezing not recommended. A lower calorie version of an all-time favourite breakfast dish; try making this for a weekend brunch treat.

1 Pour enough water into a frying-pan to come half-way up the side of the pan. Add the vinegar and bring to the boil. Carefully crack the eggs (one at a time) into a cup and then slide the egg out carefully into the water. Poach for about 3 to 4 minutes, depending on how well you like your eggs cooked. Preheat the grill.

2 Carefully lift the eggs out of the pan using a slotted spoon and drain on absorbent kitchen paper for 1 minute.

3 Meanwhile, toast the muffin under the grill for 1 to 2 minutes per side, until golden. Spread with a little low-fat spread and top with wafer-thin ham and tomato slices.

4 Lift an egg on top of each muffin half and then transfer to serving plates. Mix together the crème fraîche and mayonnaise and heat gently to just warm through but not bubble. Spoon over the eggs, sprinkle with paprika and serve at once.

Kidney bean and chilli pâté

2½	Points per serving
10½	Total Points per recipe

1 teaspoon sunflower oil

1 small onion, chopped

1 garlic clove, crushed

1 teaspoon chilli flakes

425 g (15 oz) canned kidney beans, drained

125 g (4½ oz) low-fat soft cheese

2 tablespoons freshly squeezed lemon juice

salt and freshly ground black pepper

Ⓥ *Serves 4. (120 Calories per serving) Preparation time 10 minutes. Freezing recommended. Spread on toast for a tasty starter or serve as a dip with a selection of veggies.*

1 Heat the sunflower oil in a small pan and cook the onion, garlic and chilli flakes over a low heat for 5 minutes, until softened but not browned.

2 Remove from the heat. Allow to cool a little, then transfer to a food processor with the drained kidney beans, low-fat soft cheese and lemon juice. Blend until smooth and season to taste.

3 Transfer to a serving dish and chill until ready to eat.

Variation: Other canned beans and spices can be substitued for the kidney beans and chilli such as chick-peas with ground coriander or butter beans and cumin.

Mediterranean baked peppers

2½	Points per serving
10	Total Points per recipe

2 red or green peppers, halved and de-seeded

125 g (4½ oz) soup pasta

4 drained, canned anchovy fillets, mashed

125 g (4½ oz) cherry tomatoes, halved

10 pitted black olives, roughly chopped

2 tablespoons chopped fresh basil

1 tablespoon olive oil

salt and freshly ground black pepper

Serves 4. (195 Calories per serving) Preparation time 15 minutes. Cooking time 30 minutes. Freezing not recommended. When cooked, small-shaped soup pasta swells up to the perfect size to use as stuffings and fillings for vegetables.

1 Preheat the oven to Gas Mark 4/180°C/350°F. Place the peppers in a non-stick roasting tin, cut-side up. Cook for 10 minutes.

2 Bring a pan of lightly salted water to the boil and cook the soup pasta until tender – about 5 minutes. Drain thoroughly, then toss with the mashed anchovies, cherry tomato halves, olives, basil and seasoning.

3 Pack into the part-cooked pepper halves and drizzle each with a little olive oil.

4 Roast in the oven for 15 minutes, then serve hot or cold with a salad garnish.

Variation: If you're not a lover of anchovies, replace them with a small can of tuna in brine, drained and flaked.

Ham and mustard bread and butter puddings

2	Points per serving
9	Total Points per recipe

2 slices of thin-cut bread (preferably 2 to 3 days old)

15 g (½ oz) low-fat spread, softened

1 tablespoon course-grain mustard

25g (1 oz) wafer-thin ham, cut into thin strips

25 g (1 oz) half-fat Cheddar cheese, grated

2 eggs

150 ml (¼ pint) skimmed milk

salt and freshly ground black pepper

Serves 4. (140 Calories per serving) Preparation time 15 minutes. Cooking time 20 minutes. Freezing not recommended. Serve with a sliced tomato salad.

1 Cut the crusts off the bread. Mix together the low-fat spread and mustard. Spread over one side of each slice of bread. Cut each slice into quarters and divide between four individual ramekin dishes.

2 Scatter the ham strips and grated cheese over the top.

3 Preheat the oven to Gas Mark 5/190°C/375°F.

4 Beat together the eggs, milk and seasoning and pour equally into each dish. Lift on to a baking sheet and cook for 20 minutes until the egg mixture has set and the puddings are fluffed up and golden. Serve hot.

Variation: An 80 g can of flaked tuna could be used instead of ham. The Points per serving will be the same.

Vegetarian Supper

Vegetarian meals are so tasty!
Here's a delicious menu
suggestion to prove the point.
Keep any leftover pate in a
covered container in the fridge.

✳

Kidney Bean and Chilli Pâté
page 26, (1 serving) 2½ Points

✳

Roasted Rosemary Vegetables on Ciabatta
page 32, (1 serving) 4½ Points

✳

Total Points: 7 Points

Garlic prawn and beansprout pancakes

3	Points per serving
12½	Total Points per recipe

1 teaspoon sesame oil

1 teaspoon Chinese five spice powder

1 garlic clove, crushed

125 g (4½ oz) peeled prawns

125 g (4½ oz) beansprouts

4 spring onions, trimmed and shredded

1 tablespoon light soy sauce

8 sheets filo pastry

2 tablespoons sunflower oil

1 teaspoon sesame seeds

Serves 4. (260 Calories per serving) Preparation time 20 minutes. Cooking time 15 minutes. Freezing recommended. These are rather like spring rolls, but with a lot less calories. Serve with a drizzle of soy sauce.

1 Place the sesame oil, five spice seasoning and garlic in a bowl. Add the prawns and toss together well.

2 Place the beansprouts and shredded spring onions in a small pan with 1 tablespoon of soy sauce. Cover with a tight-fitting lid and cook for 2 to 3 minutes until "wilted". Drain and toss with the prawn mixture.

3 Preheat the oven to Gas Mark 5/190°C/375°F. Line a baking sheet with non-stick baking parchment.

4 Brush each sheet of filo pastry with sunflower oil. Place a spoonful of the prawn mixture on to one side, fold the edges over and then roll up to enclose the filling. Transfer to the lined baking sheet, seam-side down.

5 Sprinkle with sesame seeds and then bake for 10 to 12 minutes, until the pastry is crisp. Serve hot.

Cook's note: If you prefer, make a vegetarian version by using a mixture of thin strips of carrot, courgette and baby corn instead of prawns. The Points per serving will be 2½.

Smoked salmon mousse with cucumber and dill relish

2½	Points per serving
10½	Total Points per recipe

For the mousse

150 g (5½ oz) smoked salmon

finely grated zest of 1 lemon

2 tablespoons fresh lemon juice

1 tablespoon horseradish sauce

200 g (7 oz) low-fat soft cheese

1 teaspoon powdered gelatine

salt and freshly ground black pepper

For the relish

225 g (8 oz) cucumber

1 tablespoon chopped fresh dill

1 tablespoon white wine vinegar

1 tablespoon caster sugar

Serves 4. (150 Calories per serving) Preparation and cooking time 15 minutes + chilling. Freezing recommended for the mousse only. So easy and delicious. When entertaining guests, serve this as a starter and no one will ever know it's a Weight Watchers dish!

1 To prepare the mousse, snip the salmon into small pieces and place in a food processor with the lemon zest, juice, horseradish sauce and low-fat soft cheese. Blend until smooth and then transfer to a mixing bowl.

2 Place 2 tablespoons of cold water in a small bowl. Sprinkle the gelatine over and leave to stand for 5 minutes until it looks spongy. Place over a pan of gently simmering water and heat for about 2 minutes until the gelatine mixture goes clear and runny. Remove from the heat and beat into the salmon mixture. Season to taste, then transfer to a suitable container and chill for at least 2 hours.

3 To prepare the relish, peel the cucumber and slice in half lengthways. Use a small spoon to scoop the seeds out. Slice the cucumber as thinly as you can. You can use the slicing side of a grater for this job. Transfer to a bowl and toss with the chopped dill, wine vinegar and sugar. Chill until required.

4 To serve, arrange some of the cucumber relish on to individual serving plates and top with a scoopful of smoked salmon mousse.

Cook's note: Most deli counters sell smoked salmon pieces that are a lot cheaper than sliced smoked salmon and perfect to use in this recipe.

Toasted courgette and ricotta wraps

4½	Points per serving
19	Total Points per recipe

4 large courgettes, wiped and trimmed

2 tablespoons olive oil

3 shallots, finely chopped

1 garlic clove, crushed

2 tomatoes, skinned, de-seeded and diced

200 g (7 oz) ricotta cheese

1 egg, beaten

25 g (1 oz) fresh wholemeal breadcrumbs

1 tablespoon fresh basil, roughly torn

salt and freshly ground black pepper

15 g (½ oz) fresh parmesan, grated

Serves 4. (230 Calories per serving) Preparation time 20 minutes. Cooking time 20 minutes. Freezing recommended. Impress your guests with these moreish bite-sized wraps. Make sure you choose large courgettes since they're easier to work with.

1 Bring a large pan of lightly salted water to the boil. Thinly slice the courgettes horizontally to make long thin strips and cook in the boiling water for 2 minutes to soften them. Drain on to sheets of double thickness kitchen paper.

2 Heat 1 tablespoonful of oil in a pan and add the shallots and garlic. Cover and cook over a low heat for 10 minutes, until very soft but not browned.

3 Remove from the heat and add the tomatoes, ricotta cheese, egg, breadcrumbs, basil and seasoning. Mix together thoroughly, then take spoonfuls of the mixture and place on one end of each courgette strip and roll up, enclosing the filling.

4 Preheat the oven to Gas Mark 5/190°C/375°F. Lift the courgette wraps on to a non-stick baking sheet, brush with remaining oil and sprinkle with grated parmesan. Bake for 15 to 20 minutes, until piping hot.

Cook's note: You can eat these tasty wraps hot or cold, they're delicious either way.

Chicken soup with noodles

4½	Points per serving
18½	Total Points per recipe

4 medium boneless, skinless chicken thighs

2 teaspoons sunflower oil

1 garlic clove, crushed

2.5 cm (1-inch) piece of root ginger, peeled and grated

1 red chilli, de-seeded and finely chopped

850 ml (1½ pints) chicken stock

2 tablespoons soy sauce

2 tablespoons fresh lime juice

125 g (4½ oz) baby corn, trimmed and halved

1 red pepper, de-seeded and cut into thin strips

6 spring onions, trimmed and shredded

125 g (4½ oz) thread egg noodles

2 tablespoons chopped fresh coriander

Serves 4. (345 Calories per serving) Preparation time 10 minutes. Cooking time 20 minutes. Freezing recommended.

1 Grill the chicken thighs under a medium heat for 10 minutes until thoroughly cooked through. Allow to cool a little and then shred the meat finely by pulling at it with two forks.

2 Heat the sunflower oil in a large pan and add the garlic, ginger and chilli. Cook for 1 minute and then add the shredded chicken, stock, soy sauce, lime juice, baby corn and red pepper.

3 Bring to the boil, reduce the heat and then simmer for 5 minutes. Add the spring onions and noodles to the pan. Cook for a further 5 minutes until the noodles are tender.

4 To serve, ladle into soup bowls and sprinkle with the chopped coriander.

Cook's note: The success of this soup really relies on the fresh herbs and spices that give a wonderful freshness to the soup. However, you can use a teaspoonful of dried chilli flakes if you don't have a fresh chilli to hand.

spicy chips with lime and coriander salsa

4	Points per serving
17	Total Points per recipe

For the salsa

450 g (1 lb) ripe tomatoes

1 small red onion, finely chopped

3 tablespoons chopped fresh coriander

finely grated zest and juice of 1 lime

1 tablespoon olive oil

1 teaspoon balsamic vinegar

1 tablespoon lime marmalade

For the chips

700 g (1 lb 9 oz) potatoes (such as Desirée, Maris Piper)

2 tablespoons sunflower oil

2 tablespoons chilli seasoning

1 teaspoon salt

menu plan

Fast Food for Friends

When friends pop round for drinks or a chat, serve these tasty low-fat nibbles instead of biscuits.

Spicy Chips with Lime and Coriander Salsa
page 30, (1 serving) 4 Points

Chilli Corn Fritters
page 38, (1 serving) 3 Points

Total Points: 7 Points

Serves 4. (305 Calories per serving) Preparation time 15 minutes. Cooking time 30 minutes. Freezing recommended. If you leave the skins on the potatoes, they will become wonderfully crispy in the oven. You can of course peel them if you prefer to but they're not half as nice!

1 To make the salsa, place the tomatoes in a bowl and cover with boiling water. Leave for 2 minutes and then drain. Peel away the skins. Quarter the tomatoes, discard the seeds and dice the flesh roughly.

2 Add the red onion and coriander and toss together well. Mix together the lime zest and juice, olive oil, vinegar and lime marmalade. Drizzle over the tomato mixture and toss well. Cover and chill until required.

3 To prepare the chips, preheat the oven to Gas Mark 6/200°C/400°F. Scrub the potatoes and cut into fat chips. Place in a large container with a tight-fitting lid and add the oil, chilli seasoning and salt. Cover tightly and shake the container well so each potato chip gets coated.

4 Arrange in an even layer on a non-stick baking parchment. Bake for 25 to 30 minutes, until cooked through and crunchy. Serve at once with the salsa.

Cook's note: If you have time, prepare the salsa at least 4 hours ahead of time. As it sits, the flavours marry together for a better result.

Broad bean and mint risotto

5½	Points per serving
21½	Total Points per recipe

1 tablespoon olive oil

4 shallots, thinly sliced

1 garlic clove, peeled and crushed

225 g (8 oz) risotto rice

30 ml (1 fl oz) vermouth (optional)

700 ml (1¼ pints) vegetable stock

350 g (12 oz) broad beans, shelled

25 g (1 oz) fresh parmesan, grated

2 tablespoons chopped fresh mint

Ⓥ *Serves 4. (315 Calories per serving) Preparation time 15 minutes Cooking time 30 minutes. Freezing recommended. Shelling the broad beans is time-consuming but the end result with the bright green beans make it really worthwhile. To save time, you could use frozen peas instead but it won't be the same. Vermouth lifts the taste of risotto from super to sublime so do try it for a treat.*

1 Heat the olive oil in a large pan and cook the shallots and garlic for 2 to 3 minutes, until just beginning to soften. Add the rice and stir well. Cook for a further 2 to 3 minutes.

2 Stir in the vermouth, if using. Then gradually add the stock a little at a time, waiting for what you add to be absorbed by the rice before adding more.

3 As you are adding the last of the stock, toss in the beans, parmesan and mint. Continue cooking until the rice is creamy and tender. A successful risotto should also be a bit sloppy. It should take about 20 minutes in all. Serve at once.

Cook's note: If you're freezing this, you may want to add some extra stock as you heat it through.

Linguine pasta with fresh tomato and lemon sauce

4	Points per serving
15½	Total Points per recipe

450 g (1 lb) fresh ripe tomatoes

300 ml (10 fl oz) tomato juice

2 tablespoons tomato purée

finely grated zest of 1 lemon

2 tablespoons fresh lemon juice

1 teaspoon caster sugar

1 vegetable stock cube, crumbled

1 tablespoon fresh chives, snipped

350 g (12 oz) fresh linguine pasta

salt and freshly ground black pepper

Ⓥ *Serves 4. (135 Calories per serving) Preparation time 10 minutes. Cooking time 15 minutes. Freezing recommended. This is really more of a light snack than a starter. For a gourmet-style lunch, serve with a fresh green salad.*

1 Place the tomatoes in a bowl and cover with boiling water. Leave to stand for 2 minutes, then drain and peel away the skins. Quarter the tomatoes, scoop out the seeds and discard. Roughly dice the flesh.

2 Place the tomatoes in a pan with the tomato juice, tomato purée, lemon zest and juice, caster sugar and crumbled stock cube. Bring to the boil, reduce the heat and simmer for 10 minutes, stirring from time to time. Stir in the chives and season to taste.

3 Cook the pasta in a pan of lightly salted boiling water until tender. It's best to follow the instructions on the packet for this but roughly it takes about 3 to 5 minutes. Drain thoroughly and toss with the tomato and lemon sauce.

4 Pile on to warmed serving dishes and serve hot with an extra grinding of black pepper.

Roasted rosemary vegetables on ciabatta

4½	Points per serving
18½	Total Points per recipe

1 red pepper, de-seeded and roughly diced

1 green pepper, de-seeded and roughly diced

1 courgette, wiped and thickly sliced

175 g (6 oz) open-cap mushrooms, wiped and halved

1 tablespoon olive oil

1 teaspoon balsamic vinegar

2 sprigs of fresh rosemary

2 whole garlic cloves

4 tomatoes, quartered

1 ciabatta loaf, halved horizontally

2 tablespoons sundried tomato purée

salt and freshly ground black pepper

Ⓥ Serves 4. (385 Calories per serving) Preparation time 10 minutes. Cooking time 25 minutes. Freezing recommended. This is a bit like a posh pizza and is delicious served warm or cold. Wrap well in plenty of greaseproof paper and foil for an excellent lunchtime snack.

1 Preheat the oven to Gas Mark 6/200°C/400°F. Place the peppers, courgette and mushrooms in a bowl. Add the oil, vinegar, salt and black pepper and toss together well.

2 Arrange on a baking sheet and add the rosemary and garlic cloves. Roast in the oven for 20 minutes. Add the tomato quarters and return to the oven for 5 minutes.

3 Cut each ciabatta half in half again and spread with sundried tomato purée. Warm through in the oven for 5 minutes.

4 To serve, pile the roasted vegetables on to ciabatta, discarding the rosemary and whole garlic cloves. Serve hot.

Variation: You can use almost any vegetable you prefer as a topping and without sacrificing Points! Next time, try adding baby corn, wedges of red onion, aubergine or celery.

Spicy Thai prawn kebabs

2	Points per serving
8	Total Points per recipe

450 g (1 lb) king prawns

finely grated zest and juice of 2 limes

2 tablespoons fish sauce

1 tablespoon tomato purée

1 garlic clove, peeled and crushed

1 teaspoon Thai seven spice seasoning

2 tablespoons chopped fresh coriander

1 tablespoon sunflower oil

1 teaspoon demerara sugar

Serves 4. (140 Calories per serving) Preparation and cooking time 15 minutes + marinating. Freezing recommended if using fresh prawns. Choose large plump king prawns and leave the tail on for an attractive finish if entertaining.

1 Peel the king prawns, leaving their tails on if desired and place in a shallow non-metallic dish.

2 Mix together the grated lime zest and juice, fish sauce, tomato purée, garlic, Thai seven spice, coriander, sunflower oil and sugar. Drizzle over the prawns. Toss well, cover and leave to marinate for 30 minutes.

3 Soak 8 wooden skewers in water for 20 minutes (this will prevent them burning when you grill the kebabs).

4 Thread the prawns evenly on to the wooden skewers and grill for 5 minutes, turning half-way through. Serve hot.

Variation: Cubes of skinless salmon tail fillet can be used instead of prawns if preferred. The Points per serving will be 3½.

vegetable rosti cakes with rocket

2	Points per serving
8	Total Points per recipe

350 g (12 oz) potatoes, peeled

1 teaspoon salt

225 g (8 oz) carrots, peeled

175 g (6 oz) fennel bulb, very finely shredded

1 egg, beaten

1 tablespoon olive oil

1 tablespoon chopped fresh parsley

150 g (5½ oz) fresh rocket, washed

freshly ground black pepper

Ⓥ Serves 4. (165 Calories per serving) Preparation time 10 minutes. Cooking time 25 minutes. Freezing recommended.

1 Coarsely grate the potatoes and place in a bowl. Sprinkle with a teaspoon of salt and leave to stand for 10 minutes (this helps draw out any excess moisture from the potatoes). Squeeze the potatoes, discarding the salty liquid and place in a clean bowl.

2 Coarsely grate the carrots and add to the potato together with the fennel, beaten egg, oil, parsley and black pepper. Mix together thoroughly.

3 Wipe out a heavy-based non-stick pan with a little of the olive oil and heat. Cooking in two batches, drop 4 spoonfuls of the rosti mixture on to the pan and cook over a medium low heat for 6 to 7 minutes per side. Repeat with the remaining mixture.

4 Pile equal amounts of rocket on to 4 serving plates and top each with 2 crispy cooked rosti and serve at once.

Cook's note: For a more even-shaped rosti, place a metal cooking ring or pastry cutter in the frying-pan. Press in a little of the rosti mixture and carefully remove the ring. Repeat with the remaining mixture.

Potato and artichoke frittata

3	Points per serving
13	Total Points per recipe

225 g (8 oz) potatoes, peeled and thinly sliced

1 tablespoon vegetable oil

1 red onion, peeled and sliced

425 g (15 oz) canned artichoke hearts, drained and quartered

5 eggs

5 tablespoons skimmed milk

½ teaspoon dried thyme

salt and freshly ground black pepper

Ⓥ Serves 4 (230 Calories per serving) Preparation time 15 minutes. Cooking time 20 minutes. Freezing not recommended. Any leftovers are delicious eaten cold the next day or packed into your lunchbox.

1 Bring a pan of lightly salted water to the boil and cook the potato slices for 5 minutes. Drain thoroughly.

2 Meanwhile, heat the oil in a 20 cm (8-inch) non-stick frying-pan and add the onion. Cook for 5 minutes until softened. Add the cooked potato slices and artichoke hearts to the pan. Carefully toss with a wooden spatula so they are evenly distributed.

3 Beat together the eggs, milk, thyme and seasoning and pour into the pan. Cook over a low heat for about 5 minutes until you see the edges beginning to set.

4 Transfer the pan to a moderate grill and cook the top for a further 2 to 3 minutes until set and golden. Leave to stand in the pan for 5 minutes, then carefully transfer to a serving plate and cut into wedges to serve.

Cook's note: Omelettes are the perfect way to use up leftover veggies; basically anything goes.

Salmon and horseradish fish cakes

3½	Points per serving
14	Total Points per recipe

Serves 4. (230 Calories per serving) Preparation time 20 minutes. Cooking time 25 minutes. Freezing recommended.

450 g (1 lb) potatoes, peeled and diced

213 g can of pink salmon, drained and flaked

1 egg, beaten

1 tablespoon horseradish sauce

finely grated zest of 1 lemon

1 tablespoon freeze-dried parsley

plain flour, for dusting

1 tablespoon sunflower oil

salt and freshly ground black pepper

1 Bring a pan of lightly salted water to the boil and cook the potatoes until tender. Drain and mash thoroughly.

2 Add the flaked salmon, beaten egg, horseradish sauce, lemon zest, parsley and seasoning. Mix together thoroughly.

3 Shape the mixture into 8 cakes using lightly floured hands. Heat the oil in a heavy-based frying-pan and cook the fish cakes for 3 to 4 minutes per side, until golden.

Cook's note: Stir a little horseradish into low-fat plain fromage frais as a tasty dip but don't forget to add the extra Points.

Variation: Substitute red salmon or canned tuna if you prefer. The Points per serving will be 4.

Stuffed mushrooms

3	Points per serving
11½	Total Points per recipe

Ⓥ Serves 4. (120 Calories per serving) Preparation time 15 minutes. Cooking time 25 minutes. Freezing not recommended. Try to choose even-sized mushrooms.

8 large flat mushrooms

1 tablespoon soy sauce

2 garlic cloves, crushed

200 g (7 oz) ricotta cheese

1 egg

2 tablespoons chopped fresh parsley

salt and freshly ground black pepper

1 Remove the centre stalks from the mushrooms and place in a frying-pan with the soy sauce, garlic and 2 tablespoons of water. Cover the pan and poach the mushrooms for 5 minutes. Drain from the pan reserving the juices.

2 Preheat the oven to Gas Mark 4/180°C/350°F. Arrange four of the mushrooms in a non-stick roasting tin.

3 Beat together the ricotta cheese, egg, parsley and seasoning. Divide equally between the four mushrooms in the tin. Top with the other mushrooms, drizzle with a little of the pan juices and bake for 20 minutes. Serve hot with an extra sprinkling of chopped fresh parsley.

Variation: A low-fat garlic and herb soft cheese can be used instead of ricotta for an even more garlicky flavour. Points per serving will be 1½.

Spinach, black olive and tomato pizzas

2½	Points per serving
9½	Total Points per recipe

Ⓥ Serves 4. (235 Calories per serving) Preparation and cooking time 20 minutes. Freezing not recommended.

2 English muffins, halved

2 tablespoons sun-dried tomato paste

½ teaspoon dried mixed herbs

150 g (5½ oz) baby spinach

1 beefsteak tomato, sliced

25 g (1 oz) pitted black olives, halved

50 g (1¾ oz) reduced-fat mozzarella cheese, thinly sliced

salt and freshly ground black pepper

1 Lightly toast the muffin halves on both sides. Mix together the tomato paste and mixed herbs. Spread on to one side of each muffin half.

2 Rinse the spinach and place in a pan. Cover tightly and cook for 2 minutes until wilted. Drain, squeezing out any excess moisture and arrange on top of the pizza with a slice of tomato, a few olive halves and sliced mozzarella.

3 Season well and return to the grill for 2 to 3 minutes, until the cheese has melted.

Spinach, black olive and tomato pizza

Baked leeks with ham

2	Points per serving
8½	Total Points per recipe

Serves 4. (130 Calories per serving) Preparation time 20 minutes. Cooking time 30 minutes. Freezing not recommended.

450 g (1 lb) leeks, trimmed and halved

50 g (1¾ oz) wafer-thin ham

2 tablespoons cornflour

150 ml (¼ pint) skimmed milk

200 g (7 oz) low-fat plain fromage frais

25 g (1 oz) reduced-fat red Leicester cheese, grated

2 tablespoons dried breadcrumbs

salt and freshly ground black pepper

1 Place the leeks in a frying-pan. Cover with boiling water and simmer gently for 5 minutes. Drain on to absorbent kitchen paper.

2 Wrap each piece of leek in slices of wafer-thin ham and arrange in a shallow ovenproof dish. Preheat the oven to Gas Mark 6/200°C/400°F.

3 Mix together the cornflour with a little of the milk to form a thin paste. Heat the remaining milk with the fromage frais until almost boiling and then stir in the cornflour paste. Cook, stirring until the sauce thickens. Season to taste and then pour over the leeks and ham.

4 Mix together the cheese and breadcrumbs and sprinkle over the top. Bake for 20 minutes until the cheese has melted and the sauce is bubbling.

Cook's note: Make sure you drain the leeks thoroughly otherwise the liquid will seep out during cooking and the sauce will become too runny.

Curried root vegetable and couscous lunch pot

4	Points per serving
16½	Total Points per recipe

225 g (8 oz) couscous

finely grated zest of 1 lemon

300 ml (½ pint) boiling water

1 tablespoon olive oil

1 onion, sliced

225 g (8 oz) carrots, peeled and sliced

350 g (12 oz) swede, peeled and diced

225 g (8 oz) parsnips, peeled and sliced

1 tablespoon medium curry powder

¼ teaspoon ground cinnamon

400 g (14 oz) canned chopped tomatoes

150 ml (¼ pint) vegetable stock

2 tablespoons chopped fresh coriander

salt and freshly ground black pepper

Ⓥ *Serves 4. (355 Calories per serving) Preparation time 20 minutes. Cooking time 35 minutes. Freezing recommended. Pack into pots for a healthy lunchtime treat.*

1 Place the couscous and lemon zest in a bowl and pour the boiling water over. Fluff the couscous up with a fork, cover the bowl with a clean tea towel. Leave to stand for 10 minutes, fluffing it up from time to time.

2 Meanwhile, heat the oil in a pan and cook the onion, carrots, swede and parsnips for 5 minutes. Stir in the curry powder and cinnamon and cook for a further 2 minutes.

3 Add the chopped tomatoes, stock and seasoning and bring to the boil. Cover and simmer for 20 minutes, until the vegetables are tender. Remove the lid, raise the heat and allow the juices to bubble and evaporate to a thick sauce.

4 Combine the couscous with the vegetable mixture, seasoning and coriander. Eat hot or allow to cool and chill until required.

Aubergine and tomato layer

2	Points per serving
7½	Total Points per recipe

1 aubergine, sliced into 8 rings
2 tablespoons fresh lemon juice
1 small onion, finely chopped
1 garlic clove, crushed
2 tablespoons tomato purée
1 teaspoon dried oregano
225 g (8 oz) canned chopped tomatoes
25 g (1 oz) fresh parmesan, grated
2 tablespoons dried breadcrumbs
1 tablespoon olive oil
salt and freshly ground black pepper

Ⓥ Serves 4. (90 Calories per serving) Preparation time 20 minutes. Cooking time 35 minutes. Freezing recommended. A delightful Italian-style starter. Delicious served with a rocket salad.

1 Bring a pan of lightly salted water to the boil and cook the aubergine slices for 5 minutes with the lemon juice. Drain on absorbent kitchen paper.
2 Place the chopped onion, garlic, tomato purée, oregano and chopped tomatoes in a small pan. Bring to the boil, reduce the heat and simmer for 10 minutes. Season to taste.
3 Preheat the oven to Gas Mark 4/180°C/350°F. Line a baking sheet with non-stick baking parchment. Place 4 slices of aubergine on the baking sheet and spoon some tomato sauce over each one. Top with another aubergine slice and the remainder of the tomato sauce.
4 Mix together the parmesan, breadcrumbs and olive oil. Scatter equal amounts over each aubergine layer. Bake for 25 minutes and serve hot.

Asparagus, spring onion and bacon hash

3½	Points per serving
13½	Total Points per recipe

450 g (1 lb) new potatoes
4 rashers lean back bacon, trimmed of fat
100 g (3½ oz) fine asparagus, trimmed
6 spring onions, trimmed and sliced
1 tablespoon olive oil
1 teaspoon wholegrain mustard
salt and freshly ground black pepper

Serves 4. (220 Calories per serving) Preparation time 15 minutes. Cooking time 35 minutes. Freezing not recommended. Real comfort food. Be sure not to over-mash the potatoes; this dish should have a chunky texture. Serve with some tomato ketchup if you wish. This will add a ½ Point per 2 tablespoons.

1 Scrub the new potatoes and place in a pan of lightly salted boiling water. Simmer for 20 minutes until cooked through. Drain well, then crush roughly with a potato masher.
2 Meanwhile, grill the bacon until crispy, then snip into small pieces. Cook the asparagus in boiling water for 2 minutes and then drain thoroughly. Toss with the snipped bacon, spring onions and crushed potatoes to make the hash.
3 Heat the olive oil and mustard in a frying-pan, add the hash and stir-fry for 10 minutes over a medium heat, turning with a wooden spatula from time to time.
4 Season to taste, then serve hot.
Cook's note: Mix 1 tablespoonful of tomato purée with 1 skinned, seeded and diced fresh tomato, salt and freshly ground black pepper for a no-Point sauce.

Chilli corn fritters

3	Points per serving
13	Total Points per recipe

50 g (1¾ oz) polenta
200 g (7 oz) canned sweetcorn
1 teaspoon chilli flakes
3 tablespoons chopped fresh coriander
1 tablespoon Thai green curry paste
1 tablespoon fish sauce
1 egg
1 tablespoon sunflower oil

Serves 4. (170 Calories per serving) Preparation and cooking time 15 minutes. Freezing recommended. You can prepare these tasty cakes up to 2 days before you want to eat them, then just heat through to serve.

1 Place the polenta in a mixing bowl and stir in the canned sweetcorn, chilli flakes, coriander, curry paste, fish sauce and egg. Mix together thoroughly until you have a combined sloppy mixture.
2 Heat a little oil in a frying-pan, then drop spoonfuls of the mixture into the pan. Cook over a medium low heat for 3 to 4 minutes per side, until cooked through and golden.
Variation: You can serve these cakes with a cucumber salad to compliment their spiciness. Peel and halve a cucumber lengthways. Scoop out the seeds, dice the flesh and mix with 1 tablespoon of rice wine vinegar and a pinch of caster sugar.

Scrambled eggs with prawns and beansprouts

5	Points per serving
5	Total Points per recipe

1 teaspoon sunflower oil
50 g (1¾ oz) beansprouts
1 spring onion, trimmed and shredded
50 g (1¾ oz) peeled prawns
2 eggs
1 tablespoon light soy sauce
1 tablespoon chopped fresh coriander

Serves 1. (150 Calories per serving) Preparation and cooking time 10 minutes. Freezing not recommended. A 10 minute snack for those hurried lunch hours.

1 Heat the sunflower oil in a small pan and stir-fry the beansprouts, spring onion and prawns for 2 minutes.
2 Beat together the eggs, soy sauce and coriander. Pour over the prawns and beansprouts. Cook over a medium heat for 2 to 3 minutes, until egg just sets and scrambles. Don't overcook or the eggs will become rubbery and begin to separate.
Cook's note: To use the microwave for this dish, toss together the oil, beansprouts, spring onions and prawns in a microwave-proof bowl. Microwave on 100% high for 1 minute. Stir in the beaten eggs and microwave for a further 2 minutes, stirring every 30 seconds. Stand for 2 minutes before serving.

Soy-glazed chicken livers

3½	Points per serving
15	Total Points per recipe

1 tablespoon sunflower oil
2 garlic cloves
350 g (12 oz) chicken livers, halved
1 tablespoon cornflour
1 teaspoon Chinese five-spice powder
3 tablespoons soy sauce
1 tablespoon clear honey
1 tablespoon sherry
1 tablespoon tomato purée
fresh salad leaves, to serve

Serves 4. (160 Calories per serving) Preparation and cooking time 20 minutes. Freezing not recommended. Chicken livers are relatively inexpensive and take very little preparation and cooking. Try out this recipe; it may become a firm favourite.

1 Heat the sunflower oil in a large frying-pan and fry the garlic for a few seconds.
2 Toss the chicken livers with the cornflour and five spice powder. Add to the pan and stir-fry for 5 minutes. Don't overcook them or they'll toughen up.
3 Mix together the soy sauce, honey, sherry and tomato purée. Add to the pan. Cook until the juices bubble and then spoon on to a bed of crisp fresh salad leaves. Serve at once.

Macaroni cheese gratins

4½	Points per serving
19	Total Points per recipe

150 g (5½ oz) quick cook macaroni

2 tablespoons cornflour

300 ml (½ pint) skimmed milk

a pinch of ground nutmeg

75 g (2¾ oz) half-fat Cheddar cheese, grated

1 teaspoon olive oil

1 tablespoonful Worcestershire sauce

175 g (6 oz) carrots, peeled and grated

1 red onion, peeled and thinly sliced

1 courgette, wiped and grated

1 tablespoon dried breadcrumbs

1 tablespoon grated parmesan

salt and freshly ground black pepper

(V) if using vegetarian cheese Serves 4. (300 Calories per serving) Preparation time 20 minutes. Cooking time 35 minutes. Freezing recommended.

1 Bring a pan of lightly salted water to the boil and cook the macaroni as directed on the packet. Drain well.

2 Meanwhile, mix the cornflour with a little of the milk to form a thin paste. Heat the remaining milk until boiling and pour over the cornflour paste. Mix well and return to the heat. Cook, stirring for 2 to 3 minutes until you have a smooth thickened sauce.

3 Stir the nutmeg and grated cheese into the sauce. Then add the drained macaroni and stir well.

4 Preheat the oven to Gas Mark 5/190°C/375°F.

5 Heat the olive oil in a pan with the Worcestershire sauce. Add the grated carrot, onion and courgette and cover. Cook for 2 to 3 minutes to just soften. Season to taste and then divide between 4 individual ramekins. Top with macaroni cheese.

6 Mix together the breadcrumbs and parmesan and sprinkle over the top. Bake for 15 minutes, then serve hot with a salad garnish.

Cook's note: Children will love these cheesy little pots. And since they're made in individual pots, they get to have one each!

Pink grapefruit, mint and smoked trout cocktail

3	Points per serving
12	Total Points per recipe

2 medium pink grapefruit, peeled and
    segmented

225 g (8 oz) smoked trout fillet, flaked

225 g (8 oz) cucumber, peeled and halved
    lengthways

2 tablespoons chopped fresh mint

salt and freshly ground black pepper

For the sauce

4 tablespoons half-fat crème fraîche

1 teaspoon clear honey

1 teaspoon tomato purée

1 tablespoon fresh lemon juice

Serves 4. (160 Calories per serving) Preparation time 15 minutes. Freezing not recommended. A deliciously refreshing starter or handy lunchpot snack. You can use ordinary grapefruit if you prefer to but the pink grapefruit is much more attractive.

1 Place the grapefruit segments in a mixing bowl with the flaked smoked trout and toss together well.

2 Use a teaspoon to scrape away the seeds from the cucumber. Slice thinly and add to the grapefruit and trout along with the mint and seasoning. Toss together thoroughly and then divide equally between 4 serving plates.

3 For the sauce, beat together the crème fraîche, honey, tomato purée and lemon juice in a small bowl. Drizzle a little over each salad just before serving.

Cook's note: If you want to use this as a lunchtime snack pot, toss the salad ingredients together and pile into a plastic container. Mix together the dressing ingredients and spoon into a small plastic bag, seal well. Drizzle over salad just before eating.

3 chapter

salads

These days, salads are a world apart from the way they used to be. There's a huge array of fresh ingredients and exciting new flavours to choose from, making each recipe a new experience. The range of flavoured oils and vinegars, yogurts, herbs and seasonings mean that we can make lively, interesting dressings to perk up the most mundane of salad leaves.

So don't ever think of salads as being dull and boring. With a little imagination, they can be the most interesting food on your plate.

Hot turkey salad

1½	Points per serving
6½	Total Points per recipe

1 head of Chinese leaves, shredded

3 celery sticks, finely sliced

1 red or yellow pepper, de-seeded and cut
    into fine strips

6 spring onions or 1 small red onion,
    finely sliced

2 tablespoons stir-fry oil or sesame oil

1–2 teaspoons chilli sauce

1 tablespoon lemon juice

1 tablespoon soy sauce

350 g (12 oz) cooked turkey, torn into shreds

freshly ground black pepper, to season

snipped chives or cress, to garnish

Serves 4. (235 Calories per serving) Preparation and cooking time 20 minutes. Freezing not recommended. If you're faced with an abundance of cold turkey, why not transform it into a delicious turkey salad, zapped up with a lively chilli dressing to give it a bit of a kick?

1 Mix together the Chinese leaves, celery, pepper, spring onions or onion. Divide between four serving bowls or plates.

2 Make the dressing by mixing together 1 tablespoon of stir-fry oil or sesame oil with the chilli sauce, lemon juice and soy sauce. Season with pepper; you won't need any salt because the soy sauce is salty.

3 Heat the remaining oil in a wok or frying pan. Add the strips of cooked turkey, stir-frying them over a high heat until crispy and brown. Pile on top of the salads.

4 Sprinkle the salads with the dressing, then serve, garnished with snipped chives or cress.

Cook's note: Stir-fry oil is flavoured with ginger and garlic, and it makes a tasty base for the spicy salad dressing, so don't just think of it for stir-frying.

Variation: Instead of Chinese leaves, use a little Gem lettuce and a head of chicory, or use a bag of mixed salad leaves.

Italian rice salad

4½	Points per serving
19	Total Points per recipe

2 tablespoons olive oil

2 tablespoons red wine vinegar

1 tablespoon lemon juice

pinch of caster sugar

5 cm (2-inch) piece of cucumber, chopped

12 baby plum or cherry tomatoes, halved

25 g (1 oz) pitted black olives, halved

100 g (3½ oz) reduced-fat mozzarella
    cheese, cut into chunks

225 g (8 oz) long grain rice, cooked

4 beef tomatoes, thinly sliced

1 small red (or ordinary) onion, sliced into
    thin rings

salt and freshly ground black pepper

To serve

4 thin slices of genuine Parma ham

about 12 basil leaves, torn into shreds

Serves 4. (410 Calories per serving) Preparation time 15 minutes. Freezing not recommended.

1 Make the salad dressing by whisking together the oil, vinegar, lemon juice and caster sugar. Season to taste with salt and pepper.

2 Mix together the cucumber, plum or cherry tomatoes, olives, mozzarella and rice. Add the dressing and mix well.

3 Arrange the sliced beef tomatoes and onion around the edge of four serving plates. Pile the rice salad in the middle, then serve, garnishing each portion with a slice of Parma ham and basil leaves.

Weight Watchers note: If you don't like olives, simply omit them from the recipe. The Points will be the same.

Warm chicken salad with lemon dressing

3½	Points per serving
15	Total Points per recipe

4 medium skinless, boneless chicken breasts

175 g (6 oz) fine green beans, trimmed

1 bag rocket leaves (or watercress)

a large handful of young spinach leaves, rinsed

½ Iceberg lettuce, shredded

1 teaspoon finely grated lemon zest

1 tablespoon lemon juice

1 tablespoon white wine or rice vinegar

2 tablespoons olive oil

1 teaspoon Dijon mustard

salt and freshly ground black pepper

Serves 4. (195 Calories per serving) Preparation time 10 minutes. Cooking time 15 minutes. Freezing not recommended. You can buy so many delicious salad leaves these days which give such great flavour to your salads.

1 Preheat the grill.

2 Grill the chicken breasts, turning once, until tender; they will take about 15 minutes to cook. At the same time, lightly cook the green beans in boiling, salted water until just tender, about 4 minutes.

3 Meanwhile, rinse all the salad leaves and arrange in four serving bowls. Mix together the lemon zest and juice, vinegar, olive oil, mustard and seasoning.

4 Drain the green beans, then refresh them in cold water and drain well.

5 Slice the hot chicken and divide between the salads with the beans. Spoon the dressing over each portion, and serve at once.

Variation: Use a couple of bags of mixed salad leaves instead of the rocket, spinach and iceberg lettuce.

Warm sesame chicken salad

3	Points per serving
11½	Total Points per recipe

2 tablespoons stir-fry oil or vegetable oil

350 g (12 oz) skinless chicken breasts, sliced into strips

4 celery sticks, finely sliced

1 red or yellow pepper, de-seeded and finely sliced

1 large carrot, cut into fine strips

1 small leek, finely sliced

2 teaspoons sesame seeds

1 tablespoon rice or white wine vinegar

a few drops of chilli sauce

4 generous handfuls of lamb's lettuce

salt and freshly ground black pepper

Serves 4. (210 Calories per serving) Preparation and cooking time 20 minutes. Freezing not recommended

1 Heat 1 tablespoon of the oil in a wok or large frying-pan. Add the chicken and stir-fry for 4–5 minutes, until browned and cooked.

2 Add the celery, pepper, carrot and leek to the wok or frying-pan and stir-fry for 1–2 more minutes, then stir in the sesame seeds.

3 In a salad bowl, whisk together the remaining oil, vinegar and chilli sauce. Season with salt and pepper.

4 Add the lamb's lettuce, chicken and vegetables to the salad bowl. Toss together, then serve at once.

Cook's note: Stir-fry oil is flavoured with ginger, garlic and spices, and it gives an excellent flavour to this recipe.

Variation: If you can't find lamb's lettuce, use watercress or young spinach leaves instead.

vegetable salad with lime and coriander vinaigrette

½	Point per serving
2½	Total Points per recipe

175 g (6 oz) baby corn, halved
100 g (3½ oz) sugar snap peas or
    mangetout, trimmed
100 g (3½ oz) green beans, sliced
2 celery sticks, sliced
1 small carrot, finely sliced
1 courgette, sliced
100 g (3½ oz) small asparagus spears
12 cherry tomatoes, halved

For the dressing

1 tablespoon olive oil
½ teaspoon finely grated lime zest
1 tablespoon lime juice
1 tablespoon rice or white wine vinegar
1 tablespoon chopped fresh coriander
    or chives
salt and freshly ground black pepper

Serves 4. (90 Calories per serving) Preparation and cooking time 20 minutes. Freezing not recommended. This warm vegetable salad tastes wonderful with its light vinaigrette dressing flavoured with lime juice and chopped coriander.

1 Steam all the vegetables, except the cherry tomatoes, over gently boiling water until just tender, about 5–8 minutes, making sure that they retain a slightly crunchy texture.
2 Meanwhile, mix together the oil, lime zest, lime juice and vinegar. Add the chopped fresh coriander or chives. Season with salt and pepper.
3 When the vegetables are cooked, transfer them to four individual serving plates. Divide the cherry tomatoes between them, then drizzle a little dressing over each one.
Cook's note: You don't have to serve this salad warm. Just allow it to cool in its dressing to take on a delicious flavour.
Variation: Use lemon zest and juice instead of lime, if you prefer.

Lamb's lettuce niçoise

3	Points per serving
12½	Total Points per recipe

150 g (5½ oz) fine green beans
2 tablespoons olive oil
1 teaspoon finely grated lemon zest
1 tablespoon lemon juice
1 teaspoon Dijon or wholegrain mustard
1 tablespoon white wine or rice vinegar
4 generous handfuls of lamb's lettuce
4 tomatoes, cut into wedges
20 pitted black olives
4 small eggs, hard-boiled and quartered
185 g can of tuna chunks in water or
    brine, drained
salt and freshly ground black pepper
chopped fresh parsley, to garnish

Serves 4. (230 Calories per serving) Preparation and cooking time 15 minutes. Freezing not recommended

1 Cook the beans in lightly salted boiling water until just tender – about 5 minutes.
2 While the beans are cooking, make up the dressing by whisking together the olive oil, lemon zest and juice, mustard and vinegar. Season with a little salt and pepper.
3 Drain the beans and add the dressing, tossing to coat. Allow to cool for a few minutes.
4 Meanwhile, arrange the lamb's lettuce and tomatoes on four serving plates. Divide the warm beans between them, then top each salad with 5 olives, 1 egg and an equal amount of tuna. Sprinkle with parsley, then serve.
Variation: If you're not keen on olives, simply leave them out. The Points per serving will be the same.

Roasted vegetable salad with toasted almonds

4	Points per serving
17	Total Points per recipe

Serves 4. (225 Calories per serving) Preparation time 10 minutes. Cooking time 25 minutes. Freezing not recommended

1 red pepper, de-seeded and cut into chunks

1 yellow pepper, de-seeded and cut into chunks

2 courgettes, cut into chunks

1 small onion, roughly chopped

4 small tomatoes, quartered

2 tablespoons olive oil

4 generous handfuls of baby spinach leaves

125 g (4½ oz) feta cheese, cut into chunks

25 g (1 oz) flaked almonds

2 tablespoons lemon juice

salt and freshly ground black pepper

1 Preheat the oven to Gas Mark 6/ 200°C/400°F.

2 Put all the vegetables into a roasting pan. Sprinkle with the olive oil, season with salt and pepper and roast for 20–25 minutes, turning once.

3 Put the spinach leaves into four serving bowls and divide the roasted vegetables and feta cheese between them.

4 Heat a small frying-pan, add the almonds and cook for a few seconds until they are lightly browned. Spoon over the salads, then sprinkle with the lemon juice. Serve at once.

Boursin, tomato and turkey salad

2	Points per serving
3½	Total Points per recipe

Serves 2. (145 Calories per serving) Preparation and cooking time 15 minutes. Freezing not recommended.

1 bag of mixed salad leaves, rinsed

2 plum tomatoes, sliced into thin wedges

75 g (2¾ oz) Boursin Light

1 rasher of lean back bacon

3 tablespoons skimmed milk

1 tablespoon chopped fresh herbs
     (e.g. chives, parsley, basil)

freshly ground black pepper

1 Divide the mixed leaves between two serving plates. Add a sliced tomato to each.

2 Reserve about one third of the Boursin, then divide the remainder between the salads, scooping it into small spoonfuls.

3 Grill the bacon rasher until crisp.

4 Meanwhile, mix the remaining Boursin with the skimmed milk and chopped herbs to make a dressing. Season with a little black pepper.

5 Snip the bacon into pieces over the salads, drizzle with the dressing and serve at once.

Variation: Use a low-fat soft cheese instead of Boursin, if you like, and simply use ordinary tomatoes if plum tomatoes are not available. The Points will be the same.

Caesar salad with smoked mackerel and parmesan

8	Points per serving
32	Total Points per recipe

Serves 4. (455 Calories per serving) Preparation time 10 minutes. Freezing not recommended.

1 cos or Romaine lettuce, washed

4 peppered smoked mackerel fillets, skinned

8 tablespoons low-fat plain yogurt

1 teaspoon wholegrain or Dijon mustard

1 teaspoon horseradish sauce (optional)

4 tablespoons croûtons

4 teaspoons grated parmesan cheese

salt and freshly ground black pepper

1 Tear the lettuce leaves roughly and divide between four serving plates. Break up the mackerel fillets into large chunks, removing any bones. Divide the pieces between the salads.

2 Mix together the yogurt, mustard and horseradish sauce, if using. Season with salt and pepper, then drizzle over the salads and toss together.

3 Scatter 1 tablespoon of croûtons over each salad, then sprinkle each portion with 1 teaspoon of parmesan cheese.

Variation: Use smoked mackerel without the pepper, if you like.

Roasted vegetable salad
Caesar salad

Mango, watercress and wensleydale salad

4	Points per serving
16	Total Points per recipe

1 bag of mixed salad leaves, rinsed

1 bunch of watercress, trimmed

fresh herb sprigs (e.g. marjoram, thyme
    or mint)

125 g (4½ oz) red or green seedless
    grapes, halved

1 large ripe mango

125 g (4½ oz) Wensleydale cheese

4 tablespoons fat-free mustard and honey or
    vinaigrette-style dressing

salt and freshly ground black pepper

V if using vegetarian cheese Serves 4. (195 Calories per serving) Preparation time 10 minutes. Freezing not recommended. Mango is a wonderful fruit and it's delicious in this refreshing salad where it perfectly complements the flavour of mild, honey-tasting Wensleydale cheese.

1 Arrange the salad leaves and watercress on four serving plates and scatter with a few fresh herbs. Sprinkle with the grapes.

2 To prepare the mango, slice on each half of its large flat stone, then peel and chop the flesh. Scatter over the salads.

3 Crumble the cheese and divide equally between the plates. Drizzle a tablespoon of the dressing over each portion and sprinkle with a little salt and pepper. Garnish with a few extra herbs and serve at once.

Cook's note: To choose a ripe mango, it should "give" a little when pressed gently with your thumb.

Variation 1: Try using Lancashire cheese or a white Cheshire instead of Wensleydale – either will be excellent in this salad. The Points per serving will be the same.

Variation 2: If you like, use papaya instead of mango.

Salad in seconds

2	Points per serving
9	Total Points per recipe

8 medium turkey rashers

1 large bag mixed salad leaves with
    herbs, rinsed

12 cherry tomatoes, halved

400 g (14 oz) canned whole red pimientos
    (canned sweet red peppers)

finely grated zest and juice of 1 lemon

2 tablespoons olive oil

a few drops of Tabasco pepper sauce

salt and freshly ground black pepper

Serves 4. (150 Calories per serving) Preparation and cooking time 10 minutes. Freezing not recommended. Pre-packed mixed salad leaves are very convenient and they give you bags of ideas for stylish salads.

1 Preheat a hot grill.

2 Arrange the turkey rashers on the grill rack. Grill for 2 minutes on each side. Remove and drain on kitchen paper.

3 Divide salad leaves and cherry tomatoes between four serving plates. Snip the turkey rashers into pieces and sprinkle them over leaves. Drain the pimientos, tear them into strips and divide between the salads.

4 Mix the lemon zest and juice with the olive oil. Add a few drops of Tabasco sauce and season with salt and pepper. Sprinkle over the salads and serve at once.

Variation: If you're vegetarian, leave out the turkey rashers and substitute 75 g (2¾ oz) of crumbled vegetarian feta cheese. The Points per serving will be 2½.

Mango, watercress and Wensleydale salad

Summer Picnic

Accompany with some fresh
fruit and chilled drinks for a
real outdoor treat.

✳

Tuna and Three-bean Salad
page 51, (1 serving) 3½ Points

✳

Slimline Potato Salad
page 57, (1 serving) 1½ Points

✳

Mango, Watercress and Wensleydale Salad
page 48, (1 serving) 4 Points

✳

Total Points: 9 Points

Prawn, crab and baby new potato salad

3½	Points per serving
15	Total Points per recipe

750 g (1 lb 10 oz) baby new potatoes,
    scrubbed

2 tablespoons sun-dried tomato paste

2 tablespoons lime or lemon juice

6 spring onions, trimmed and finely chopped

175 g (6 oz) cherry tomatoes, halved

125 g (4½ oz) canned red pimiento (sweet
    red pepper), drained and sliced

170 g can of crab in brine, drained

225 g (8 oz) large prawns, defrosted
    if frozen

1 tablespoon capers

a few basil leaves

lime or lemon wedges, to serve

salt and freshly ground black pepper

Serves 4. (300 Calories per serving) Preparation time 15 minutes + 10 minutes cooling time. Cooking time 20 minutes. Freezing not recommended. Make the most of new potatoes by including them in wonderful salads like this one.

1 Put the potatoes into a large saucepan and simmer gently in lightly salted boiling water until just tender, about 15–20 minutes.

2 Meanwhile, in a serving bowl, mix together the sun-dried tomato paste with the lime or lemon juice.

3 Drain the cooked potatoes and add to the bowl, tossing them in the dressing. Allow them to cool for about 10 minutes.

4 When the potatoes have cooled, add the spring onions, tomatoes, pimiento and crab meat, stirring gently to mix. Season with salt and pepper, then pile on to serving plates and top with the prawns.

5 Sprinkle the salads with capers and basil leaves, then serve with lime or lemon wedges.

Cook's note: Coating the hot potatoes with the dressing means that they will absorb more of its flavour.

Greek summer vegetable salad

2	Points per serving
7½	Total Points per recipe

2 tablespoons olive oil

1 garlic clove, crushed

1 small aubergine, very finely chopped

1 red or ordinary onion, very finely chopped

1 red pepper, de-seeded and sliced

1 large courgette, sliced

125 g (4½ oz) baby corn, halved

125 g (4½ oz) fine green beans, trimmed
    and halved

3 tomatoes, finely chopped

2 tablespoons sun-dried tomato paste

2 tablespoons red wine vinegar

8 cherry tomatoes, halved

8 stoned black olives, sliced

2 tablespoons chopped fresh parsley

salt and freshly ground black pepper

Ⓥ *Serves 4. (165 Calories per serving) Preparation and cooking time 25 minutes + 5 minutes cooling time. Freezing not recommended. Enjoy a stunning plateful of lightly cooked vegetables, coated with a delicious Greek-style dressing.*

1 Heat the olive oil in a frying-pan and add the garlic, aubergine and onion, sautéing them over a medium-low heat until very soft, about 10 minutes.

2 Meanwhile, cook the red pepper, courgette, baby corn and green beans in a little boiling, lightly salted water for about 5 minutes, until just tender.

3 Transfer the aubergine mixture to a very large bowl and stir in the chopped tomatoes and tomato paste. Add the vinegar and season with salt and pepper.

4 Drain the simmered vegetables thoroughly, then tip them, whilst they are hot, into the bowl with the aubergine mixture.

5 Add the cherry tomatoes and stir to coat. Leave to cool for about 5 minutes before serving, sprinkled with the black olives and parsley.

Cook's note: Make sure that you don't overcook the vegetables; they should retain their crunch and colour.

Avocado, tomato and cucumber salad

2½	Points per serving
10	Total Points per recipe

12 Cos or Romaine lettuce leaves

225 g (8 oz) tomatoes, chopped

1 small avocado, peeled and diced

½ cucumber, diced

2 tablespoons olive oil

½ teaspoon finely grated lemon zest

2 tablespoons lemon juice

1 small garlic clove, crushed

2 teaspoons Dijon mustard

salt and freshly ground black pepper

2–3 tablespoons chopped fresh coriander,
   mint or basil (or all three), to garnish

Ⓥ Serves 4 (140 Calories per serving) Preparation time 10 minutes. Freezing not recommended. This refreshing salad is healthy and delicious and it's a great way of making the smooth, delicate flavour of avocado go a long way. I love it finished off with lots of chopped fresh coriander but you could also try mint or basil. This salad makes an excellent starter for a special meal.

1 Arrange three lettuce leaves on to each of four serving plates.

2 Mix together the tomatoes, avocado and cucumber and pile into the lettuce leaves.

3 Make the dressing by mixing together the olive oil, lemon zest and juice, garlic and mustard. Season to taste with salt and pepper.

4 Spoon the dressing over the salads and serve at once, scattered with the herbs.

Cook's note 1: Use a mixture of tomatoes for a variety of flavours – Sungold, cherry and vine tomatoes taste delicious together.

Cook's note 2: Good quality olive oil will always improve the flavour of a dressing. Because you're only using a small amount, you might as well make sure it has a fine, fruity flavour.

Variation: If you can't get Cos or Romaine lettuce, use chicory instead.

Tuna and three bean salad

3½	Points per serving
14	Total Points per recipe

75 g (2¾ oz) fine green beans, trimmed
   and chopped

2 tablespoons tomato purée

1 tablespoon lemon juice

1 tablespoon white wine or cider vinegar

1 small red or ordinary onion, finely chopped

400 g can of red kidney beans, rinsed
   and drained

400 g can of cannellini beans, rinsed and
   drained

180 g can of tuna chunks in brine or water,
   drained

2 tablespoons chopped fresh parsley

salt and freshly ground black pepper

Serves 4. (180 Calories per serving) Preparation and cooking time 15 minutes. Freezing not recommended.

1 Cook the green beans in a small amount of lightly salted boiling water until just tender – about 5 minutes.

2 Meanwhile, in a large salad bowl, mix together the tomato purée, lemon juice and vinegar. Add the onion, then the drained canned beans. Mix together thoroughly.

3 Add the tuna chunks and parsley. Season with salt and pepper, stir together gently to mix, then refrigerate until ready to serve.

Cook's note: Avoid mixing the salad vigorously once the tuna has been added – it's best if it doesn't break up too much.

Variation: Use 2 × 400 g cans of mixed beans instead of the red kidney and cannellini beans. The Points per serving will be the same.

Weight Watchers note: To add more bulk to the salad without adding further Points, stir in a couple of chopped tomatoes and a 10 cm (4-inch) piece of chopped cucumber.

menu plan

Store Cupboard Lunch

Just reach into the cupboard to
make this tasty two-course meal.
For extra colour and flavour,
serve a mixed leaf salad with
the main course, drizzled with
Point-free dressing.

Cracked Wheat Salad with Feta,
Mint and Apricots
page 53, (1 serving) 6½ Points

Three Minute Trifle
page 184, (1 serving) 4 Points

Total Points: 10½ Points

Cracked wheat salad with feta, mint and apricots

6½	Points per serving
27	Total Points per recipe

175 g (6 oz) bulgar wheat (cracked wheat)

grated zest and juice of 1 orange

1 tablespoon clear honey

1 tablespoon walnut oil or olive oil

1 tablespoon chopped fresh mint

2 heaped tablespoons raisins or sultanas

75 g (2¾ oz) ready-to-eat dried apricots,
  chopped

2 celery sticks, thinly sliced

75 g (2¾ oz) seedless red or green grapes,
  halved

100 g (3½ oz) feta cheese, cut into
  small cubes

salt

mint sprigs, to garnish

V if using vegetarian cheese Serves 4. (360 Calories per serving) Preparation time 10 minutes + 30 minutes soaking time. Freezing not recommended. Try cracked wheat, otherwise known as bulghar wheat if you're not familiar with it. It's delicious in this Moroccan-style salad.

1 Put the bulgar wheat into a large bowl and add a generous pinch of salt. Pour over enough boiling water to cover, then eave to soak for about 20–30 minutes, until swollen and tender.

2 Mix together the orange zest and juice, honey, walnut oil or olive oil and chopped mint.

3 Drain any excess water from the soaked bulgar wheat, then add the orange juice dressing, stirring well. Add the raisins or sultanas, apricots, celery, grapes and cheese, tossing well to mix.

4 Divide between four serving plates or bowls, garnish with mint sprigs, then serve.
Variation: If you like, make this salad with rice instead of bulgar wheat. The Points per serving will be 9.

Sunshine chicken salad

3½	Points per serving
14½	Total Points per recipe

2 tablespoons lime or lemon juice

125 g (4½ oz) red or green seedless
  grapes, halved

10 cm (4-inch) piece of cucumber, chopped

450 g (1 lb) cooked chicken, cut into strips

150 ml (5 fl oz) low-fat plain yogurt

1 teaspoon ground cumin

1 tablespoon chopped fresh mint

salt and freshly ground black pepper

To serve

mixed lettuce leaves

1 red pepper, de-seeded and sliced

1 yellow pepper, de-seeded and sliced

2 teaspoons sesame seeds, toasted

Serves 4. (240 Calories per serving) Preparation time 15 minutes. Freezing not recommended. Make this tasty recipe with bought roast chicken or if you have leftovers from a large bird, why not use them up to delicious effect in this vibrant, fruity salad.

1 Put the lime or lemon juice into a large serving bowl and add the grapes and cucumber, tossing to coat. Add the chicken and season with a little salt and black pepper.

2 To make the dressing, combine the yogurt, cumin and mint, seasoning with a dash of salt and pepper. Chill the salad and dressing separately until ready to serve.

3 Pile the mixed lettuce leaves and peppers on to four plates, then divide the chicken mixture between them. Drizzle with the dressing, sprinkle with toasted sesame seeds and serve at once.
Cook's note: To toast sesame seeds, heat a small frying-pan without fat, add the seeds and heat, stirring often until lightly browned.

Blue cheese salad with crispy rashers and croûtons

3½	Points per serving
13½	Total Points per recipe

4 medium turkey rashers

2 tablespoons lemon juice

1 teaspoon wholegrain mustard

1 bag of rocket leaves, rinsed

175 g (6 oz) young spinach leaves, rinsed

75 g (2¾ oz) Blue Stilton, crumbled

4 tablespoons low-fat plain yogurt

2 teaspoons chopped fresh herbs (e.g. chives, parsley or oregano)

4 tablespoons garlic and herb croûtons

salt and freshly ground black pepper

Serves 4. (185 Calories per serving) Preparation and cooking time 15 minutes. Freezing not recommended. Rocket has the most wonderful flavour, and tastes delicious with crumbled blue cheese and crispy-cooked turkey rashers.

1 Preheat the grill. Arrange the turkey rashers on the grill pan. Mix 1 tablespoon of lemon juice with the mustard and brush over the rashers. Grill for 2 minutes on each side, until browned. Allow to cool slightly.

2 Meanwhile, divide the rocket and spinach leaves between four serving bowls and sprinkle with the remaining lemon juice.

3 Snip the turkey rashers into fine shreds and sprinkle over the leaves. Add the crumbled blue cheese.

4 Mix the yogurt with the herbs and use to dress the salads. Sprinkle the croûtons on top and season with salt and pepper.

Cook's note: Turkey rashers are a lightly smoked low-fat alternative to bacon and they are 98% fat-free, so look for them in the chiller cabinet.

Spiced Indian salad

2½	Points per serving
10½	Total Points per recipe

150 g (5½ oz) long grain rice

1 tablespoon vegetable oil

1 garlic clove, crushed

1 small red onion, thinly sliced

1 large green chilli, de-seeded and finely chopped

1 courgette, chopped

1 teaspoon cumin seeds

4 tomatoes, chopped

2 tablespoons chopped fresh coriander

5 tablespoons low-fat plain yogurt

2 tablespoons chopped fresh mint

salt and freshly ground pepper

Ⓥ Serves 4. (210 Calories per serving) Preparation time 15 minutes. Cooking time 20 minutes. Freezing not recommended. Fresh green chilli and coriander add fragrant flavours to this simple salad. It would be excellent with curry.

1 Cook the rice in plenty of boiling, lightly salted water until tender, about 12 minutes. Rinse with cold water and drain thoroughly.

2 Meanwhile, heat the oil and fry the garlic, onion, green chilli and courgette and sauté for about 4–5 minutes, until softened. Add the cumin seeds and cook for a further 30 seconds or so.

3 Remove from the heat and stir through the tomatoes, rice and chopped coriander. Season to taste with salt and pepper, then transfer to a serving bowl.

4 Mix together the yogurt and mint. Serve, drizzled over the salad.

Variation 1: Serve the rice salad in 4 warm medium pitta breads, topped with 50 g (1¾ oz) grilled or barbecued chicken. Remember to add the extra Points.

Variation 2: If you don't have cumin seeds, substitute ground cumin instead.

Mixed leaf salad with tofu

2	Points per serving
8½	Total Points per recipe

2 tablespoons light soy sauce

1 tablespoon sesame oil

1 teaspoon finely grated fresh root ginger

1 tablespoon lime juice

300 g (10½ oz) firm tofu, cut into chunks

1 bag of watercress

4 generous handfuls of lamb's lettuce

½ head of Chinese leaves, shredded

6 spring onions, trimmed and finely sliced

25 g (1 oz) salted roast peanuts

freshly ground black pepper

Serves 4. (145 Calories per serving) Preparation time 10 minutes + 30 minutes to marinate. Cooking time 15 minutes. Freezing not recommended.

1 In a non-metallic bowl, whisk together the soy sauce, sesame oil, ginger and lime juice. Season with a little black pepper.

2 Add the tofu cubes to the soy sauce mixture. Stir to coat, then cover and leave to marinate for at least 30 minutes.

3 Mix together the watercress, lamb's lettuce and Chinese leaves. Divide them between four serving plates, then spoon an equal amount of the tofu pieces on top of each salad.

4 Use any remaining marinade as a dressing for the salads. Sprinkle with the spring onions and peanuts, then serve at once.

Cook's note: If you are allergic to nuts, simply leave out the peanuts which will reduce the Points to 1½ per serving – and use olive oil instead of sesame oil.

Sweetcorn and bean salad

3	Points per serving
12½	Total Points per recipe

100 g (3½ oz) fine green beans, trimmed and chopped

4 teaspoons olive oil

2 tablespoons lemon juice

1 tablespoon chopped fresh mint

326 g can of sweetcorn, drained

400 g can of red kidney beans, rinsed and drained

1 small red onion, finely chopped

2 large tomatoes, chopped

1 bag of mixed salad leaves

salt and ground black pepper

Serves 4. (225 Calories per serving) Preparation and cooking time 20 minutes. Freezing not recommended.

1 Cook the fine green beans in a small amount of lightly salted boiling water for about 3–4 minutes, until just tender. Drain well.

2 Meanwhile, mix together the olive oil, lemon juice and mint in a large bowl.

3 Add the cooked green beans, sweetcorn, red kidney beans, onion and tomatoes. Stir well to combine. Season to taste with salt and pepper.

4 Arrange the lettuce leaves on four serving plates and divide the salad equally between them. Serve at once.

Cook's note: The salad will keep in a covered container in the refrigerator for 2–3 days.

Variation: Use cherry tomatoes in this salad, if you like. You'll need about 12–16, halved.

Pasta and sweet pepper salad

3	Points per serving
12½	Total Points per recipe

175 g (6 oz) pasta shapes

1 courgette, chopped

1 red pepper, de-seeded and sliced

1 yellow pepper, de-seeded and sliced

1 small red onion, thinly sliced

4 spring onions, trimmed and finely chopped

12 cherry tomatoes, halved

12 pitted black olives

salt and freshly ground black pepper

a few sprigs of fresh oregano or parsley,
    to garnish

For the dressing

1 tablespoon olive oil

1 tablespoon red or white wine vinegar

1 tablespoon sun-dried tomato paste

2 tablespoons chopped fresh oregano or
    parsley

V *Serves 4. (260 Calories per serving) Preparation and cooking time 20 minutes. Freezing not recommended.*

1 Cook the pasta in plenty of boiling, lightly salted water until just tender, about 8–10 minutes.

2 Meanwhile, cook the courgette in a small amount of boiling, lightly salted water for 3–4 minutes. Drain and refresh under cold running water to cool quickly.

3 To make the dressing, mix together the olive oil, vinegar, sun-dried tomato paste and chopped herbs. Season well with salt and pepper.

4 Drain the pasta and tip it into a large serving bowl. Add the dressing and toss well. Add the courgette, peppers, red onion, spring onions, cherry tomatoes and olives, stirring to mix.

5 Serve, garnished with fresh sprigs of oregano or parsley.

Variation 1: You could use tomato purée instead of sun-dried tomato paste.

Variation 2: Add more vegetables if you like. Try chopped cucumber, tiny cauliflower florets or sliced mushrooms.

Tomato and basil platter

½	Point per serving
2½	Total Points per recipe

4 beef tomatoes, thinly sliced

12 baby plum or cherry tomatoes, halved

1 bunch of spring onions, trimmed and
   finely chopped

a handful of basil leaves, torn into shreds

salt and freshly ground black pepper

For the dressing

1 tablespoon olive oil

2 teaspoons lemon juice

1 garlic clove, chopped

(V) Serves 4. (75 Calories per serving) Preparation time 10 minutes + 30 minutes standing time. Freezing not recommended.

1 Arrange the beef tomatoes on to a large serving platter, fanning out the slices. Top with the plum or cherry tomato halves, then sprinkle with the spring onions.
2 Mix together the olive oil, lemon juice and garlic. Season with salt and pepper.
3 Sprinkle the dressing over the individual salads. Cover with clingfilm and leave at room temperature for about 30 minutes to allow time for the flavours to develop.
4 Serve, scattered with the basil leaves.

Cook's note: When all the different varieties of tomatoes are in season, it's a good idea to use them to make this fabulous salad.

Fruity rice salad

4½	Points per serving
18	Total Points per recipe

150 g (5½ oz) long-grain rice

1 teaspoon finely grated lemon zest

2 tablespoons lemon juice

1 tablespoon walnut or hazelnut oil

1 red apple, cored and chopped

25 g (1 oz) sultanas or raisins

100 g (3½ oz) seedless green grapes

100 g (3½ oz) seedless red grapes

1 medium banana, sliced

25 g (1 oz) chopped walnuts

(V) Serves 4. (295 Calories per serving) Preparation time 10 minutes. Cooking time 15 minutes. Freezing not recommended. The nut oil adds a lovely flavour.

1 Cook the rice in plenty of boiling, lightly salted water until tender, about 12 minutes.
2 Meanwhile, mix together the lemon zest and juice and walnut or hazelnut oil in a large serving bowl. Add all the fruit and mix together gently.
3 Drain the rice, rinse with cold water and drain thoroughly. Add to the fruit and stir to mix. Sprinkle with the walnuts and serve.

Variation: For added crunch, add a couple of sticks of chopped celery.

Slimline potato salad

1½	Points per serving
6½	Total Points per recipe

450 g (1 lb) small new potatoes, scrubbed

125 g (4½ oz) low-fat plain fromage frais

5 tablespoons low-fat plain yogurt

1 bunch of spring onions, trimmed and
   finely chopped

2 tablespoons chopped fresh parsley

a pinch of paprika

salt and freshly ground black pepper

(V) Serves 4. (130 Calories per serving) Preparation time 10 minutes. Cooking time 20 minutes. Freezing not recommended.

1 Cook the potatoes in plenty of boiling, lightly salted water until tender, about 20 minutes. Drain well and cool for a few minutes.
2 Mix together the fromage frais and plain yogurt in a serving bowl. Add the spring onions and parsley, then season well with salt, pepper and a good pinch of paprika.
3 Add the warm potatoes and stir them through the dressing. Cover and chill until ready to serve, then sprinkle with a little more paprika.

Variation: Add a couple of teaspoons of mild curry powder to the fromage frais dressing to give the potatoes a lovely spicy flavour.

Spiced carrot and sultana salad

1½	Points per serving
6	Total Points per recipe

Serves 4. (145 Calories per serving) Preparation and cooking time 20 minutes. Freezing not recommended.

1 tablespoon sesame oil
½ tablespoon poppy seeds
1 teaspoon cumin seeds
15 g (½ oz) pine kernels
450 g (1 lb) carrots, peeled and
　　coarsely grated
50 g (1¾ oz) raisins or sultanas
2 tablespoons seasoned rice vinegar
salt and freshly ground black pepper

1 Heat the sesame oil in a large saucepan that has a lid. Add the poppy seeds and cumin seeds. Put the lid on and heat until the seeds start to pop. Take care that the seeds do not burn.

2 Remove the saucepan from the heat and add the pine kernels, stirring to mix.

3 Put the grated carrots into a serving bowl and add the seeds, nuts and any remaining oil. Add the raisins or sultanas and vinegar, then season with salt and pepper. Toss together well, then serve.

Cook's note 1: If you have a food processor, use it to make light work of grating the carrots.

Cook's note 2: This is an excellent dish for a buffet, served with a selection of other salads.

Variation: If you can't find seasoned rice vinegar, use white wine vinegar instead.

Chicory and ham salad

3	Points per serving
11½	Total Points per recipe

Serves 4. (155 Calories per serving) Preparation time 10 minutes. Freezing not recommended. Chicory leaves are very crisp and they have a pleasant, slightly bitter flavour that perfectly complements the ham and cheese in this salad.

4 heads of chicory, broken into separate
　　leaves
10 cm (4-inch) piece of cucumber, chopped
1 bunch of radish, trimmed and halved
175 g (6 oz) lean cooked ham, cut into
　　small cubes
50 g (1¾ oz) Edam cheese, cut into
　　small cubes
salt and freshly ground black pepper
For the dressing
150 g (5½ oz) low-fat plain yogurt
1 teaspoon finely grated orange or
　　lemon zest
1 tablespoon chopped fresh parsley or
　　chives

1 Arrange the chicory leaves on four serving plates.

2 In a mixing bowl, combine the cucumber, radish, ham and cheese. Spoon an equal amount on to each plate.

3 Mix together the yogurt, orange or lemon zest and parsley or chives. Add a little salt and pepper, then spoon over the salads.

Weight Watchers note: To reduce the Points to 2½ per serving, use a half-fat Cheddar-type cheese instead of the Edam.

4 fish

Fish is fantastic and we should all eat more of it. Low in fat, yet high in valuable protein and vitamins, fish should play a more important part in many of our diets. So don't be daunted by cooking with fish; select the recipe you fancy, and give it a try!

Fish is marvellous for anyone who's trying to lose weight. You can make so many delicious meals with it, and it's very quick to prepare and cook. You can buy it fresh and cook it the same day, or buy it frozen or canned, ready for use at a moment's notice.

Grilled cod with spring herbs

2½	Points per serving
5	Total Points per recipe

2 × 175 g (6 oz) cod steaks

juice and finely grated zest of ½ lemon

1 teaspoon olive oil

3 tablespoons chopped fresh herbs such as
     dill, chives, parsley, chervil

salt and freshly ground black pepper

Serves 2. (185 Calories per serving) Preparation and cooking time 15 minutes. Freezing not recommended. Serve with freshly cooked vegetables or a green salad.

1   Rinse the cod and pat dry with absorbent kitchen paper. Line a grill pan with foil and place the steaks in it.

2   Mix together the lemon juice, zest, olive oil, herbs and seasoning and drizzle half over the fish. Turn the fish over and drizzle with the remainder of the herb mixture.

3   Grill the fish for 2 to 3 minutes per side, until cooked through and piping hot.

Cook's note: You can use other fish if preferred: salmon steaks (the Points per serving will be 7) or swordfish (the Points per serving will be 3½) all work well. Just adjust the Points as necessary.

Cod fillets pizza-style

2	Points per serving
8	Total Points per recipe

4 × 100 g (3½ oz) cod fillets

225 g (8 oz) canned chopped tomatoes

2 tablespoons tomato purée

50 g (1¾ oz) pitted black olives, halved

2 tablespoons fresh basil, torn

25 g (1 oz) freshly grated parmesan

salt and freshly ground black pepper

Serves 4. (120 Calories per serving) Preparation time 10 minutes. Cooking time 25 minutes. Freezing recommended. Serve with freshly cooked vegetables or a side salad.

1   Rinse the cod steaks and pat dry with absorbent kitchen paper. Line a roasting tin with non-stick baking parchment and lift the fish steaks into the tin. Preheat the oven to Gas Mark 5/190°C/375°F.

2   Mix together the chopped tomatoes, tomato purée, olives, basil and seasoning and spread equal amounts over each cod steak. Sprinkle the parmesan over the top and bake for 20 to 25 minutes, until the fish is cooked through and the cheese has melted.

Cook's note: A crushed garlic clove can be added to the tomatoes if liked.

Thai green curry with cod

4½	Points per serving
18½	Total Points per recipe

300 ml (½ pint) reduced-fat coconut milk

150 ml (¼ pint) fish stock

1 garlic clove, crushed

4 lime leaves

1 tablespoon Thai fish sauce

2 tablespoons Thai green curry paste

4 shallots, halved

125 g (4 oz) fine green beans, halved

350 g (12 oz) cod fillet, skinned and cubed

125 g (4 oz) cherry tomatoes, halved

2 tablespoons chopped fresh coriander

Serves 4. (160 Calories per serving) Preparation time 10 minutes. Cooking time 15 minutes. Freezing recommended. Look out for Bart's reduced-fat coconut milk; it's 88% fat-free and a real find when you're trying to lose weight.

1   Place the coconut milk, fish stock, garlic, lime leaves, fish sauce and curry paste in a pan and bring to the boil. Add the shallots. Allow the mixture to bubble for 10 minutes.

2   Add the green beans and cod and cook for a further 5 minutes. Toss in the tomatoes and coriander and simmer for a further 2 to 3 minutes. Serve at once.

Cook's note: Thai cooking uses fish sauce a little like Chinese cooking uses soy sauce. Take care when adding it as it is very salty. Add a little and taste. Then add more if required.

Fish pie with herby mash

4½	Points per serving
17½	Total Points per recipe

450 g (1 lb) potatoes, peeled and quartered

225 g (8 oz) leeks

50 g (1¾ oz) frozen peas

2 tablespoons cornflour

300 ml (½ pint) milk

450 g (1 lb) smoked haddock fillet

2 tablespoons vermouth, dry white wine or
dry sherry

75 g (2¾ oz) low-fat soft cheese

3 tablespoons skimmed milk

4 tablespoons chopped fresh herbs, such as
parsley, chives, dill

salt and freshly ground black pepper

Serves 4. (335 Calories per serving) Preparation time 25 minutes. Cooking time 35 minutes. Freezing recommended. It really is worth using fresh herbs in the mash; the flavour is so much better.

1 Bring a pan of lightly salted water to the boil and cook the potatoes until tender.

2 Trim the leeks and slice thinly. Cook in boiling water for 5 minutes, add the peas, and then cook for a further 2 minutes. Drain thoroughly.

3 Mix the cornflour with a little of the milk to form a thin paste. Heat the remaining milk until boiling and then add the cornflour paste. Stir well and cook, stirring until the sauce thickens.

4 Remove any skin from the fish and cut into bite-sized pieces. Place in a pan, pour the vermouth, wine or sherry over and cover and steam the fish for 5 minutes. Add the sauce, cooked leeks and peas and stir well.

5 Preheat the oven to Gas Mark 5/190°C/375°F. Spoon the fish mixture into a shallow ovenproof dish.

6 Drain the cooked potatoes and mash with the low-fat soft cheese, milk, herbs and seasoning and spoon over the fish. Bake for 25 minutes until piping hot.

Provençal fish stew

1½	Points per serving
6	Total Points per recipe

1 teaspoon olive oil

1 red onion, sliced

1 garlic clove, crushed

1 red pepper, de-seeded and diced

1 green pepper, de-seeded and diced

175 g (6 oz) courgettes, wiped and sliced

1 teaspoon dried oregano

2 tablespoons tomato purée

400 g (14 oz) canned chopped tomatoes

4 tablespoons white wine

225 g (8 oz) cod or haddock fillet, skinned
and cubed

125 g (4½ oz) prepared squid rings

75 g (2¾ oz) peeled prawns

salt and freshly ground black pepper

Serves 4. (170 Calories per serving) Preparation time 10 minutes. Cooking time 25 minutes. Freezing not recommended. Serve with boiled baby new potatoes or crusty bread.

1 Heat the olive oil in a pan and stir-fry the onion and garlic for 5 minutes, until softened. Add the peppers and courgettes and cook for a further 2 to 3 minutes.

2 Stir in the oregano, tomato purée, chopped tomatoes and wine and bring to the boil. Simmer for 10 minutes then toss in the fish, squid rings and prawns.

3 Season to taste and cook for about 5 minutes until the fish is cooked through.

Fish 'n' Chips

6½	Points per serving
25½	Total Points per recipe

900 g (2 lb) potatoes

1 teaspoon salt

2 tablespoons sunflower oil

4 × 200 g (7 oz) skinless cod fillets

1 small egg, beaten

100 g (3½ oz) white breadcrumbs

low-fat cooking spray

lemon slices, to serve

Serves 4. (510 Calories per serving) Preparation time 10 minutes. Cooking time 25 minutes. Freezing not recommended.

1 Preheat the oven to Gas Mark 6/200°C/400°F. Line two baking sheets with non-stick baking parchment.

2 Peel the potatoes and cut into chips. Place in a large container with a tight-fitting lid and add the salt and oil. Place the lid on the container and shake thoroughly so the potatoes get coated with a thin film of oil. Arrange on a baking sheet and cook for about 25 minutes.

3 Meanwhile, make sure there are no bones in the fish fillets. Dip the fish into beaten egg and then into the breadcrumbs to coat evenly. Place on to the other baking sheet and spray with the cooking spray, turning it over so that both sides get coated.

4 Bake on the oven shelf below the chips for 20 minutes. Serve hot with the lemon slices and crunchy oven chips!

Cook's note: Leave the skins on the potatoes if you wish.

Variation: Serve with a tomato salsa. To make it, just de-seed and dice 2 ripe tomatoes. Mix with 1 teaspoon chopped fresh herbs and 1 teaspoon of balsamic vinegar.

Seafood paella

4½	Points per serving
18½	Total Points per recipe

1 teaspoon olive oil

1 small onion, finely chopped

1 garlic clove, crushed

5 saffron strands

1 red pepper, de-seeded and diced

225 g (8 oz) risotto rice

850 ml (1½ pints) fish or vegetable stock

125 g (4½ oz) frozen peas

225 g (8 oz) skinless cod fillet, cut into
    bite-sized pieces

125 g (4½ oz) peeled prawns

2 tablespoons fresh chopped parsley

salt and freshly ground black pepper

Serves 4. (350 Calories per serving) Preparation time 15 minutes. Cooking time 25 minutes. Freezing not recommended. There are many varieties of this popular dish; this fish paella is a simplified version but just as delicious.

1 Heat the olive oil in a frying-pan and add the onion and garlic. Cook over a low heat, stirring until onion has softened but not browned.

2 Place the saffron in a small dish and cover with 2 tablespoons of boiling water, leave to stand so saffron infuses and colours the water a bright yellow.

3 Add the red pepper and rice to the pan with the saffron and its soaking liquid and the stock. Bring to the boil and simmer for 15 minutes, until most of the liquid has been absorbed.

4 Add the peas and fish and continue cooking for 5 minutes. Toss in the prawns and parsley, season to taste and cook for a further 2 to 3 minutes until piping hot.

Pan-fried salmon with sun-dried tomato couscous

7	Points per serving
29	Total Points per recipe

50 g (1¾ oz) sun-dried tomatoes

225 g (8 oz) couscous

a pinch of garlic salt

1 teaspoon balsamic vinegar

1 tablespoon olive oil

4 × 150 g (5½ oz) salmon fillets

2 tablespoons fresh basil, torn

salt and freshly ground mixed pepper

Serves 4. (515 Calories per serving) Preparation and cooking time 25 minutes + 50 minutes standing. Freezing not recommended.

1 Place the tomatoes in a small dish and pour 300 ml (1/2 pint) boiling water over them. Cover and leave to soak for 30 minutes. Drain, reserving the liquid and chop very finely.

2 Place the couscous in a bowl and stir in the chopped tomatoes, garlic salt and balsamic vinegar. Bring the reserved tomato liquid to the boil in a small pan and pour over the couscous. Fluff up with a fork, cover the bowl with clingfilm and leave to stand for 20 minutes, fluffing up with a fork again half-way through.

3 Heat the oil in a griddle pan or heavy-based frying-pan. Rinse the salmon fillets and pat dry with the absorbent kitchen paper. Season well with pepper and then lift into the pan, skin-side down. Cook for 5 minutes. Turn over carefully and cook for a further 1 to 2 minutes, until just cooked through.

4 Toss the basil into the couscous mixture and season to taste. Divide the couscous between four serving plates and top with a salmon fillet. Serve hot.

Cook's note: Use sun-dried tomatoes that aren't packed in oil. They are a little more difficult to find but should be available in most delicatessens and health food stores.

menu plan

Valentine's Special

The love of your life will adore this special meal. Serve a Point-free salad for starters - such as a platter of tomatoes with basil leaves, black pepper and a little balsamic or red wine vinegar.

Pan-fried Salmon with Sun-dried Tomato Couscous
page 64, (1 serving) 7 Points

Fresh Apricot and Passion Fruit Fool
page 175, (1 serving) 2½ Points

Total Points: 9½ Points

Haddock stuffed with mushrooms

2½	Points per serving
10½	Total Points per recipe

1 teaspoon sunflower oil

225 g (8 oz) open cap mushrooms, wiped
    and finely chopped

1 garlic clove, crushed

1 tablespoon soy sauce

1 teaspoon freeze-dried parsley

1 teaspoon freeze-dried tarragon

2 × 350 g (12 oz) fillets of haddock, skinned

50 g (2 oz) thinly sliced pancetta, Prosciutto
    or Parma ham

salt and freshly ground black pepper

Serves 4. (200 Calories per serving) Preparation time 10 minutes. Cooking time 25 minutes. Freezing recommended. This can be a real dinner party centrepiece. Prepare it ahead of time so all you have to do is pop it in the oven half an hour before you're ready to eat.

1 Heat the sunflower oil in a pan and add the mushrooms, garlic and soy sauce. Cover and cook over a low heat for 5 minutes, until softened. Stir in the parsley and tarragon and season.

2 Preheat the oven to Gas Mark 6/200°C/400°F. Line a roasting tin with non-stick baking parchment.

3 Lift the fish on to a clean board and use a small tweezers to remove any bones. Top one piece with the cooked mushroom mixture, then cover with the other piece of fish to sandwich together.

4 Wrap the pancetta, Prosciutto or Parma ham slices around the fish to help enclose the filling, then lift into the roasting tin and cook for 30 minutes. Allow to stand for 5 minutes before slicing thickly to serve.

Balsamic monkfish

2	Points per serving
4½	Total Points per recipe

225 g (8 oz) monkfish

finely grated zest of 1 lemon

½ teaspoon freeze-dried tarragon

15 g (½ oz) thinly sliced Parma ham
    (about 2 slices)

1 teaspoon olive oil

1 tablespoon balsamic vinegar

salt and freshly ground black pepper

225 g (8 oz) cherry tomatoes on the vine,
    to serve

Serves 2. (130 Calories per serving) Preparation time 15 minutes. Cooking time 25 minutes. Freezing recommended. A perfect dish for an intimate dinner for two. If Points allow, try serving with boiled baby new potatoes tossed with a little fresh mint.

1 Preheat the oven to Gas Mark 6/200°C/400°F.

2 Rinse the monkfish and pat dry with absorbent kitchen paper. Make a horizontal split almost all the way through the fish.

3 Mix together the lemon zest, a little seasoning and the tarragon. Spread into the slit of the fish. Use the Parma ham to wrap around the fish and then lift into a non- stick roasting tin.

4 Mix together the olive oil and balsamic vinegar and brush over the fish. Roast in the oven for 15 minutes. Arrange the tomatoes around the fish and return to the oven for 10 minutes. Warm the serving plates.

5 To serve, transfer the tomatoes to warmed serving plates. Thinly carve the fish into diagonal slices and arrange in a slightly fanned pattern next to the tomatoes. Drizzle over any juices left in the roasting tin.

Thai fish cakes

2½	Points per serving
10	Total Points per recipe

350 g (12 oz) skinless cod fillet

1 garlic clove, crushed

1 tablespoon green Thai curry paste

2 tablespoons fish sauce

2 tablespoons chopped fresh coriander

1 tablespoon cornflour

1 egg

75 g (2¾ oz) fine green beans, trimmed

1 tablespoon sunflower oil

Serves 4. (155 Calories per serving) Preparation and cooking time 20 minutes. Freezing recommended. These spicy fish cakes are delicious served with a chilli sauce for dipping.

1 Cut the cod into bite-sized pieces and place in a food processor with the garlic, curry paste, fish sauce, coriander, cornflour and egg. Blend until thoroughly combined.

2 Finely slice the green beans into thin discs and fold into the fish mixture. Using clean hands, shape the mixture into about 12 small cakes

3 Heat the oil in a large frying-pan and fry the cakes for 10 minutes, turning half-way through cooking. Drain on to absorbent kitchen paper and serve hot .

Cook's note: A little canned white crab meat can be used in place of some of the cod. Use 225 g (8 oz) cod and 125 g (4½ oz) canned drained white crab meat. The Points per serving would be the same.

Thai shellfish broth

2	Points per serving
8½	Total Points per recipe

1 teaspoon sunflower oil

4 shallots, peeled and chopped

1 garlic clove, peeled and crushed

1 red chilli, de-seeded and thinly sliced

2.5 cm (1-inch) piece of root ginger, peeled and grated

2 stalks of lemon grass, trimmed and very thinly sliced

4 kaffir lime leaves (optional)

2 tablespoons fish sauce

1. 2 litre (2 pint) fish stock

350 g (12 oz) mixed shellfish, such as prawns, mussels, scallops and squid

175 g (6 oz) cherry tomatoes, halved

50 g (1¾ oz) rice noodles

3 tablespoons chopped fresh coriander

Serve 4. (185 Calories per serving) Preparation time 20 minutes. Cooking time 15 minutes. Freezing not recommended. Look out for packets of mixed seafood cocktail containing mussels, squid rings, crab sticks, prawns and scallops; they're perfect for this recipe.

1 Heat the oil in a large pan and add the shallots, garlic and chilli, cook over a low heat for 2 to 3 minutes until just softened but not browned. Add the ginger, lemon grass, lime leaves, if using, fish sauce and stock and bring to the boil, reduce the heat and simmer for 10 minutes.

2 Add the shellfish, tomatoes and noodles to the pan and cook for a further 5 minutes, until noodles are tender. Scatter the coriander over and ladle into deep bowls to serve.

Cook's note 1: Look out for the small red Thai chillies for an authentic result. Take care though – they may be small but they're very fiery! Always wash your hands after cutting them up and never rub your eyes just after.

Cook's note 2: If you want to use lime leaves, look for them in the supermarket beside the herbs and spices where you'll find a dried version. You can also get them fresh. They add a wonderfully refreshing flavour to Thai dishes.

Trout with asparagus and mushrooms

3½	Points per serving
14	Total Points per recipe

8 × 75 g (2¾ oz) trout fillets

1 teaspoon Chinese five-spice powder

1 teaspoon sunflower oil

2 tablespoons teriyaki sauce

100 g (3½ oz) fine asparagus, blanched

175 g (6 oz) shiitake mushrooms, wiped
    and halved

6 spring onions, trimmed and sliced

50 g (1¾ oz) radish, trimmed and sliced

1 teaspoon sesame oil

Serves 4. (255 Calories per serving) Preparation time 15 minutes. Cooking time 20 minutes. Freezing not recommended.

1   Coat each trout fillet with a little of the Chinese five-spice powder, rubbing it in with your fingertips. Wipe out a large non-stick frying pan with the oil and heat. Cook the trout fillets for 1 to 2 minutes per side over a high heat, until cooked through and browning, set aside and keep warm.

2   Add the teriyaki sauce to the pan with the asparagus, mushrooms, spring onions and radish. Lower the heat, cover the pan and cook for 5 minutes, until the vegetables are just tender, but retain a little bite. Keep the pan covered to keep warm until ready to serve.

3   Remove the lid and drizzle with sesame oil. Raise the heat and cook on high for 1 minute.

4   Pile the cooked vegetables on to serving plates and top with the trout fillets.

Cook's note 1: Sesame oil has a wonderfully rich nutty flavour and a little goes a very long way. However it's not good for cooking with since it can't tolerate a high heat. Use it sparingly as a flavouring for Oriental sauces, salads and stir-fries.

Variation: You could substitute button mushrooms for the shiitake mushrooms but the flavour won't be quite the same.

Salmon and sweetcorn pie

5	Points per serving
21	Total Points per recipe

300 ml (½ pint) skimmed milk

2 tablespoons cornflour

2 tablespoons chopped fresh parsley

50 g (1¾ oz) half-fat Cheddar cheese, grated

1 teaspoon sunflower oil

1 leek, trimmed and sliced

150 g (5½ oz) mushrooms, wiped and sliced

100 g (3½ oz) canned or frozen sweetcorn

300 g (10½ oz) canned pink salmon,
    drained and flaked

3 sheets filo pastry

25 g (1 oz) low-fat spread, melted

salt and freshly ground black pepper

Serves 4. (385 Calories per serving) Preparation time 20 minutes. Cooking time 35 minutes. Freezing recommended.

1   Pour the milk, reserving 4 tablespoons, into a small pan and bring to the boil. Pour the reserved 4 tablespoons over the cornflour and mix to a paste. Pour the hot milk over and stir well. Return to the heat and cook, stirring until the sauce thickens.

2   Stir in the parsley and cheese and cook for 1 minute until the cheese melts.

3   Meanwhile, heat the sunflower oil in a pan and cook the leek and mushrooms until softened. Stir into the sauce with the sweetcorn, salmon and seasoning. Mix well.

4   Preheat the oven to Gas Mark 5/190°C/375°F. Spoon the salmon mixture into a shallow ovenproof dish. Brush the filo pastry sheets with the melted spread and crumple loosely. Cover the salmon mixture with the filo sheets and bake for 20 minutes, until the pastry is crisp and golden.

Variation 1: Canned tuna could be used instead of salmon as a tasty alternative. You could also substitute the sweetcorn for frozen peas. The Points per serving would be 4½.

Variation 2: If you want to use canned red salmon, the Points per serving will be 6 and the total Points for the recipe will be 23½.

Friday Fish Supper

Try this delicious combination for a fish supper with a difference. To deduct 2½ Points per serving, leave the feta cheese out of the salad.

❋

Baked Trout with Lemon and Parsley Pesto
page 69, (1 serving) 7 Points

❋

Roasted Vegetable Salad with Feta and Toasted Almonds
page 46, (1 serving) 4 Points

❋

Total Points: 11 Points

Baked trout with lemon and parsley pesto

7	Points per serving
14½	Total Points per recipe

2 × 350 g (12 oz) fresh trout (but not
　　rainbow trout), cleaned and gutted

2 large parsley sprigs

1 tablespoon dry white wine

salt and freshly ground black pepper

For the pesto

1 garlic clove, chopped

25 g (1 oz) fresh parsley, roughly chopped

1 tablespoon olive oil

2 anchovy fillets

1 tablespoon fresh lemon juice

finely grated zest of 1 lemon

1 tablespoon pine kernels

Serves 2. (450 Calories per serving) Preparation time 15 minutes. Cooking time 20 minutes. Freezing recommended for the pesto only. Ask your fishmonger to prepare the trout for you; if buying from a supermarket, they are normally ready-cleaned.

1　Preheat the oven to Gas Mark 5/190°C/375°F. Line a baking sheet with non-stick baking parchment.

2　Rinse the fish and pat dry with absorbent kitchen paper. Season the cavity with salt and pepper and insert a sprig of parsley into each one. Lift into the roasting tin and drizzle with the wine. Bake for 20 minutes.

3　Meanwhile, to make the pesto, place the garlic, parsley, olive oil, anchovy fillets, lemon juice and zest and pine kernels in a food processor. Blend until well chopped and evenly combined. Transfer to a small bowl and season to taste.

4　Serve the baked trout with a spoonful of the lemon and parsley pesto and a green salad.

Prawn and butternut squash risotto

5½	Points per serving
21½	Total Points per recipe

1 teaspoon olive oil

1 tablespoon tomato purée

1 tablespoon white wine vinegar

1 small onion, chopped

1 garlic clove, crushed

300 g (10½ oz) risotto rice

350 g (12 oz) butternut squash, peeled
　　and cubed

850 ml (1½ pints) fish or chicken stock

175 g (6 oz) peeled prawns

2 tablespoons fresh chopped parsley

25 g (1 oz) fresh parmesan, grated

salt and freshly ground black pepper

Serves 4. (425 Calories per serving) Preparation time 15 minutes. Cooking time 25 minutes. Freezing not recommended.

1　In a large non-stick pan, heat together the oil, tomato purée and vinegar. Stir in the onion and garlic and cook for 1 minute. Stir in the rice and squash and cook for 2 minutes.

2　Gradually add the stock a little at a time, waiting for it to be absorbed before adding more.

3　As you add the last of the stock, toss in the prawns, parsley and parmesan. Continue cooking until the rice is just tender and has a creamy texture. Season to taste and serve at once.

Cook's note: Risotto is at its best when served immediately; that ensures that you get the creamy texture it is renowned for. When left to go cold, the rice will absorb any juices and become a little stodgy.

Variation: You can use the same amount of diced pumpkin or sweet potato instead of squash if you prefer. The Points per serving will be the same with pumpkin. The Points per serving will be 6½ with sweet potato.

Moroccan fish tagine

2½	Points per serving
9½	Total Points per recipe

1 tablespoon olive oil

1 onion, sliced

150 g (5½ oz) carrots, peeled and sliced

225 g (8 oz) potatoes, peeled and cubed

2 celery stalks, trimmed and sliced

100 g (3½ oz) mushrooms, wiped and sliced

½ teaspoon ground cinnamon

½ teaspoon paprika

½ teaspoon dried chilli flakes

1 teaspoon ground coriander

½ teaspoon cumin seeds

2 bay leaves

25 g (1 oz) sultanas

400 g (14 oz) canned chopped tomatoes

2 tablespoons tomato purée

300 ml (½ pint) fish stock

350 g (12 oz) skinless cod fillet, cubed

salt and freshly ground black pepper

2 tablespoons chopped fresh coriander,
    to garnish

Serves 4. (235 Calories per serving) Preparation time 15 minutes. Cooking time 35 minutes. Freezing recommended. A warmly spiced casserole, full of the flavours of the mysterious East. For a really traditional meal, serve with couscous, adding extra Points.

1   Heat the oil in a large flameproof casserole with 2 tablespoons of water and add the onion, carrots, potatoes, celery and mushrooms. Cook, stirring for 2 minutes and then stir in the spices, bay leaves and sultanas.

2   Add the chopped tomatoes, tomato purée and stock and bring to the boil. Cover and simmer for 20 minutes, until the vegetables are tender. Remove the lid, add the fish and cook for a further 10 minutes, until the fish is cooked through. Season to taste.

3   Spoon into warmed serving bowls and scatter with coriander to serve.

Thai noodles with crab meat (Pad Thai)

4½	Points per serving
18	Total Points per recipe

2 tablespoons fish sauce

1 tablespoon tomato purée

1 tablespoon rice wine vinegar or white
    wine vinegar

1 tablespoon demerara sugar

1 tablespoon fresh lime juice

1 teaspoon cornflour

1 garlic clove, crushed

225 g (8 oz) Thai flat rice noodles

1 tablespoon sunflower oil

100 g (3½ oz) white cabbage, shredded

6 spring onions, trimmed and sliced

1 carrot, peeled and grated

100 g (3½ oz) beansprouts

1 teaspoon dried chilli flakes

200 g (7 oz) canned white crab meat,
    drained

2 tablespoons chopped fresh coriander

*Serves 4. (330 Calories per serving) Preparation and cooking time 25 minutes.
Freezing not recommended*

1 Mix together the fish sauce, tomato purée, vinegar, sugar, lime juice, cornflour and
   garlic and set aside.
2 Place the rice noodles in a bowl and cover with boiling water. Leave to soak for
   10 minutes. Drain thoroughly.
3 Meanwhile, heat the oil in a large pan or wok and add the cabbage, spring onions,
   carrot, beansprouts and chilli flakes. Stir-fry for 2 to 3 minutes until beginning to
   soften and then add the noodles. Stir-fry for a further 5 minutes.
4 Mix the drained crabmeat with the coriander and prepared sauce and add to the pan.
   Toss well and heat through for a further 2 to 3 minutes.

Variation: If you wish, you could garnish this dish with 15 g (½ oz) chopped, salted
peanuts. The Points per serving would be the same.

Lemon chicken with leeks and rice

4	Points per serving
16½	Total Points per recipe

1 tablespoon olive oil

1 leek, finely chopped

125 g (4½ oz) risotto rice

1 chicken stock cube dissolved in 600 ml
    (1 pint) hot water

1 tablespoon plain flour

1 teaspoon ground ginger

finely grated zest of 1 lemon

4 medium skinless, boneless chicken breasts

juice of 1 lemon

2 tablespoons light soy sauce

50 g (1¾ oz) frozen peas

salt and freshly ground black pepper

To serve

lemon slices

fresh herbs (optional)

Serves 4 (350 Calories per serving). Preparation time 15 minutes. Cooking time 30 minutes. Freezing not recommended. Lemon and ginger-flavoured chicken breasts on a bed of creamy risotto taste fantastic – you must try them!

1 Heat the olive oil in a large frying-pan and add the leek and rice. Cook gently, stirring, until the rice looks translucent – about 3 minutes. Add the stock a ladleful at a time, allowing the rice to absorb the liquid before adding the next ladle.

2 Meanwhile, mix together the flour, ginger and lemon zest and season with salt and pepper. Roll the chicken breasts in this mixture.

3 Preheat the grill. Mix together the lemon juice and soy sauce. Arrange the chicken on the grill pan and brush with the lemon juice mixture. Cook for about 8 minutes on each side.

4 Check that the rice is cooked – it should be creamy and tender. Add the peas and cook for 2–3 minutes to heat them through.

5 Pile the rice on to warm serving plates and arrange the chicken breasts on top. Garnish with lemon slices and herbs, if using, then serve.

Cook's note: Make sure that you use a genuine risotto rice for the best results. Long grain rice will not work because it does not absorb enough liquid to become soft and creamy.

Sizzled chicken with parsley mash

5	Points per serving
19½	Total Points per recipe

25 g (1 oz) plain flour

2 teaspoons dried sage

450 g (1 lb) skinless, boneless chicken,
    cut into chunks

1 tablespoon vegetable oil

2 garlic cloves, finely sliced

1 onion, sliced

2 apples, cored and chopped but unpeeled

1 chicken stock cube dissolved in 150 ml
    (¼ pint) hot water

150 ml (¼ pint) unsweetened apple juice

125 g (4½ oz) mushrooms, sliced

700 g (1 lb 9 oz) potatoes, cut into chunks

4 tablespoons skimmed milk

2 tablespoons chopped fresh parsley

salt and freshly ground black pepper

chopped fresh parsley, to garnish

Serves 4. (400 Calories per serving) Preparation time 20 minutes. Cooking time 35 minutes. Freezing recommended. This dish is ideal for the whole family including children.

1 Sprinkle the flour and dried sage on to a plate and add salt and pepper. Roll the pieces of chicken in this mixture.

2 Heat the oil in a large flameproof casserole or saucepan and add the chicken, cooking over a medium heat until browned on all sides. Push to one side, then add the garlic, onion and apples and sauté for about 3 minutes.

3 Add the stock and apple juice, bring up to the boil, then cover and cook over a low heat for 20–25 minutes, adding the mushrooms after 15 minutes.

4 Meanwhile, cook the potatoes until tender. Mash well, adding the milk and parsley. Season with salt and pepper and serve with the chicken, garnished with extra chopped parsley.

Cook's note: Check out the herb and spice racks for some excellent seasonings. Schwartz make Garlic and Herb or Onion and Chive mashed potato seasoning.

Chicken, ham and sweetcorn bake

6½	Points per serving
26½	Total Points per recipe

750 g (1 lb 10 oz) potatoes

350 ml (12 fl oz) skimmed milk

25 g (1 oz) polyunsaturated margarine

50 g (1¾ oz) plain flour

300 ml (½ pint) chicken stock

350 g (12 oz) cooked chicken, cut into
   chunks

50 g (1¾ oz) cooked ham, chopped

100 g (3½ oz) canned or frozen sweetcorn

1 tablespoons chopped fresh parsley plus
   extra, to garnish

salt and freshly ground black pepper

Serves 4. (475 Calories per serving) Preparation time 25 minutes. Cooking time 45 minutes. Freezing recommended. Chicken, ham and sweetcorn, topped with sliced cooked potatoes, make a satisfying main course dish.

1 Cook the potatoes in plenty of lightly salted boiling water until just tender, about 15 minutes. Mash well, adding 50 ml (2 fl oz) of milk and season with a little pepper.

2 Preheat the oven to Gas Mark 6/200°C/400°F. Grease a 2 litre (3½ pint) shallow ovenproof dish with a teaspoon of the margarine.

3 Melt the remaining margarine in a medium-sized saucepan. Add the flour, stirring to blend. Cook gently for 1 minute, then remove from the heat. Gradually blend in the remaining milk, then stir in the chicken stock. Heat, stirring continuously until the sauce boils and thickens.

4 Add the chicken, ham, sweetcorn and parsley to the sauce. Season with salt and pepper.

5 Pour the chicken and ham mixture into the baking dish and top with the mashed potatoes. Bake for 25–30 minutes, or until the potatoes are lightly browned. Serve sprinkled with the extra chopped parsley.

Variations: Use cooked turkey instead of chicken, if you prefer, and try chopped fresh tarragon instead of parsley. The Points per serving would be 7.

Chicken cordon bleu

5	Points per serving
19½	Total Points per recipe

4 × 150 g (5½ oz) skinless, boneless
   chicken breasts

50 g (1¾ oz) wafer-thin ham

50 g (1¾ oz) Gruyère or Cheddar cheese,
   finely grated

1 small egg

50 g (1¾ oz) dried breadcrumbs

salt and freshly ground black pepper

lemon wedges, to serve

Serves 4. (270 Calories per serving) Preparation time 20 minutes. Cooking time 1 hour. Freezing recommended. Serve with the Point-free vegetables of your choice!

1 Preheat the oven to Gas Mark 5/190°C/375°F.

2 Using a sharp knife, cut a pocket into each chicken breast. Stuff each pocket with an equal amount of ham and cheese. Season with salt and pepper. Close the pockets and secure with cocktail sticks.

3 Beat the egg in a shallow dish with 2 tablespoons of cold water. Sprinkle the breadcrumbs on to a plate. Dip each chicken breast first into the egg, then into the breadcrumbs, pressing them in well.

4 Arrange the chicken breasts in a roasting pan and cook for 30–35 minutes until tender. Test with a sharp knife, there should be no traces of pink. Serve with lemon wedges.

Autumn Sunday Lunch

When the weather's chilly outside, tuck into something comforting with this deliciously satisfying meal. Serve baked potatoes with the chicken, remembering to add the extra Points.

✳

Roast Chicken with Autumn Fruits
page 83, (1 serving) 4 Points

✳

Grape Cheesecakes
page 160, (1 serving) 3½ Points

✳

Total Points: 7½ Points

Roast chicken with autumn fruits

4	Points per serving
15½	Total Points per recipe

25 g (1 oz) plain flour

2 teaspoons sage and apple seasoning

    (or use dried mixed herbs)

4 medium skinless, boneless chicken breasts

1 tablespoon olive oil

2 apples

1 pear

1 tablespoon lemon juice

salt and freshly ground black pepper

Serves 4. (255 Calories per serving) Preparation time 10 minutes. Cooking time 35 minutes. Freezing not recommended. Chicken is coated in sage and apple seasoning, then roasted with apples and pears. This is a great recipe for the whole family and ideal for Sunday lunch.

1 Preheat the oven to Gas Mark 5/190°C/375°F.

2 Sprinkle the flour on to a plate and add the sage and apple seasoning or mixed herbs. Season with salt and pepper and mix well.

3 Rinse the chicken breasts, but do not pat dry. Roll in the seasoned flour. Place in a roasting tin, sprinkle with the oil, transfer to the oven and cook for 15 minutes.

4 Quarter and core the apples and pear, without peeling them. Sprinkle with lemon juice and place them next to the chicken. Roast for a further 20 minutes, or until the chicken is cooked and the fruit is tender.

Variation 1: Use garlic-flavoured olive oil if you like; it adds a delicious taste to the chicken.

Variation 2: If you want to use a medium whole chicken, in step two, brush the chicken with olive oil and then roll in the seasoned flour. Sprinkle the chicken with 1 teaspoon of oil and then cook in the oven for 1 hour. The Points will remain the same for a 150 g (5½ oz) portion of chicken.

Mediterranean chicken

5½	Points per serving
21½	Total Points per recipe

1 tablespoon olive or vegetable oil

1 red onion, sliced

2 celery sticks, sliced

4 medium skinless, boneless chicken breasts

125 ml (4 fl oz) red wine

1 chicken stock cube dissolved in 150 ml

    (5 fl oz) hot water

12 small pitted black olives, halved

    (optional)

25 g (1 oz) raisins or sultanas

2 sprigs fresh rosemary

2 sprigs fresh thyme

125 g (4½ oz) long grain rice

salt and freshly ground black pepper

sprigs of fresh rosemary and thyme, to

    garnish (optional)

Serves 4. (370 Calories per serving) Preparation time 15 minutes. Cooking time 35 minutes. Freezing not recommended. Lean chicken breasts take on an Italian flavour in this easy to cook dish.

1 Heat the oil in a large frying-pan and sauté the onion and celery for 2 minutes. Add the chicken breasts and cook for 3 or 4 minutes more, turning once, to brown.

2 Add the wine, stock, olives, if using, raisins or sultanas, rosemary and thyme. Season with salt and pepper. Bring to the boil, then reduce the heat. Cover and simmer for about 25 minutes, until the chicken is tender.

3 Meanwhile, cook the rice in plenty of lightly salted, boiling water, according to pack instructions.

4 Drain the rice and serve with the chicken, garnished with sprigs of rosemary and thyme, if using.

Weight Watchers note: Without the olives, the Points per serving will be the same.

Variation: Use white wine instead of red if you prefer.

Marinated chicken breasts

5	Points per serving
20½	Total Points per recipe

4 medium skinless, boneless chicken breasts

150 ml (5 fl oz) low-fat plain yogurt

2 tablespoons tandoori spice mix

finely grated zest and juice of 1 lemon

3 carrots, scrubbed and sliced

2 leeks, trimmed and sliced

2 medium parsnips, trimmed and cut
     into chunks

1 onion, cut into chunks

2 medium potatoes, scrubbed and thinly
     sliced

2 tablespoons olive oil

salt and freshly ground black pepper

parsley or coriander sprigs, to garnish

Serves 4. (395 Calories per serving) Preparation time 15 minutes + 1 hour marinating. Cooking time 40–45 minutes. Freezing not recommended. For a tasty main course, simply marinate some chicken breasts in a spicy yogurt mixture, then roast them alongside a selection of seasonal vegetables.

1 Rinse the chicken breasts and put them into a shallow dish. Mix together the yogurt, tandoori spice, lemon zest and juice. Season with salt and pepper and pour over the chicken, stirring to mix. Cover and refrigerate for at least 1 hour.

2 Preheat the oven to Gas Mark 7/200°C/400°F.

3 Put all the vegetables into a baking dish and sprinkle with 1½ tablespoons of olive oil, tossing to coat. Roast on the top shelf of the oven for 20 minutes, then toss the vegetables and return to the middle shelf of the oven.

4 Grease a roasting tin with the remaining olive oil, then put the chicken into it. Roast on the top shelf of the oven above the vegetables for 20–25 minutes, until golden brown. Check that the chicken is thoroughly cooked by testing with a sharp knife – there should be no traces of pink.

5 Spoon the roasted vegetables on to warm serving plates and top with the spiced chicken. Garnish with sprigs of parsley or coriander.

Variation: You could also use a selection of Mediterranean-style vegetables, such as peppers, red onion, courgette and aubergine instead of the carrots, leeks, parsnips and potatoes. These vegetables will not take as long to cook, so put them into the oven at the same time as the chicken.

Easy chicken casserole

3	Points per serving
11½	Total Points per recipe

1 tablespoon vegetable oil

2 leeks, sliced

2 celery sticks, sliced

2 carrots, chopped

1 onion, chopped

1 medium parsnip, chopped

450 g (1 lb) skinless, boneless chicken,
     cut into large chunks

600 ml (1 pint) chicken stock

1 tablespoon chopped fresh parsley

1 bay leaf

1 tablespoon cornflour

salt and freshly ground black pepper

Serves 4. (240 Calories per serving) Preparation time 15 minutes. Cooking time 1½ hours. Freezing recommended. Casseroles are so deliciously simple. They are the perfect recipe for a tasty supper, even though you may have to wait a little while before it's ready to eat.

1 Preheat the oven to Gas Mark 4/180°C/350°F.

2 Heat the vegetable oil in a large flameproof casserole and sauté the leeks, celery, carrots, onion and parsnip for 3 or 4 minutes, until softened.

3 Add the chicken to the casserole and cook until sealed on all sides. Add the chicken stock, parsley and bay leaf. Season with salt and pepper.

4 Cover the casserole and transfer it to the oven. Cook for 1–1¼ hours.

5 Lift the casserole from the oven and remove the bay leaf. Blend the cornflour with a little cold water and add to the casserole, stirring to mix. Cover, return to the oven and cook for 5 more minutes.

6 Serve the casserole on warmed serving plates.

Coq au vin

4½	Points per serving
17½	Total Points per recipe

1 tablespoon olive or vegetable oil

2 rashers of lean back bacon, snipped
   into pieces

8 shallots or small onions, halved

2 garlic cloves, crushed

4 × 150 g (5½ oz) skinless, boneless
   chicken breasts

125 ml (4 fl oz) red wine

300 ml (½ pint) chicken stock

175 g (6 oz) button mushrooms, halved

1 bay leaf

1 tablespoon chopped fresh parsley

1 tablespoon cornflour

salt and freshly ground black pepper

parsley, to garnish

Serves 4. (290 Calories per serving)
Preparation time 15 minutes.
Cooking time 45 minutes. Freezing
recommended.

1 Heat the olive or vegetable oil in a large frying pan or saucepan and sauté the bacon, shallots or onions and garlic for about 5 minutes, until beginning to turn brown. Lift them out and set aside.

2 Add the chicken breasts to the pan and seal them quickly on each side. Add the wine to the pan and bring it to the boil, allowing it to bubble for a few seconds. Pour the chicken stock into the pan.

3 Return the bacon, shallots or onion and garlic to the pan and add the mushrooms, bay leaf and parsley. Cover and simmer gently for about 30 minutes, until the chicken is tender.

4 Blend the cornflour with about 2 tablespoons of cold water and stir into the pan juices. Heat, stirring, until thickened and smooth. Cook for 2–3 minutes, then check the seasoning, adding salt and pepper to taste. Remove the bay leaf and serve, garnished with extra chopped fresh parsley.

Chicken biriyani

5	Points per serving
20	Total Points per recipe

1 tablespoon vegetable oil

2 garlic cloves, crushed

2 teaspoons finely grated fresh root ginger

1 large onion, chopped

350 g (12 oz) skinless, boneless chicken

½ teaspoon ground cinnamon

2 teaspoons ground coriander

1 teaspoon ground cumin

½ teaspoon ground turmeric

225 g (8 oz) long grain rice

900 ml (1½ pints) hot chicken stock

4 tomatoes, cut into quarters

salt and freshly ground black pepper

To serve

4 tablespoons low-fat plain yogurt

chopped fresh coriander

Serves 4. (395 Calories per serving) Preparation time 10 minutes. Cooking time
30 minutes. Freezing recommended. Chicken, spices and long grain rice make a
quick and tasty Indian-inspired dish.

1 Heat the oil in a large frying-pan. Add the garlic, ginger and onion and sauté gently for 2 minutes.

2 Chop the chicken and add. Cook for 3–4 more minutes, until browned. Stir in the cinnamon, coriander, cumin, turmeric and rice. Cook, stirring, for 1–2 minutes.

3 Pour in the stock and add the tomatoes. Cook over a low heat, stirring occasionally, until the liquid has been absorbed and the rice is tender. If the rice is not tender when all the liquid has evaporated, add a little extra stock or water and cook for a few more minutes.

4 Season to taste with salt and pepper, then serve, garnished with yogurt and chopped fresh coriander.

Variation: If you are vegetarian, make this recipe with Quorn instead of chicken and use vegetable stock. The Points per serving will be the same.

Quick Thai chicken curry with rice noodles

6	Points per serving
24½	Total Points per recipe

1 tablespoon stir-fry oil or vegetable oil

1 bunch of spring onions, chopped

350 g (12 oz) skinned and boned chicken
    breast, cut into large chunks

1 cm (½ inch) piece of fresh root ginger,
    finely grated

finely grated zest of 1 lime or lemon

100 ml (3½ fl oz) Bart Spices 88% fat-free
    coconut milk

125 ml (4 fl oz) chicken stock

2 tablespoons Thai red or green curry paste

1 tablespoon light soy sauce

1 tablespoon chopped fresh basil or coriander

175 g (6 oz) rice noodles

salt and freshly ground black pepper

chopped spring onions, lime slices and basil
    or coriander leaves, to garnish

Serves 4. (330 Calories per serving) Preparation time 15 minutes. Cooking time 25 minutes. Freezing recommended without the noodles. This Thai-style chicken curry is made in no time and it's full of wonderful flavours.

1 Heat the oil in a large frying-pan and sauté the spring onions until softened, about 2 minutes. Add the chicken and cook for 3 more minutes, until sealed on the outside.

2 Add the ginger, lime or lemon zest, coconut milk, stock, curry paste, soy sauce and chopped basil or coriander. Heat until almost boiling. Cover and simmer gently over a low heat for 15–20 minutes, until the chicken is cooked.

3 Meanwhile, soak the rice noodles in boiling, lightly salted water for about 6 minutes, or according to pack instructions.

4 Season the chicken curry with salt and pepper, then serve with the drained, cooked noodles. Garnish with chopped spring onions, lime slices and sprigs of fresh basil or coriander.

Cook's note: Look out for Thai red or green curry paste, coconut milk and rice noodles in the Oriental foods section of your supermarket, or ask for them at your local delicatessen.

Sweet and sour chicken with noodles

3½	Points per serving
15	Total Points per recipe

175 g (6 oz) instant noodles

2 tablespoons light soy sauce

2 tablespoons rice, white wine or cider vinegar

2 tablespoons sherry

2 teaspoons light muscovado sugar

1 tablespoon cornflour

1 teaspoon Chinese five-spice powder

210 g can of pineapple chunks in
    natural juice

1 tablespoon stir-fry oil or vegetable oil

350 g (12 oz) chicken stir-fry strips

1 onion, finely sliced

1 large carrot, finely sliced

1 courgette, finely sliced

3 tomatoes, de-seeded and chopped

salt and freshly ground black pepper

fresh coriander or parsley, to garnish (optional)

Serves 4. (375 Calories per serving) Preparation time 20 minutes. Cooking time 10 minutes. Freezing not recommended. Stir-fry strips of chicken taste fabulous in this quick and easy dish which the whole family, including the kids, will enjoy.

1 Soak the noodles in boiling water for 6 minutes, or follow the pack instructions.

2 Mix together the soy sauce, vinegar, sherry, sugar, cornflour and five-spice powder. Drain the pineapple, adding the juice to the soy sauce mixture. Set to one side.

3 Heat the oil in a wok or a very large frying-pan. Add the chicken, a handful at a time, and stir-fry over a high heat for 3–4 minutes.

4 Add the onion, carrot and courgette to the chicken. Stir fry for another 3–4 minutes, then add the tomatoes and pineapple chunks. Stir the soy sauce mixture and add to the chicken and vegetables, stirring until hot and thickened. Season to taste.

5 Drain the noodles and divide between 4 warmed serving plates. Pile the stir fry on top, then serve, garnished with fresh coriander or parsley, if desired.

Variation: For speed and convenience, use a bag of ready-prepared stir-fry vegetables, either fresh or frozen.

Moroccan chicken with papaya raita

6½	Points per serving
25½	Total Points per recipe

225 g (8 oz) couscous or bulgar wheat

3 spring onions, finely sliced

50 g (1¾ oz) ready-to-eat dried apricots,
   chopped

1 tablespoon stir-fry oil or vegetable oil

450 g (1 lb) skinless, boneless chicken,
   diced

1–2 tablespoons harissa paste or 3 teaspoons
   chilli sauce

1 red pepper, de-seeded and chopped

1 yellow pepper, de-seeded and chopped

1 large courgette, chopped

salt, to taste

For the raita (optional)

1 papaya (paw paw), finely chopped
   (see Cook's note)

5 tablespoons low-fat plain yogurt

1 tablespoon chopped fresh mint

Serves 4. (455 Calories per serving) Preparation time 20 minutes. Cooking time 15 minutes. Freezing not recommended. A spicy Moroccan-style paste, known as harissa, makes this recipe especially delicious.

1   Put the couscous or bulghar wheat into a heatproof bowl with a generous pinch of salt, the spring onions and apricots. Cover with 400 ml (14 fl oz) of boiling water and leave to soak for 10 minutes.

2   Meanwhile, heat the oil in a wok or frying-pan and add the chicken, cooking and stirring it for 4–5 minutes, until browned. Add the harissa paste: 1 tablespoon if you prefer a milder flavour, 2 tablespoons if you like your food spicy. Cook over a medium heat, stirring, for another 2–3 minutes.

3   Add the peppers and courgette and cook for another 5–6 minutes, stirring often, until the vegetables are cooked, but not mushy.

4   Meanwhile, make the raita by mixing together the papaya, yogurt and mint. Cover and chill until ready to serve.

5   Reheat the couscous or bulghar wheat, either by microwaving it for about 1 minute on High or by steaming it over a pan of simmering water. Fluff up with a fork, then divide between four serving plates. Top with the chicken mixture and serve with the raita.

Weight Watchers note: To reduce the Points to 5½, leave out the raita.

Cook's note: To prepare a papaya (paw paw), slice it in half, scoop out the inedible black seeds, then peel. Harissa paste is a Moroccan blend of garlic, chillies, caraway and salt and is now readily available in many supermarkets.

Variation: Not keen on papaya? Then use a 10 cm (4-inch) piece of cucumber, finely chopped, for the raita. The Points per serving will be 6.

Thai grilled chicken

5½	Points per serving
23	Total Points per recipe

1 large garlic clove, crushed

2 teaspoons prepared minced lemon grass

2 teaspoons finely grated fresh root ginger

1 tablespoon Thai red curry paste

finely grated zest and juice of 2 limes

2 tablespoons chopped fresh coriander

4 medium skinless, boneless chicken breasts

225 g (8 oz) jasmine or basmati rice

lime slices and fresh coriander, to garnish

salt and freshly ground black pepper

Serves 4. (370 Calories per serving) Preparation time 10 minutes + 30 minutes marinating. Cooking time 20 minutes. Freezing not recommended.

1   In a glass or plastic bowl, mix together the garlic, lemon grass, ginger, curry paste, lime zest, lime juice and coriander. Season with a little salt and pepper. Add the chicken breasts, turn to coat in the mixture, then cover and refrigerate for at least 30 minutes.

2   Preheat a medium-hot grill. Put the chicken breasts on to the grill rack and cook for about 15–20 minutes, turning once and basting with the marinade from time to time.

3   Meanwhile, cook the rice in plenty of boiling, lightly salted water for about 12 minutes, or until tender. Drain well.

4   Check that the chicken breasts are thoroughly cooked by piercing the thickest part with a sharp knife. The juices should run clear. If not, cook for a little longer. Serve the chicken and rice, garnished with lime slices and sprigs of coriander.

Cook's note: You can buy prepared "fresh" lemon grass, minced ginger, coriander, garlic and red Thai curry paste in handy small jars from most supermarkets. Keep refrigerated once opened.

Chicken and mushroom risotto

7	Points per serving
27½	Total Points per recipe

2 tablespoons olive oil

225 g (8 oz) risotto rice

225 g (8 oz) skinless, boneless chicken, chopped into chunks

2 garlic cloves, crushed

1 onion, chopped

1 yellow or green pepper, de-seeded and sliced

100 g (3½ oz) mushrooms, wiped and sliced

2 teaspoons dried mixed Italian herbs

1 litre (1¾ pints) chicken or vegetable stock

25 g (1 oz) sun-dried tomatoes in olive oil, rinsed and sliced

salt and freshly ground black pepper

To serve

4 tablespoons finely grated parmesan cheese

a few sprigs of fresh basil

Serves 4. (415 Calories per serving) Preparation time 15 minutes. Cooking time 15 minutes. Freezing recommended. Choose Italian arborio rice and freshly grated parmesan cheese to make the best risotto; flavour is everything when you're trying to lose weight! Children will like the creamy texture.

1 Heat the oil in a large frying-pan or wok. Add the rice and sauté gently for 2 minutes. Add the chunks of chicken and cook gently for a further 2–3 minutes, stirring constantly.

2 Add the garlic, onion and pepper. Cook over a low heat, stirring frequently, for 5 minutes. Add the mushrooms and cook for another minute or so.

3 Stir in the dried herbs, half the stock and the sun-dried tomatoes. Bring to the boil, then reduce the heat. Cover and simmer gently for about 20 minutes, adding further stock as needed, until the rice is tender and all the stock has been absorbed.

4 Season the risotto with salt and pepper, then ladle on to warmed plates and sprinkle each portion with 1 tablespoon of parmesan cheese. Garnish with sprigs of fresh basil.

Cook's note: If all the stock has been absorbed before the rice is tender, add a little more stock or hot water.

Variation 1: For a special occasion, replace 150 ml (¼ pint) of the stock with 150 ml (¼ pint) dry white wine. This will add a further ½ Point to each portion.

Variation 2: You could add 2 skinned and chopped fresh tomatoes in step 3, just 5 minutes before the end of the cooking time.

Moroccan spiced chicken

5	Points per serving
21	Total Points per recipe

2 oranges

100 g (3½ oz) long grain rice

2 teaspoons stir-fry oil or vegetable oil

350 g (12 oz) chicken stir-fry strips

1 onion, sliced

50 g (1¾ oz) ready-to-eat dried apricots, sliced

25 g (1 oz) sultanas

½ teaspoon ground allspice

½ teaspoon cumin seeds (or ground cumin)

225 g (8 oz) canned chick-peas, rinsed and drained

2 tablespoons chopped fresh coriander, plus sprigs to garnish

15 g (½ oz) pistachio nuts or flaked almonds, lightly toasted

salt and freshly ground black pepper

Serves 4. (350 Calories per serving) Preparation time 15 minutes. Cooking time 15 minutes. Freezing not recommended. Oranges, apricots, sultanas, spices, chick-peas, rice and nuts are all typical ingredients of Moroccan cookery. Try them combined in this easy chicken dish.

1 Finely grate the zest and squeeze the juice from 1 orange. Slice the second orange into 8 segments.

2 Cook the rice in plenty of lightly salted boiling water.

3 Heat the oil in a wok or large frying-pan and add the chicken strips and onion, frying briskly for 3–4 minutes, until the chicken is browned.

4 Reduce the heat a little and add the apricots, sultanas, allspice, cumin, orange zest and juice. Cook gently for 5 minutes, then season to taste.

5 Add the chick peas to the rice for the final 2–3 minutes of cooking time to heat them thoroughly. Drain well, then stir through the chopped coriander.

6 Divide the rice and chick-peas between four warm plates. Spoon the chicken mixture on top, sprinkle with the nuts and garnish with sprigs of fresh coriander. Serve at once, with the segments of orange.

Cook's note: Don't confuse allspice with ground mixed spice. Allspice is the name of a single spice, sometimes known as pimiento.

Variations: You can use raisins instead of sultanas, parsley instead of coriander and turkey strips instead of chicken.

Fiery chicken pitta pockets

5½	Points per serving
22	Total Points per recipe

2 teaspoons olive oil

1 tablespoon paprika

1 teaspoon mild chilli powder

2 teaspoons finely grated fresh root ginger

3 tablespoons lime or lemon juice

1 tablespoon chopped fresh coriander or mint

4 medium skinless, boneless chicken breasts

4 medium pitta breads

salt and freshly ground black pepper

To serve

salad leaves, shredded

chopped cucumber, radish and tomato

sprigs of fresh coriander or mint and lime
        or lemon wedges

Serves 4. (340 Calories per serving) Preparation time 15 minutes + 1 hour marinating. Cooking time 15 minutes. Freezing recommended for the uncooked chicken with marinade. Spice up some chicken breasts, then serve in pitta bread with chopped fresh salad and a good squeeze of lime juice. Children will love this if they like spicy things.

1   In a shallow glass or plastic bowl, mix together the olive oil, paprika, chilli powder, ginger, lime or lemon juice and chopped herbs. Season with salt and pepper.

2   Lay the chicken breasts in the mixture. Cover and leave to marinate for about 1 hour.

3   Preheat the grill, then cook the chicken for about 12–15 minutes, turning once and basting often, until tender. When tested with a fork, the juices should run clear.

4   Warm the pitta breads, either by wrapping in foil and heating under the grill, or by toasting lightly.

5   Slice the chicken and serve in the warm pitta bread with shredded salad leaves, cucumber, radish and tomato. Garnish with fresh coriander or mint and serve with lime or lemon wedges.

Cook's note 1: If you haven't the time to marinate the chicken, just use the mixture for basting.

Cook's note 2: Try this dish in summer, it's perfect when barbecued over hot coals.

Grilled chicken with orange and ginger

4	Points per serving
15½	Total Points per recipe

4 medium chicken breasts

2 tablespoons stir-fry oil or sesame oil

1 large leek, shredded

1 carrot, finely sliced

100 g (3½ oz) mange-tout peas or sugar
        snap peas, trimmed

juice of 1 orange

2.5 cm (1-inch piece) fresh root ginger,
        peeled and finely grated

1 teaspoon Chinese five-spice powder

salt and freshly ground black pepper

To serve

1 teaspoon sesame seeds

a few sprigs of fresh coriander

finely grated zest of 1 orange

Serves 4. (275 Calories per serving) Preparation time 15 minutes. Cooking time 15 minutes. Freezing not recommended. A simple chicken dish tastes really special when served with interesting flavours.

1   Preheat the grill. Cover the grill pan with foil. Arrange the chicken breasts on the grill pan and brush with a little oil. Grill under a medium-high heat for about 5–6 minutes on each side, or until tender. (There should be no trace of pink when tested with a sharp knife).

2   Meanwhile, heat the remaining oil in a wok or frying-pan and stir-fry the leek, carrot and mange-tout peas or sugar snap peas for about 3 minutes, until cooked, yet still crunchy.

3   Mix together the orange juice, ginger and five-spice powder. Add to the vegetables and stir until heated. Season to taste with salt and pepper.

4   Divide the vegetable mixture between 4 warmed serving plates and top with the chicken. Scatter with sesame seeds, fresh coriander and orange zest, then serve at once.

Variation: Use 4 × 150 g (5½ oz) turkey steaks instead of chicken for a change. The Points will remain the same.

Summer Barbecue

Serve a huge bowlful of salad
leaves dressed with lemon juice
and fresh herbs. And lay out fresh
crusty bread for hungry guests.

✳

Fiery Chicken Pitta Pockets
page 90, (1 serving) 5½ Points

✳

Fruity Rice Salad
page 57, (1 serving) 4½ Points

✳

Tropical Mango and Lime Fruit Salad
page 184, (1 serving) 1½ Points

✳

Total Points: 11½ Points

Chicken, sage and basil parcels

5	Points per serving
20½	Total Points per recipe

4 × 175 g (6 oz) skinless chicken breasts

2 garlic cloves, crushed

1 tablespoon chopped fresh sage

1 tablespoon chopped fresh basil

4 tablespoons fresh breadcrumbs

1 tablespoon red or green pesto sauce

12 sage leaves

12 basil leaves

2 tablespoons olive oil

1 red and 1 yellow pepper, de-seeded and
    cut into large chunks

2 courgettes, cut into chunks

8 small tomatoes

salt and freshly ground black pepper

Serves 4. (320 Calories per serving) Preparation time 15 minutes. Cooking time 15 minutes. Freezing not recommended.

1 Preheat the oven to Gas Mark 5/190°C/375°F.

2 Lay the chicken breasts on a work surface and use a sharp knife to cut a pocket into them. Season with salt and pepper.

3 Mix together the garlic, chopped sage and basil, breadcrumbs and pesto sauce, adding a little water to mix to a stiff paste. Spread into the pockets in the chicken, then lay a few sage and basil leaves on top. Close the pockets and secure with string or cocktail sticks.

4 Heat one tablespoon of olive oil in a frying pan and add the chicken parcels, cooking and turning them over a medium-high heat for about 3 minutes to brown and seal them.

5 Add the remaining oil to a roasting pan and put the peppers and courgettes into it. Arrange the chicken breasts on top and transfer to the oven. Roast for 30 minutes, or until the chicken is tender, adding the tomatoes to the roasting tin for the final 10 minutes.

6 Serve the chicken parcels with the vegetables.

Chicken, chestnut and winter vegetable stir-fry

4	Points per serving
16½	Total Points per recipe

2 teaspoons cornflour

1 tablespoon soy sauce

2 tablespoons sherry or wine

1 tablespoon stir-fry oil or vegetable oil

350 g (12 oz) stir-fry chicken strips

1 garlic clove, crushed

1 red (or ordinary) onion, finely sliced

1 large leek, finely sliced

3 celery sticks, finely sliced

1 medium parsnip, cut into fine strips

1 large carrot, cut into fine strips

100 g (3½ oz) red or white cabbage,
    shredded

240 g can of peeled chestnuts

1 teaspoon sesame seeds (optional)

salt and freshly ground black pepper

Serves 4. (310 Calories per serving) Preparation time 15 minutes. Cooking time 10 minutes. Freezing not recommended. Make the most of seasonal vegetables in this delicious stir-fry.

1 Blend the cornflour with the soy sauce and sherry or wine. Set aside.

2 Heat the oil in a wok or large frying-pan. Add the chicken and stir-fry for about 3–4 minutes, until browned.

3 Add the garlic, onion, leek, celery, parsnip and carrot. Stir-fry over a medium-high heat for 3–4 minutes, then add the cabbage and chestnuts. Stir-fry for about 3 more minutes.

4 Stir the soy sauce mixture and add to the wok or frying-pan. Heat, stirring, until thickened. Season to taste, then serve, sprinkled with sesame seeds (if using).

Variation 1: Use up leftover cooked turkey or chicken in this recipe – just add it at the same time as the cabbage, making sure that it is thoroughly reheated.

Variation 2: Stock can be used instead of sherry or wine if you prefer and the Points will remain the same.

Weight Watchers note: Omit the chestnuts and the Points will be reduced to 2½ per serving.

Chilli-garlic chicken and rice

5	Points per serving
20	Total Points per recipe

225 g (8 oz) long grain rice

1 tablespoon toasted sesame oil, stir-fry oil
or vegetable oil

350 g (12 oz) chicken stir-fry strips

1 bunch of spring onions, trimmed and
finely sliced

175 g (6 oz) mange-tout peas or sugar snap
peas, trimmed and sliced

2 tablespoons chilli-garlic sauce

salt and freshly ground black pepper

1 tablespoon chopped fresh chives,
to garnish

Serves 4. (345 Calories per serving) Preparation time 10 minutes. Cooking time 15 minutes. Freezing not recommended. You can buy some excellent sauces these days, which give a quick and tasty finish to a simple dish. This one uses a chilli sauce flavoured with garlic.

1 Put the rice on to cook in plenty of lightly salted boiling water. It will take about 12 minutes, so start cooking the stir-fry about 8 minutes before the rice is ready.

2 Heat the oil in a wok or large frying-pan and add the chicken strips. Stir-fry for about 3–4 minutes, then add spring onions and mange-tout peas or sugar snap peas. Stir-fry for another 2–3 minutes.

3 Add the chilli-garlic sauce and cook for a further minute. Season to taste with salt and pepper.

4 Drain the rice, divide between four warm bowls or plates and pile the chicken and vegetable mixture on top. Garnish with chives and serve at once.

Cook's note 1: Use a combination of white and wild rice for extra interest.

Cook's note 2: If you can't find chilli-garlic sauce, add a crushed garlic clove to the stir-fry and use ordinary chilli sauce instead.

Weight Watchers note: You can add extra vegetables such as peppers or beansprouts without adding any extra Points.

Quick fruity chicken supper

7	Points per serving
28	Total Points per recipe

225 g (8 oz) long grain rice

1 tablespoon sesame or vegetable oil

1 small leek or 5 spring onions, finely sliced

350 g (12 oz) skinless roast chicken, chopped

100 ml (3½ fl oz) Bart Spices 88% fat-free
coconut milk

150 ml (¼ pint) chicken stock

1 tablespoon Jamaican jerk seasoning or
Thai red curry paste

210 g can of pineapple pieces in natural
juice, drained

1 medium banana, sliced

2 clementines or 1 small orange, segmented

salt and freshly ground black pepper

shredded leek or spring onion, to garnish
(optional)

Serves 4. (460 Calories per serving) Preparation time 10 minutes. Cooking time 15 minutes. Freezing not recommended. If you've run out of ideas for using leftover chicken, try it in this very tasty, fruity curry with its slightly unusual ingredients and see how well children like it too.

1 Cook the rice in lightly salted boiling water until just tender, about 12 minutes.

2 Meanwhile, heat the oil in a wok or frying-pan. Add the leek or spring onions and sauté for 2 minutes. Add the chicken and cook, stirring, for 2 more minutes.

3 Add the coconut milk, stock and jerk seasoning or Thai curry paste to the chicken mixture. Heat until just boiling, then reduce heat and simmer, uncovered, for 5–6 minutes.

4 Add the pineapple, banana and clementines or orange to the chicken mixture. Heat through for 2 minutes, then season to taste.

5 Drain the rice and divide between 4 warmed serving plates. Spoon the chicken mixture on top, then garnish with shredded leek or spring onion, if desired. Serve at once.

Cook's note: Jamaican jerk seasoning tends to be quite hot so add it according to taste.

Easy chicken tikka

4	Points per serving
15½	Total Points per recipe

450 g (1 lb) skinned and boned chicken, cubed

150 ml (5 fl oz) white wine vinegar

1 teaspoon salt

2 garlic cloves, crushed

2 teaspoons chilli powder

1 teaspoon finely grated fresh root ginger

1 teaspoon chopped fresh mint

1 teaspoon garam masala or other curry powder

½ teaspoon cumin seeds or ground cumin

1 tablespoon vegetable oil

150 ml (5 fl oz) low-fat plain yogurt

For the tomato and red onion salad

1 red onion, thinly sliced

1 small garlic clove, crushed

3 tomatoes, skinned, de-seeded and chopped

2 tablespoons lemon juice

2 tablespoons chopped fresh mint

For the coriander relish

150 g (5½ oz) low-fat plain yogurt

2 tablespoons chopped fresh coriander

salt and freshly ground black pepper

Serves 4. (215 Calories per serving) Preparation time 20 minutes + 3½ – 4½ hours marinating. Cooking time 15 minutes. Freezing recommended without side dishes. Children will enjoy this if they like spicy food. It's an easy-to-make authentic chicken tikka recipe, perfect for preparing ahead. Serve with a couple of side dishes – chopped tomatoes with mint and red onion and chopped fresh coriander in low-fat plain yogurt.

1   Put the chicken into a non-metallic bowl and add the vinegar and salt. Stir well, then cover and refrigerate for 20–30 minutes.

2   Mix together all the remaining ingredients. Drain the chicken, discarding the vinegar. Add the yogurt mixture, stirring well, then cover and refrigerate for at least 3 or 4 hours, or overnight if preferred.

3   To cook, thread the chicken on to 6 skewers and grill or for 12–15 minutes, turning frequently.

4   To make the tomato and red onion salad, mix the onion with the garlic, tomatoes, lemon juice and mint. Season with salt and pepper and transfer to a small bowl. Chill well.

5   To make the coriander relish, mix together the yogurt, coriander and seasoning. Transfer to a small bowl, then cover and chill. Serve with the chicken tikka and salad.

Cook's note: This is the perfect recipe for a barbecue. Prepare the chicken the day before, so that it can absorb the flavours of the marinade overnight.

Turkey ciabatta grills

| 4½ | Points per serving |
| 18 | Total Points per recipe |

1 ciabatta loaf with sun-dried tomatoes
    or olives
2 tablespoons sun-dried tomato paste
150 g (5½ oz) grilled red and yellow
    pepper strips
8 medium turkey rashers, uncooked
salt and freshly ground black pepper
a few basil leaves

Serves 4. (225 Calories per serving) Preparation and cooking time 10 minutes. Freezing not recommended. Turkey rashers make a tasty topping.

1 Preheat the grill to high.
2 Slice the loaf in half lengthways and spread with the tomato paste.
3 Top both pieces of ciabatta with the pepper strips, then the uncooked turkey rashers. Grill for 1½ minutes, then turn the rashers over and grill for another 1½ minutes, until the rashers are cooked.
4 Slice each piece of bread in half, then serve, seasoned with salt and pepper and scattered with a few basil leaves.
Cook's note: Look for grilled pepper strips in jars, preserved in vinegar, then rinse and drain them. Alternatively, you can buy canned red peppers (sometimes called pimientos) which simply need to be drained and sliced.
Variation: Buy plain ciabatta loaves if you can't find ciabatta with sun-dried tomatoes or olives. The Points per serving will be the same.

Tandoori turkey bites

| 2½ | Points per serving |
| 5½ | Total Points per recipe |

1 tablespoon tandoori paste
1 teaspoon lemon juice
3 tablespoons low-fat plain yogurt
1 tablespoon chopped fresh mint
225 g (8 oz) turkey steaks, cut into 2.5 cm
    (1-inch) chunks

Serves 2. (140 Calories per serving) Preparation time 10 minutes + 1 hour marinating. Cooking time 15 minutes. Freezing recommended.

1 Mix together the tandoori paste, lemon juice, yogurt and mint in a non-metallic bowl.
2 Add the turkey, stir well, then cover and refrigerate for 1–4 hours. The longer the meat is left to marinate, the more intense the flavour will be.
3 Thread the cubes of turkey on to four skewers. Cook under a medium-high preheated grill or barbecue for about 15 minutes, turning occasionally, and serve.
Cook's note: Wooden kebab sticks should be soaked in hot water for about 10 minutes before use, to prevent them from burning when grilling.
Variation: Balti curry paste can be used instead of tandoori paste.

Glazed turkey steaks

| 4 | Points per serving |
| 16 | Total Points per recipe |

1 aubergine, sliced
1 red (or ordinary) onion, roughly chopped
1 courgette, sliced
1 red pepper, de-seeded and thickly sliced
1 yellow pepper, de-seeded and thickly sliced
2 tablespoons olive oil
4 × 150 g (5½ oz) turkey steaks
2 tablespoons soy sauce
finely grated zest and juice of 1 lemon
1 tablespoon dark or light muscovado sugar
salt and freshly ground black pepper

Serves 4. (285 Calories per serving) Preparation time 15 minutes. Cooking time 25 minutes. Freezing not recommended.

1 Preheat the oven to Gas Mark 6/200°C/400°F. Put the aubergine, onion, courgette and peppers into a roasting pan. Sprinkle with the oil and toss to coat. Season.
2 Transfer to the oven and roast for 10 minutes. Turn the vegetables over and roast for 10–15 more minutes, until the vegetables are tender and just beginning to char.
3 Start to cook the turkey steaks just after you have turned the vegetables over. First preheat a hot grill. Arrange the turkey steaks onto the grill rack.
4 Mix together the soy sauce, lemon zest and juice and muscovado sugar. Season with salt and pepper, then brush over the turkey steaks and grill for 5–6 minutes. Turn the steaks over, brush with the marinade and cook for a further 5–6 minutes. Serve on warm plates, accompanied by the roasted vegetables.

Turkey shepherd's pie

5	Points per serving
20	Total Points per recipe

720 g (1 lb 10 oz) potatoes, peeled and
    quartered
450 g (1 lb) minced turkey
1 large onion, chopped finely
2 carrots, sliced
300 ml (½ pint) chicken or vegetable stock
6 tablespoons skimmed milk
1 tablespoon cornflour
salt and freshly ground black pepper

Serves 4. (340 Calories per serving) Preparation time 20 minutes. Cooking time 1 hour. Freezing recommended. Extra vegetables add padding to this variation on a traditional favourite, without adding any Points!

1   Put the potatoes into a large saucepan and cover with cold water. Add ½ teaspoon of salt and bring to the boil. Cover and reduce the heat, then simmer for about 20 minutes, until tender.
2   Meanwhile, heat a non-stick saucepan and dry-fry the minced turkey with the onion for about 3 minutes. Add the carrots, then pour in the stock. Bring to the boil, then cover and simmer for about 20 minutes.
3   Drain the potatoes and mash well. Add the milk and seasoning, then beat vigorously with a wooden spoon until they are light and fluffy. Alternatively, use a hand-held electric beater to whisk the potatoes for a few moments.
4   Blend the cornflour with about 2 tablespoons of cold water and add to the minced turkey mixture, stirring to blend. Cook until thickened, then remove from the heat.
5   Preheat the oven to Gas Mark 5/190°C/375°F.
6   Transfer the turkey mixture to an ovenproof dish and top with the mashed potato. Bake for 25–30 minutes until thoroughly heated and the surface is brown.

Turkey tomato pasta

3½	Points per serving
14	Total Points per recipe

2 teaspoons olive oil
1 bunch of spring onions, finely sliced
1 garlic clove, crushed
1 green pepper, de-seeded and chopped
4 plum or ordinary tomatoes, chopped
50 g (1¾ oz) sun-dried tomatoes in olive oil,
    rinsed and sliced
200 ml (7 fl oz) tomato juice or passata
    (sieved tomatoes)
1 tablespoon dried oregano or Italian mixed
    dried herbs
175 g (6 oz) pasta shapes
150 g pack of turkey rashers
salt and freshly ground black pepper
oregano or basil leaves, to garnish (optional)

Serves 4. (270 Calories per serving) Preparation time 10 minutes. Cooking time 20 minutes. Freezing not recommended. Turkey rashers are very low in fat and they're tasty too. They make an excellent addition to this easy pasta dish which the whole family, including children, will love.

1   Heat the oil in a large saucepan and sauté the spring onions and garlic until softened, about 2 minutes. Add the green pepper and cook, stirring, for 2 more minutes.
2   Add the fresh and sun-dried tomatoes, tomato juice or passata and dried herbs. Heat until bubbling, then turn the heat to low and simmer for 10 minutes without a lid.
3   Meanwhile, cook the pasta in a large pan of boiling, lightly salted water for 8–10 minutes, until just tender.
4   At the same time, grill the turkey rashers for 1½ minutes on each side, then snip into small pieces.
5   Drain the pasta well, then add the sauce and most of the turkey rashers. Season to taste. Divide between four warmed plates and garnish with oregano or basil leaves (if using) and the reserved turkey rashers. Sprinkle with black pepper and serve at once.

Variation: If you like, you can replace the fresh tomatoes and tomato juice or passata with a 400 g can of chopped tomatoes.

Tasty turkey kebabs with lemon and garlic

2½	Points per serving
10½	Total Points per recipe

450 g (1 lb) fresh turkey steaks, cut into
    chunks

16 large peeled prawns, de-frosted if frozen

16 cherry tomatoes

1 yellow or green pepper, de-seeded and
    cut into chunks

1 garlic clove, crushed

2 teaspoons olive oil

1 teaspoon finely grated lemon zest

3 tablespoons lemon juice

2 teaspoons chopped fresh thyme or parsley

salt and freshly ground black pepper

mixed salad, to serve

Serves 4. (205 Calories per serving). Preparation and cooking time 15 minutes. Freezing not recommended. Barbecued food needn't be fatty or full of calories. Try these delicious turkey kebabs to prove the point. Children will enjoy these kebabs as long as they aren't fussy about prawns.

1 Preheat the barbecue or grill to high.
2 On to each of 8 skewers or soaked wooden kebab sticks, thread 3 or 4 pieces of turkey with 2 prawns, 2 cherry tomatoes and 2 or 3 pieces of pepper.
3 Mix together the remaining ingredients, except the salad leaves, to make the baste.
4 Arrange the kebabs on the barbecue rack or grill pan and brush with the baste. Cook, turning and basting often, for 5–6 minutes. Serve with the mixed salad.

Variation 1: Spice up the marinade by adding 1 finely chopped fresh red or green chilli. Remember to de-seed it first and rinse your hands thoroughly afterwards.

Variation 2: Omit the prawns if you're not keen on seafood. This will reduce the Points to 2 per serving.

Turkey jambalaya

4	Points per serving
15½	Total Points per recipe

1 tablespoon vegetable oil

1 red (or ordinary) onion, finely chopped

2 celery sticks, chopped

2 garlic cloves, crushed

350 g (12 oz) turkey steaks, cut into chunks

1 large green pepper, de-seeded and
    chopped

100 g (3½ oz) button mushrooms

4 tomatoes, skinned and chopped

350 g (12 oz) cooked long grain rice

2 tablespoons chopped fresh parsley

2–3 teaspoons Cajun seasoning

½ teaspoon chilli powder (optional)

salt and freshly ground black pepper

Serves 4. (470 Calories per serving) Preparation time 10 minutes. Cooking time 15 minutes. Freezing not recommended. This delicious turkey dish is made with a blend of spices called Cajun seasoning.

1 Heat the oil in a frying-pan and sauté the onion, celery and garlic until softened, about 2–3 minutes. Add the turkey and cook for 3–4 more minutes.
2 Add the pepper, mushrooms and tomatoes and continue to cook for 2–3 minutes, stirring often.
3 Stir in the cooked rice, parsley, Cajun seasoning and chilli powder (if using). Cook for 6–8 more minutes, stirring frequently until the turkey is cooked.
4 Check the seasoning, adding salt and pepper and a little more chilli powder if required. Spoon on to warm plates and serve at once.

Variation: If you can't find Cajun seasoning, use 2 teaspoons of dried thyme and 2–3 teaspoons of paprika instead.

Turkey tagliatelle with asparagus and peas

6	Points per serving
25	Tota Points per recipe

225 g (8 oz) tagliatelle or spaghetti

2 teaspoons olive oil

225 g (8 oz) turkey stir-fry strips

1 bunch spring onions, trimmed and finely
   chopped

100 g (3½ oz) asparagus spears, trimmed
   and chopped

100 g (3½ oz) frozen petit pois or garden peas

200 g (7 oz) very low-fat plain fromage frais

200 g (7 oz) low-fat garlic and herb-flavoured
   soft cheese

a few basil leaves, torn into shreds

salt and freshly ground black pepper

Serves 4. (435 Calories per serving) Preparation time 10 minutes. Cooking time 15 minutes. Freezing not recommended.

1 Cook the tagliatelle or spaghetti in plenty of boiling, lightly salted water for about 8–10 minutes, until just tender.

2 Meanwhile, heat the olive oil in a large saucepan and sauté the turkey strips for about 5–6 minutes, until golden. Add the spring onions and cook for another 2–3 minutes, then add the asparagus and frozen peas. Cook, stirring, for 2–3 minutes.

3 Add the fromage frais, soft cheese and basil leaves to the saucepan. Heat, stirring gently, for about 3 minutes until melted and blended. Season with salt and pepper.

4 Drain the pasta well. Add the sauce and stir gently to mix. Transfer to four warmed plates and serve at once, garnished with basil leaves.

Variation: Use chicken stir-fry strips instead of turkey, if you prefer - the Points will remain the same. If asparagus is out of season or very expensive, use fine green beans instead.

Turkey steaks with orange and watercress

4	Points per serving
16½	Total Points per recipe

4 × 150 g (5½ oz) turkey steaks

1 tablespoon olive oil

finely grated zest and juice of 1 orange

2 tablespoons clear honey

2 teaspoons cumin seeds

175 g (6 oz) sugar snap peas or mange-tout
   peas, trimmed

175 g (6 oz) carrots, cut into very thin slices

175 g (6 oz) asparagus or fine green beans

salt and freshly ground black pepper

watercress sprigs and shreds of orange zest,
   to garnish

Serves 4. (275 Calories per serving) Preparation time 10 minutes. Cooking time 15 minutes. Freezing not recommended

1 Preheat the grill to high.

2 Arrange the turkey steaks on the grill rack and season with a little salt and pepper.

3 Mix together the oil, orange zest and juice, honey and cumin seeds. Use half this mixture to brush over the turkey steaks. Grill them on each side for 6–8 minutes until thoroughly cooked, basting often.

4 At the same time, cook the vegetables in a small amount of lightly salted boiling water until just tender. Drain well, then add the reserved orange juice mixture. Reheat for a few moments.

5 Divide the vegetables between four warmed serving plates and serve with the turkey steaks. Garnish with watercress and shreds of orange zest.

Cook's note: If you wish, marinate the turkey steaks in the orange juice mixture to impart a more pronounced flavour.

Variation: Another time, use skinless, boneless chicken breasts instead of the turkey steaks. The Points will remain the same.

Turkey Italienne

4	Points per serving
16	Total Points per recipe

225 g (8 oz) turkey mince

4 spring onions or 2 shallots, finely chopped

1 garlic clove, crushed

2 teaspoons mixed dried Italian herbs

100 g (3½ oz) button mushrooms, sliced

300 ml (½ pint) passata (sieved plum tomatoes)

1 vegetable stock cube, dissolved in 150 ml (¼ pint) water

225 g (8 oz) pasta shapes or spaghetti

salt and freshly ground black pepper

fresh basil or oregano, to garnish

Serves 4. (295 Calories per serving) Preparation time 10 minutes. Cooking time 25-30 minutes. Freezing recommended. Another easy supper to dish up for the family. Try adding some fun pasta shapes for the kids.

1. Mix together the turkey mince, spring onions or shallots, garlic and dried herbs. Season with salt and pepper, then form the mixture into tiny meatballs.
2. Heat a large non-stick frying-pan and dry-fry the meatballs for 2–3 minutes, until lightly browned.
3. Add the mushrooms and dry-fry them for a few moments, then stir in the passata and stock. Heat until simmering, then cook gently for 20–25 minutes to reduce the liquid by about one-third, stirring occasionally.
4. Ten minutes before the end of cooking time, put the pasta on to cook in plenty of boiling, lightly salted water. Cook until just tender, about 8–10 minutes, or according to pack instructions.
5. Drain the pasta, the meatballs and sauce and stir together gently. Serve, garnished with basil or oregano.

Cook's note: Another time, use lean minced beef for this recipe. The Points per serving will be 5.

Speedy turkey burgers

4½	Points per serving
19	Total Points per recipe

450 g (1 lb) turkey mince

1 small onion, chopped very finely

2 tablespoons chopped fresh parsley or 2 teaspoons of dried parsley

a few drops of mushroom ketchup or Worcestershire sauce

1 small egg, beaten

salt and freshly ground black pepper

To serve

4 × 50 g (1¾ oz) burger buns

2 tomatoes, sliced

sliced onion rings

shredded lettuce and sliced tomato

Serves 4. (280 Calories per serving) Preparation time 10 minutes. Cooking time 15 minutes. Freezing recommended before cooking. This is a great one to treat the kids with after school and they're ready in almost no time at all.

1. In a large bowl, mix the burger ingredients together (or use a food processor to do it for you).
2. Shape the mixture into four burgers. Wrap and refrigerate until required.
3. Preheat the grill to high. Arrange the burgers on the grill rack and grill for 12–15 minutes, turning once.
4. Lightly toast the cut sides of the burger buns, top with the burgers, then garnish with slices of tomato and onion. Serve with plenty of shredded lettuce and sliced tomato.

Variation: Try a generous dollop of American mustard on top of the burgers before serving them.

6

chapter

lamb, beef, pork and bacon

In this chapter you'll find some truly delicious favourites. Look out for some of the dishes you know and love, with the Weight Watchers slant to make them lower in fat and lower in Points than regular versions. Then try something different too, it's all within these pages.

Spaghetti Bolognese (page 104), Beef Goulash (page 107), Beer-braised Beef with Dumplings (page 103); this is not necessarily the kind of food you thought you could eat when trying to lose weight. That's the thing with the wonderful Weight Watchers Programme – no foods are banned! And we have the ways and means of making sure that recipes usually high in fat are friendlier. By using very lean meat, trimmed of all fat, and by using a greater proportion of vegetables, the Points per serving can be kept to a minimum, without compromising on flavour.

Cottage pie

5	Points per serving
20½	Total Points per recipe

350 g (12 oz) extra-lean minced beef

1 onion, chopped

1 garlic clove, crushed

1 red pepper, de-seeded and diced

1 medium cooking apple, peeled and grated

175 g (6 oz) mushrooms, wiped and diced

1 teaspoon ground cumin

425 ml (¾ pint) beef stock

1 tablespoon tomato purée

225 g (8 oz) carrots, peeled and diced

450g (1 lb) potatoes, peeled and diced

3 tablespoons half-fat crème fraîche

salt and freshly ground black pepper

Serves 4. (345 Calories per serving) Preparation time 25 minutes. Cooking time 50 minutes. Freezing recommended

1 Dry-fry the mince in a non-stick pan until evenly browned and crumbly. Add the onion, garlic, red pepper, apple, mushrooms and cumin. Stir well and cook for a further 5 minutes, stirring from time to time.

2 Add the stock and tomato purée. Bring to the boil, cover and simmer for 20 minutes.

3 Meanwhile, bring a pan of lightly salted water to the boil and cook the carrots and potatoes for 20 minutes. Drain well and mash with the crème fraîche and seasoning.

4 Preheat the oven to Gas Mark 4/180°C/350°F. Spoon the mince mixture into a shallow ovenproof dish. Spread the mashed carrot and potato mixture over the top and bake for 25 minutes. Serve hot.

Lasagne

6	Points per serving
24½	Total Points per recipe

1 teaspoon olive oil

1 small onion, chopped

1 garlic clove, crushed

350 g (12 oz) extra-lean minced beef

1 green pepper, de-seeded and diced

1 carrot, peeled and finely diced

1 teaspoon freeze-dried oregano

2 tablespoons tomato purée

400 g (14 oz) canned chopped tomatoes

300 ml (½ pint) beef stock

6 sheets of oven-ready lasagne

salt and freshly ground black pepper

chopped fresh parsley, to garnish (optional)

For the sauce

25 g (1 oz) cornflour

425 ml (¾ pint) skimmed milk

25 g (1 oz) half-fat Cheddar cheese

25 g (1 oz) fresh parmesan cheese, grated

a pinch of ground nutmeg

Serves 4. (775 Calories per serving) Preparation time 25 minutes. Cooking time 1 hour 15 minutes. Freezing recommended.

1 Heat the oil in a large pan and cook the onion and garlic until softened but not browned. Stir in the mince and cook, stirring until evenly browned.

2 Add the green pepper, carrot and oregano and cook, stirring, for a further 2 minutes. Stir in the tomato purée, chopped tomatoes and stock. Bring to the boil. Season to taste and then simmer for 30 minutes .

3 While the mince is cooking, prepare the sauce. Mix the cornflour with a little of the milk to form a thin paste and heat the remaining milk until boiling. Pour over the cornflour paste and stir well. Return to a clean pan and cook, whisking well until thickened. Stir in the Cheddar, parmesan and nutmeg. Season to taste.

4 Preheat the oven to Gas Mark 4/180°C/350°F. Spoon some of the mince mixture over the base of a large rectangular ovenproof dish. Top with three sheets of lasagne and half of the sauce.

5 Repeat with the same layers, finishing with the sauce and sprinkle the top with a little freshly ground black pepper. Bake for 40 minutes. Serve hot, garnished with chopped fresh parsley, is using.

Beer-braised beef with dumplings

5½	Points per serving
23	Total Points per recipe

2 teaspoons sunflower oil

8 shallots, peeled and halved

350 g (12 oz) lean braising steak, cubed

225 g (8 oz) carrots, peeled and sliced

4 celery stalks, trimmed and sliced
   diagonally

225 g (8 oz) turnips, peeled and diced

150 ml (¼ pint) beer

150 ml (¼ pint) boiling water

1 teaspoon caster sugar

1 tablespoon tomato purée

1 beef stock cube, crumbled

For the dumplings

175 g (6 oz) self-raising flour

½ teaspoon baking powder

2 tablespoons chopped fresh mixed herbs
   such as parsley, chives, coriander,
   oregano

1 tablespoon sunflower oil

Serves 4. (495 Calories per serving) Preparation time 25 minutes. Cooking time 1¼ hours. Freezing recommended.

1 Heat the oil in a large pan and fry the shallots for 2 to 3 minutes to brown lightly.

2 Remove from the pan using a slotted spoon and set to one side. Add the beef to the pan and stir-fry for 2 to 3 minutes until sealed and browned on all sides.

3 Return the shallots to the pan with the carrots, celery and turnips. Pour the beer and boiling water over and stir in the sugar, tomato purée and crumbled stock cube. Bring to the boil, cover and simmer for 40 minutes.

4 To make the dumplings, sift the flour and baking powder into a mixing bowl. Stir in the herbs and sunflower oil and add enough cold water to mix to a soft dough. Using lightly floured hands, shape the mixture into eight small balls and arrange around the top of the stew. Cover the pan again and cook for a further 25 minutes, until the dumplings have almost doubled in size.

Cook's note: If you are unable to get hold of fresh herbs for the dumplings, use 1 tablespoon of dried mixed herbs instead. As an alternative you could also use a tablespoon of coarse grain mustard.

Spaghetti bolognese

6	Points per serving
24	Total Points per recipe

1 teaspoon olive oil

1 red onion, finely chopped

1 garlic clove, crushed

225 g (8 oz) extra-lean minced beef

2 rashers smoked streaky bacon, diced

2 celery stalks, trimmed and sliced

1 carrot, peeled and finely chopped

150 g (5½ oz) button mushrooms, wiped
    and diced

1 teaspoon dried mixed herbs

1 beef stock cube, crumbled

2 tablespoons tomato purée

100 ml (3½ fl oz) red wine

300 ml (½ pint) boiling water

400 g (14 oz) can chopped tomatoes

225 g (8 oz) dried spaghetti

2 tablespoons chopped fresh parsley
    (optional)

salt and freshly ground black pepper

*Serves 4. (420 Calories per serving)
Preparation time 20 minutes.
Cooking time
1 hour. Freezing recommended.*

1   Heat the olive oil in a large pan and cook the onion and garlic until softened. Add the mince and bacon and cook for a further 5 minutes until evenly browned.

2   Stir in the celery, carrot, mushrooms and herbs and cook for 2 minutes.

3   Mix together the crumbled stock cube, tomato purée, red wine and boiling water and pour into the pan with the chopped tomatoes. Stir well, season to taste and bring to the boil. Simmer for 50 minutes.

4   About 10 minutes before the bolognese is ready, bring a large pan of lightly salted

water to the boil. Cook the spaghetti until tender. Drain and toss with the chopped parsley if using.

5   Divide between four warmed serving plates and top with bolognese sauce to serve.

Pot roast beef with parsley broth

4	Points per serving
17	Total Points per recipe

600 g (1 lb 5oz) piece of beef silverside

225 g (8 oz) shallots

225 g (8 oz) carrots

225 g (8 oz) baby new potatoes

1 tablespoon tomato purée

300 ml (½ pint) beef stock

225 g (8 oz) canned chopped tomatoes

4 tablespoons chopped fresh flat leaf parsley

salt and freshly ground black pepper

*Serves 4. (280 Calories per serving) Preparation time 20 minutes. Cooking time
1½ hours. Freezing recommended.*

1   Heat a large flameproof casserole and dry-fry the beef on all sides to seal.
    Add the shallots, carrots, new potatoes, tomato purée and stock to the pan. Season well and stir in the tomatoes.

2   Bring to the boil, cover and simmer for 1½ hours until the beef is tender.

3   To serve, carefully lift the meat out on to a serving platter and arrange the vegetables around it. Bring the pan juices to the boil and stir in the chopped parsley. Check the seasoning, drizzle some over the meat and serve the remainder separately in a jug.

Cook's note: You could also prepare this the night before and then allow to cook slowly in a slow cooker all day. You can leave it for about 10 hours but the beauty of this method of cooking is that if you leave it for an extra hour, it won't spoil. A very welcoming meal to come home to if you've had a long day.

Thai-style red beef curry

6½	Points per serving
27	Total Points per recipe

300 ml (½ pint) Bart reduced-fat
    coconut milk

2 tablespoons Thai red curry paste

2 tablespoons Thai fish sauce

6 kaffir lime leaves

2.5 cm (1-inch) piece of root ginger, peeled
    and grated

1 garlic clove, crushed

350 g (12 oz) rump steak, cubed

175 g (6 oz) fine green beans, trimmed
    and halved

175 g (6 oz) cherry tomatoes, halved

3 tablespoons chopped fresh coriander

Serves 4. (195 Calories per serving) Preparation time 15 minutes. Cooking time 40 minutes. Freezing recommended. Serve hot with freshly boiled Thai or fragrant rice, adding extra Points as necessary.

1 Place the coconut milk in a large pan with the curry paste, fish sauce, lime leaves, ginger and garlic. Heat for 5 minutes until bubbling and then add the beef. Reduce the heat and simmer for 20 minutes.

2 Add the green beans and cook for a further 10 minutes.

3 Toss in the cherry tomatoes and coriander and heat through.

Cook's note 1: Thai cookery uses fish sauce like the Chinese use soy sauce. Most major supermarkets now stock it; look out for it beside the soy sauce or spices.

Cook's note 2: Bart Spices have brought out a reduced-fat coconut milk which means that delicious Thai-style curries can now help you to lose weight!

Variation: You can also use sirloin steak if you wish. The Points per serving will be 7.

Chilli con carne

3	Points per serving
12	Total Points per recipe

225 g (8 oz) extra-lean minced beef

1 onion, chopped

1 garlic clove, crushed

175 g (6 oz) carrots, diced

1 red pepper, de-seeded and diced

1 green pepper, de-seeded and diced

175 g (6 oz) courgettes, diced

150 g (5½ oz) button mushrooms, quartered

1 tablespoon mild chilli powder

1 teaspoon ground coriander

3 tablespoons tomato purée

4 tablespoons red wine

300 ml (½ pint) beef stock

400 g (14 oz) canned chopped tomatoes

225 g (8 oz) canned red kidney beans,
    drained

2 tablespoons chopped fresh parsley

salt and freshly ground black pepper

Serves 4. (240 Calories per serving) Preparation time 20 minutes. Cooking time 1 hour. Freezing recommended. Adding diced vegetables helps bulk out chilli so as well as adding flavour it saves you valuable Points too!

1 Dry-fry the mince in a large non-stick pan until evenly browned. Add the onion, garlic, carrots, peppers, courgettes, mushrooms, chilli powder and coriander. Stir well.

2 Cook for 5 minutes and then add the tomato purée, wine, stock and chopped tomatoes. Season to taste and bring to the boil. Cover, reduce the heat and simmer for 40 minutes.

3 Remove the lid, stir in the kidney beans and cook uncovered for a further 10 minutes. Serve hot sprinkled with chopped fresh parsley.

Cook's note: Make your own low-fat garlic bread by spraying slices of French stick with garlic-flavour low-fat cooking spray. Grill for 2 to 3 minutes, adding the extra Points.

Chilli beef burgers

3½	Points per serving
14	Total Points per recipe

1 small onion, diced

1 tablespoon Worcestershire sauce

350 g (12 oz) extra lean minced beef

1 pickled gherkin, finely chopped

1 teaspoon chilli flakes

1 egg, beaten

a few lettuce leaves, to garnish

Serves 4. (185 Calories per serving) Preparation time 10 minutes. Cooking time 15 minutes. Freezing recommended. Serve hot in a split bap with a few lettuce leaves, adding the Points as necessary.

1 Place the onion in a small pan with 2 tablespoons water and the Worcestershire sauce. Cover and cook gently for 2 to 3 minutes until softened. Drain and place in a mixing bowl. Add the minced beef, gherkin, chilli flakes and egg. Mix well. Divide the mixture into four even-sized burgers and grill under a medium heat for 5 minutes per side.

Cook's note: You could use lamb or turkey mince if preferred. The Points per serving will be 4 with lamb and 2½ with turkey. Flavour the lamb burgers with dried mint instead of chilli flakes and the turkey with wholegrain mustard.

Beef goulash

3	Points per serving
11½	Total Points per recipe

1 teaspoon olive oil

1 onion, sliced

350 g (12 oz) extra-lean stewing steak, cubed

1 tablespoon paprika

2 bay leaves

150 ml (¼ pint) red wine

400 g (14 oz) canned chopped tomatoes

150 ml (¼ pint) beef stock

1 tablespoon chopped fresh parsley

salt and freshly ground black pepper

Serves 4. (220 Calories per serving) Preparation time 20 minutes. Cooking time 1 hour. Freezing recommended. Serve with freshly boiled rice, pasta or mashed potatoes for a real winter warmer, adding extra Points as appropriate.

1 Heat the oil in a pan and fry the onion until softened. Add the steak and cook until sealed on all sides.

2 Stir in the paprika, add the bay leaves, wine, chopped tomatoes and stock and bring to the boil. Season to taste, then simmer for 1 hour or until the meat is tender.

3 Sprinkle with parsley just before serving.

Cook's note: This dish freezes very well. Make a double batch and freeze in single portions for those nights when you need something quick and easy for tea.

Beef teriyaki with noodles

6	Points per serving
24	Total Points per recipe

225 g (8 oz) medium egg noodles

1 teaspoon sunflower oil

300 g (10½ oz) sirloin steak, thinly sliced

1 onion, thinly sliced

1 garlic clove, crushed

1 carrot, cut into thin sticks

3 celery stalks, trimmed and thinly sliced

175 g (6 oz) shiitake mushrooms, sliced

5 tablespoons teriyaki sauce

1 teaspoon sesame oil

1 teaspoon sesame seeds

Serves 4. (385 Calories per serving) Preparation and cooking time 20 minutes. Freezing recommended.

1 Place the noodles in a large bowl and pour boiling water over. Leave to stand for 10 minutes, stirring from time to time.

2 Heat the oil in a large pan or wok and stir-fry the beef for 2 minutes. Add the onion, garlic, carrot, celery and mushrooms and stir-fry for a further 5 minutes.

3 Drain the noodles and toss in to the pan with the teriyaki sauce. Allow the juices to bubble for 2 minutes, drizzle the sesame oil over and toss well. Sprinkle with sesame seeds just before serving.

Variation: This stir-fry is just as delicious made with chicken breasts or skinless boneless chicken thighs. Freeze the meat for about 1 hour to firm it up so it is easier to slice thinly. The Points per serving will be 5.

Beef teriyaki with noodles
Chilli beef burgers

Moussaka

5	Points per serving
20	Total Points per recipe

225 g (8 oz) lean minced lamb

1 onion, chopped

1 garlic clove, crushed

1 teaspoon ground coriander

½ teaspoon ground cumin

1 teaspoon dried oregano

225 g (8 oz) courgettes, wiped and
    coarsely grated

150 ml (¼ pint) beef or lamb stock

1 aubergine

low-fat cooking spray

350 g (12 oz) potatoes, peeled and
    thinly sliced

300 ml (½ pint) skimmed milk

2 tablespoons cornflour

100 g (3½ oz) low-fat plain yogurt

a pinch of ground nutmeg

25 g (1 oz) fresh parmesan cheese, grated

1 beefsteak tomato, sliced

salt and freshly ground black pepper

Serves 4. (315 Calories per serving) Preparation time 40 minutes. Cooking time 1½ hours. Freezing recommended. A little time-consuming to prepare but well worth the effort. Serve with a selection of freshly cooked vegetables or a green salad for a really satisfying meal.

1 Heat a non-stick frying-pan and add the mince. Dry-fry until evenly browned and then drain off any excess fat. Add the onion, garlic, coriander, cumin, oregano and courgettes and cook for a further 5 minutes.

2 Pour the stock over, season to taste. Cover and cook for 20 minutes, stirring from time to time.

3 Meanwhile, trim and slice the aubergine into 1 cm (½ inch) rounds and spray each slice with low-fat cooking spray. Grill for 3 to 4 minutes per side until tender. Cook the potatoes in a pan of boiling water for 5 minutes and then drain.

4 Stir 3 tablespoons of the milk into the cornflour to form a paste. Heat the remaining milk until boiling and then pour over the cornflour. Stir well and return to the heat. Cook, stirring until the sauce thickens. Simmer for 2 minutes and then remove from the heat. Stir in the yogurt, nutmeg and parmesan.

5 Preheat the oven to Gas Mark 5/190°C/375°F. Spoon the mince mixture into the base of an ovenproof dish. Top with the aubergine and potato slices and then pour the sauce over. Arrange the tomato slices over the top and bake for 40 minutes.

Lamb en croûte

5	Points per serving
9½	Total Points per recipe

175 g (6 oz) lamb loin fillet

3 spring onions, trimmed and sliced

1 small garlic clove, crushed

1 teaspoon soy sauce

15 g (½ oz) butter, melted

1 teaspoon wholegrain mustard

3 sheets of filo pastry

salt and freshly ground black pepper

Serves 2 (290 Calories per serving) Preparation time 10 minutes. Cooking time 25 minutes. Freezing recommended.

1 Preheat the oven to Gas Mark 6/200°C/400°F.
2 Make a horizontal slit through the lamb. Place the spring onions and garlic in a small pan with the soy sauce and cover. Heat gently for 1 minute until the spring onions wilt. Spoon into the slit in the lamb and then season well.
3 Mix together the melted butter and mustard and use to brush over each sheet of filo pastry. Stack together and then use to wrap around the lamb fillet, tucking the edges under. Lift on to a non-stick baking sheet and brush with any remaining butter and mustard mixture.
4 Cook for 25 minutes and then serve carved into slices with freshly cooked vegetables.

Grilled lamb steaks with mint and lemon

5½	Points per serving
11	Total Points per recipe

2 × 150 g (5½ oz) lamb leg steaks

1 tablespoon mint jelly

finely grated zest of 1 lemon

25 g (1 oz) fresh wholemeal breadcrumbs

15 g (½ oz) fresh parmesan cheese, grated

salt and freshly ground black pepper

Serves 2. (355 Calories per serving) Preparation time 15 minutes. Cooking time 25 minutes. Freezing recommended.

1 Preheat the oven to Gas Mark 5/19C°C/375°F. Line a baking tray with non-stick baking parchment.
2 Rinse the lamb steaks and pat dry with absorbent kitchen paper. Arrange on to the baking sheet.
3 Mix together the mint jelly, lemon zest, breadcrumbs, parmesan and seasoning. Spread evenly over each steak.
4 Bake for 25 minutes until the lamb is cooked through.

Italian meatballs

4½	Points per serving
18	Total Points per recipe

350 g (12 oz) lean lamb mince

25 g (1 oz) fresh breadcrumbs

1 small onion, finely chopped

1 garlic clove, crushed

1 teaspoon dried oregano

1 teaspoon dried basil

1 egg, beaten

400 g (14 oz) canned chopped tomatoes

300 ml (½ pint) tomato juice

1 beef stock cube

2 tablespoons fresh basil, shredded

salt and freshly ground black pepper

Serves 4. (255 Calories per serving) Preparation time 20 minutes. Cooking time 40 minutes. Freezing recommended. Serve these tasty little meatballs with freshly cooked pasta such as tagliatelle or spaghetti, adding the extra Points for the pasta.

1 Place the mince in a mixing bowl with the breadcrumbs, chopped onion, crushed garlic, dried oregano, basil, seasoning and egg. Mix together thoroughly and then shape the mixture into 16 small balls.
2 Heat a large non-stick pan and dry-fry the meatballs for 2 to 3 minutes to lightly brown and seal on all sides. Add the chopped tomatoes and tomato juice to the pan and crumble the stock cube over.
3 Bring to the boil, stirring, and then cover. Reduce the heat and simmer for 30 minutes. Scatter with the fresh basil just before serving.

Garlic and rosemary leg of lamb

6½	Points per serving
25½	Total Points per recipe

½ leg of lamb (about 1 kg/2 lb 4 oz in weight)

4 garlic cloves, sliced

8 small sprigs of fresh rosemary

1 orange, cut into thin slices

1 tablespoon clear honey

salt and freshly ground black pepper

Serves 4. (465 Calories per serving) Preparation time 10 minutes + marinating. Cooking time 1½ hours + 15 minutes standing. Freezing recommended. A perfect Sunday lunch treat served with freshly cooked veggies.

1 Rinse the lamb and pat dry. Lift into a shallow non-metallic dish.

2 Make random slits all over the top of the lamb and insert slices of garlic and rosemary sprigs. Arrange the orange slices over the top and season well. Cover and leave to marinate for at least 3 hours or preferably overnight.

3 Preheat the oven to Gas Mark 6/200°C /400°F. Lift the lamb into a roasting tin, removing the orange slices and cook for 1 hour. Brush the top with honey and return to the oven for 30 minutes. Allow to stand for 15 minutes before carving.

Cumin-spiced lamb kebabs

3	Points per serving
12	Total Points per recipe

350 g (12 oz) lean cubed lamb (leg or
   neck fillet)

1 teaspoon cumin seeds

1 garlic clove, crushed

2 teaspoons olive oil

½ teaspoon chilli flakes

1 teaspoon balsamic vinegar

1 tablespoon tomato purée

2 red onions, sliced into thick wedges

Serves 4. (180 Calories per serving) Preparation and cooking time 20 minutes + 2 hours marinating. Freezing recommended. If using wooden skewers, soak them in water for 20 minutes before using; this will prevent them from burning.

1 Place the cubed lamb in a non-metallic dish. Mix together the cumin seeds, garlic, olive oil, chilli flakes, vinegar and tomato purée. Pour over the lamb, toss well and leave to marinate for 2 hours.

2 Thread the lamb on to skewers alternating with the red onion. Grill for about 10 minutes, turning frequently.

Ginger lamb stir-fry

4	Points per serving
16	Total Points per recipe

300 g (10½ oz) lamb neck fillet, thinly sliced

2 tablespoons soy sauce

1 garlic clove, crushed

2.5 cm (1-inch) piece of root ginger, peeled
   and grated

2 tablespoons sherry

2 tablespoons tomato ketchup

1 tablespoon sunflower oil

1 red pepper, de-seeded and sliced

1 green pepper, de-seeded and sliced

6 spring onions, trimmed and sliced

150 g (5½ oz) beansprouts

Serves 4. (245 Calories per serving) Preparation and cooking time 20 minutes. Freezing recommended. Serve with freshly boiled noodles or rice and remember to add the extra Points.

1 Place the lamb in a dish and add the soy sauce, garlic, ginger, sherry and ketchup. Mix well.

2 Heat the oil in a pan, drain the lamb from the marinade (reserving) and stir-fry for 3 minutes. Add the peppers to the pan and stir-fry for a further 2 minutes.

3 Toss in the spring onions, beansprouts and reserved marinade and stir-fry for 2 to 3 minutes.

Variation: Liven up plain boiled rice or noodles by tossing with fresh mixed herbs, lemon, orange or lime zest or a few toasted cumin and lightly crushed coriander seeds.

Sunday Lunch

Treat your friends and family
to a special spread for
Sunday lunch.

✳

Garlic and Rosemary Leg of Lamb with
Point-free vegetables (courgettes, carrots,
broccoli, grilled peppers, green beans)
Boiled new potatoes with mint
(add extra Points)
page 110, (1 serving) 6½ Points

✳

Lemon Yogurt Ice
page 188, (1 serving) 2½ Points

✳

Total Points: 9 Points

Pork escalopes with mushrooms and ricotta

5½	Points per serving
23	Total Points per recipe

8 × 100g (3½ oz) small pork escalopes

150 g (5½ oz) button mushrooms, wiped

1 garlic clove, crushed

1 tablespoon light soy sauce

25 g (1 oz) fresh breadcrumbs

finely grated zest of 1 lemon

150 g (5½ oz) ricotta cheese

1 teaspoon olive oil

400 g (14 oz) canned chopped tomatoes

3 tablespoons white wine

1 teaspoon caster sugar

1 teaspoon chopped fresh tarragon

salt and freshly ground black pepper

Serves 4. (360 Calories per serving) Preparation time 20 minutes. Cooking time 40 minutes. Freezing recommended.

1 Place each escalope between two sheets of greaseproof paper and hammer lightly with the side of a rolling pin to flatten out a little. Preheat the oven to Gas Mark 4/180°C/350°F.

2 Chop the mushrooms finely and put in a small pan with the garlic and soy sauce. Cover and cook gently until softened. Drain on to absorbent kitchen paper.

3 In a small mixing bowl, mix together the breadcrumbs, lemon zest, ricotta cheese and cooked mushrooms. Season well.

4 Spoon a little of the filling on to one side of each escalope and roll up the escalope, enclosing the filling. Secure the escalope roll with a cocktail stick if necessary.

5 Heat the oil in a frying-pan and brown the escalopes in the pan to seal on all sides. Transfer to a shallow ovenproof dish.

6 Mix together the chopped tomatoes, wine, sugar and tarragon. Season to taste. Spoon over the escalopes and bake for 30 minutes.

Sweet and sour pork chops

6	Points per serving
24	Total Points per recipe

4 medium pork loin chops, trimmed of fat

1 teaspoon sunflower oil

1 red pepper, de-seeded and thinly sliced

1 green pepper, deseeded and thinly sliced

1 carrot, cut into thin sticks

6 spring onions, trimmed and sliced

200 g (7 oz) canned pineapple chunks in juice

1 tablespoon white wine vinegar

1 tablespoon demerara sugar

2 tablespoons tomato ketchup

1 tablespoon cornflour

Serves 4. (290 Calories per serving) Preparation time 15 minutes. Cooking time 20 minutes. Freezing recommended.

1 Grill the chops on both sides under a medium heat until cooked through. This will take about 15 minutes.

2 Meanwhile, heat the oil in a pan or wok and stir-fry the peppers and carrot for 5 minutes. Add the spring onions and cook for a further 2 minutes.

3 Drain the pineapple, reserving the juice and add to the pan. Mix the reserved juice with the vinegar, sugar, ketchup and cornflour. Add to the pan and cook, stirring, until the juices thicken.

4 Serve the cooked pork chops on warmed serving plates and top with the sweet and sour sauce.

Chinese-style pork with soy-braised beansprouts

2½	Points per serving
10½	Total Points per recipe

Serves 4. (195 Calories per serving) Preparation and cooking time 25 minutes. Freezing recommended.

2 teaspoons sunflower oil

350 g (12 oz) lean pork leg steaks,
    thinly sliced

1 teaspoon Chinese five-spice powder

1 garlic clove, crushed

2 tablespoons sherry

1 tablespoon tomato purée

3 tablespoons soy sauce

2 tablespoons oyster sauce

225 g (8 oz) beansprouts

1 small head of Chinese leaves, trimmed
    and shredded

75 g (2¾ oz) canned drained water
    chestnuts, sliced

50 g (1¾ oz) frozen peas

1   Heat the oil in a wok and add the pork and five spice powder. Stir-fry for 5 minutes until sealed and just beginning to brown.

2   Mix together the garlic, sherry, tomato puree, soy sauce and oyster sauce and set aside.

3   Add the beansprouts, Chinese leaves, water chestnuts and peas to the wok and stir-fry for a further 2 to 3 minutes.

4   Drizzle the sauce over and allow the juices to bubble for 2 minutes. Serve at once.

Variation: Other green vegetables such as thinly sliced and de-seeded green pepper, mange-tout peas or spring onions can also be added to this tasty stir-fry.

Cider pork casserole with root vegetables

4	Points per serving
17	Total Points per recipe

Serves 4. (345 Calories per serving) Preparation time 20 minutes. Cooking time 55 minutes. Freezing recommended.

1 tablespoon sunflower oil

350 g (12 oz) lean pork (ie tenderloin)

175 g (6 oz) carrots, sliced

1 red onion, sliced into wedges

225 g (8 oz) baby new potatoes, scrubbed
    and halved

350 g (12 oz) swede, diced

225 g (8 oz) parsnips, cut into thick chunks

150 ml (¼ pint) dry cider

300 ml (½ pint) pork or chicken stock

1 teaspoon dried thyme

2 tablespoons cornflour

50 ml (2 fl oz) fresh orange juice

salt and freshly ground black pepper

1   Heat the oil in a large casserole and fry the pork for 2 minutes to seal on all sides. Add the carrots, onion, potatoes, swede and parsnips and cook for a further 2 to 3 minutes.

2   Stir in the cider, stock, thyme and seasoning and bring to the boil. Cover and simmer for 45 minutes.

3   Mix the cornflour with the orange juice to form a thin paste and stir into the casserole. Cook, stirring, until the juices thicken.

Pork and sweet pepper hot pot

3½	Points per serving
13½	Total Points per recipe

2 teaspoons sunflower oil

350 g (12 oz) lean diced pork

2 leeks, trimmed and sliced

1 red pepper, de-seeded and diced

1 green pepper, de-seeded and diced

1 yellow pepper, de-seeded and diced

2 sprigs of fresh thyme or 1 teaspoon
    freeze-dried thyme

a pinch of salt

300 ml (½ pint) pork or chicken stock

350 g (12 oz) potatoes, sliced

25 g (1 oz) low-fat spread, melted

1 teaspoon paprika

Serves 4. (295 Calories per serving)
Preparation time 25 minutes.
Cooking time 1 hour. Freezing
recommended.

1 Heat the sunflower oil in a large
   flameproof casserole and fry the pork to
   seal on all sides. Preheat the oven to Gas
   Mark 4/180°C/350°F.

2 Add the leeks, peppers, thyme and salt
   to the pork and pour the stock over.
   Bring to the boil, then remove from
   the heat.

3 Arrange the potato slices over the top.
   Mix together the melted low fat spread
   and paprika and brush over the top.

4 Bake for 1 hour until the potatoes are
   golden and tender.

Roast loin of pork with peaches and sage

4½	Points per serving
28	Total Points per recipe

1 kg (2 lb 4 oz) boneless pork loin

1 teaspoon olive oil

2 shallots, chopped

4 canned peach halves in natural juice,
    finely chopped

1 teaspoon freeze-dried sage

1 tablespoon flaked almonds

25 g (1 oz) fresh wholemeal breadcrumbs

1 tablespoon clear honey

salt and freshly ground black pepper

Serves 6. (435 Calories per serving) Preparation time 20 minutes. Cooking time 1
hour. Freezing recommended. Ideal for Sunday lunch. A fruity stuffing keeps
the pork beautifully moist as it roasts. Serve with freshly cooked vegetables.

1 Preheat the oven to Gas Mark 6/200°C/400°F.

2 Use a long-bladed sharp knife to cut a slit right through the centre of the pork loin,
   forming a pocket for the filling.

3 Heat the olive oil in a small pan and cook the shallots until softened. Remove from
   the heat and stir in the peaches, sage, almonds, breadcrumbs, honey and seasoning.

4 Spoon into a piping bag fitted with a large plain nozzle and push the nozzle into the
   slit in the pork. Squeeze out the stuffing so it fills the pocket.

5 Lift into a non-stick roasting tin. Season the top of the pork and roast for 1 hour.
   Leave to rest for 10 minutes before carving into slices.

Chinese-style rice and ham

4½	Points per serving
19	Total Points per recipe

225 g (8 oz) rice

1 tablespoon sunflower oil

1 onion, finely chopped

1 teaspoon Chinese five-spice powder

1 carrot, peeled and grated

75 g (2¾ oz) frozen peas

1 red pepper, de-seeded and diced

75 g (2¾ oz) wafer-thin ham, shredded

1 tablespoon soy sauce

low-fat cooking spray

2 eggs, beaten

salt

Serves 4. (350 Calories per serving) Preparation time 20 minutes. Cooking time 25 minutes. Freezing recommended without the egg.

1 Measure the rice into a cup to gauge the volume, then add 1½ times the amount of water and a generous pinch of salt. Bring to the boil, cover, reduce the heat and simmer for 10 minutes. Remove the lid, fluff up with a fork. Leave to cool and dry out a little.

2 Heat the oil in a large pan or wok and stir-fry the onion until softened. Stir in the five-spice powder, carrot, peas and red pepper. Stir-fry for a further 5 minutes. Add the rice, stir well and heat through. Toss in the ham and soy sauce.

3 Spray a small non-stick frying-pan with low-fat cooking spray and heat gently. Beat the eggs with 2 tablespoons of cold water and pour into the pan. Cook gently until the egg sets and you have a flat pancake-type omelette. Transfer to a board and slice into thin strips.

4 Pile the cooked rice into a serving dish and arrange the egg strips over the top in a lattice pattern.

Variation: As an extra treat, add 50 g (1¾ oz) peeled prawns to this recipe. The Points per serving will be 5.

Boiled bacon with spiced lentils

3	Points per serving
13	Total Points per recipe

350 g (12 oz) cooked ham hock

2 bay leaves

6 peppercorns, crushed

100 g (3½ oz) red lentils

1 onion, chopped

225 g (8 oz) carrots, diced

1 tablespoon medium curry powder

225 g (8 oz) canned chopped tomatoes

600 ml (1 pint) boiling water

Serves 4. (260 Calories per serving) Preparation time 20 minutes. Cooking time 1½ hours. Freezing recommended.

1 Place the ham hock in a large pan with the bay leaves, peppercorns, lentils, onion, carrots, curry powder and chopped tomatoes. Add the boiling water and bring to the boil.

2 Cover and cook for about 1 hour and 20 minutes, stirring from time to time. The lentils should be tender and the meat from the ham should be falling off the bone. Remove the bay leaves.

3 Remove the ham from the pan, shred the meat with two forks and discard the bone. Return to the pan and stir well. Serve hot.

Cook's note: Ask at your local deli counter or supermarket deli counter for a ham hock; they should sell one to you for very little, generally about £1.00.

Bangers and mash

6½	Points per serving
13½	Total Points per recipe

4 thick reduced-fat pork sausages

1 teaspoon sunflower oil

1 onion, sliced

1 teaspoon caster sugar

225 g (8 oz) carrots, diced

350 g (12 oz) floury potatoes, diced

3 tablespoons low-fat plain fromage frais

1 teaspoon low-fat spread

1 tablespoon chopped fresh parsley, to
garnish (optional)

salt and freshly ground black pepper

Serves 2. (545 Calories per serving) Preparation time 10 minutes. Cooking time 25 minutes. Freezing recommended. Turn this all time favourite into a healthy low-fat version that's equally as moreish.

1 Grill the sausages for 10 to 12 minutes, turning frequently, until evenly cooked. Meanwhile, heat the sunflower oil in a small pan and gently cook the onion over a low heat until softened. Stir in the sugar and cook for a further 5 minutes over a low heat.

2 Meanwhile, bring a pan of salted water to the boil and cook the carrots and potatoes until tender. Drain and mash thoroughly with the seasoning, fromage frais and low-fat spread.

3 Serve the grilled sausages with the caramelised onions and a generous mound of the mash. Sprinkle some fresh parsley over the top, if using.

Ham and bean hot pot

3½	Points per serving
13	Total Points per recipe

2 teaspoons sunflower oil

2 leeks, trimmed and sliced

175 g (6 oz) carrots, peeled and diced

300 g (10½ oz) lean gammon steak,
trimmed and diced

1 tablespoon wholegrain mustard

2 tablespoons Worcestershire sauce

300 ml (½ pint) pork or chicken stock

1 bay leaf

225 g can of Weight Watchers from Heinz
Baked Beans in Tomato Sauce

freshly ground black pepper

Serves 4. (215 Calories per serving) Preparation time 20 minutes. Cooking time 35 minutes. Freezing recommended. Canned beans are a handy store-cupboard standby; they're filling, nutritious and low in fat. Serve with French bread or a baked potato, adding the extra Points.

1 Heat the oil in a flameproof casserole and add the leeks, carrots and gammon, cook for 5 minutes. Then stir in the mustard, Worcestershire sauce, stock and bay leaf.

2 Bring to the boil, cover and simmer for 20 minutes.

3 Remove the bay leaf, season with freshly ground black pepper and stir in the beans. Cook for a further 10 minutes and serve.

Cook's note: Gammon can be quite salty so you shouldn't need to add any extra salt to this dish. When you're adding the black pepper, check to see if you want to add a little more.

Family Favourite

You can eat anything on the
Weight Watchers Programme –
even Toad in the Hole, so enjoy!

✳

Toad in the Hole
page 119, (1 serving) 3½ Points

✳

Rhubarb and Orange Fool
page 182, (1 serving) 2 Points

✳

Total Points: 5½ Points

LAMB, BEEF, PORK & BACON **119**

Toad in the hole

3½	Points per serving
14	Total Points per recipe

8 low-fat thin sausages

1 tablespoon sunflower oil

100 g (3½ oz) plain flour

300 ml (½ pint) skimmed milk

1 egg

150 g (5½ oz) open cap mushrooms, halved

2 tablespoons snipped fresh chives

salt and freshly ground black pepper

Serves 4. (290 Calories per serving) Preparation time 20 minutes. Cooking time 30 minutes. Freezing not recommended.

1 Lightly grill the sausages for 5 minutes. Preheat the oven to Gas Mark 6/200°C/400°F.

2 Drizzle the oil over the base of a 20 cm (8-inch) square non-stick tin and then heat in the oven while preparing the batter.

3 Sift the flour into a mixing bowl and make a well in the centre. Add the milk and egg and whisk thoroughly to form a smooth batter. Leave to stand for 10 minutes.

4 Add the sausages and mushrooms to the heated pan and return to the oven for 5 minutes.

5 Add the chives and seasoning to the batter and stir well. Carefully remove the tin from the oven and pour the batter over. Return to the oven for 30 minutes until well risen and golden brown. Serve at once, allowing two sausages per serving.

Honey mustard gammon with slow-roasted tomatoes

3½	Points per serving
15	Total Points per recipe

4 × 125 g (4½ oz) gammon steaks

2 teaspoons clear honey

2 teaspoons wholegrain mustard

finely grated zest of 1 orange

700 g (1 lb 9 oz) plum or vine tomatoes

salt and freshly ground black pepper

Serves 4. (225 Calories per serving) Preparation time 15 minutes + marinating. Cooking time 1½ hours. Freezing not recommended. Slowly roasting the tomatoes intensifies their flavour and they're so delicious that you can eat them on toast or on their own with a drizzle of balsamic vinegar.

1 Arrange the gammon steaks in a shallow non-metallic dish. Mix together the honey, mustard and orange zest. Drizzle over the gammon and leave to marinate for 1 hour, turning over half-way through.

2 Meanwhile preheat the oven to Gas Mark 2/150°C/300°F. Cut the tomatoes in half and place cut-side up on to a grill or cooling rack, resting on a baking sheet.

3 Sprinkle with the salt and freshly ground black pepper. Roast for 1½ hours.

4 Just before the tomatoes are ready, grill the gammon for 2 to 3 minutes on each side. Serve topped with the roasted tomatoes.

Cook's note: You can cook up a double batch of tomatoes and keep them in an airtight container in the fridge for up to 3 days.

Toad in the hole

Open-topped bacon and tomato toasties

4	Points per serving
4	Total Points per recipe

1 medium slice of wholemeal bread

1 teaspoon low-fat spread

1 rasher lean back bacon

1 small tomato, thinly sliced

2 to 3 red onion rings

1 low-fat cheese slice

salt and freshly ground black pepper

Serves 1. (255 Calories per serving) Preparation and cooking time 20 minutes. Freezing not recommended. A speedy lunchtime snack, guaranteed to fill you up.

1 Lightly toast the bread on both sides and spread with low fat spread.

2 Grill the bacon slice until just crispy and lift onto the toast. Arrange the tomato slices over the bacon with the onion rings. Top with the cheese slice and season.

3 Grill for 1 to 2 minutes until the cheese melts and serve hot.

Baked stuffed tomatoes with ham and mushrooms

2	Points per serving
4½	Total Points per recipe

100 g (3½ oz) cooked white or brown rice

25 g (1 oz) wafer-thin ham, diced

10 pitted black olives, diced

1 tablespoon tomato purée

50 g (1¾ oz) mushrooms, wiped and diced

50 g (1¾ oz) low-fat soft cheese with garlic
    and herb (Boursin)

2 large beef tomatoes

salt and freshly ground black pepper

some salad leaves, to garnish (optional)

Serves 2. (180 Calories per serving) Preparation time 20 minutes. Cooking time 25 minutes. Freezing recommended.

1 Preheat the oven to Gas Mark 5/190°C/375°F.

2 Mix together the rice, ham, olives, tomato purée, mushrooms and soft cheese.

3 Slice the tops off the tomatoes and using a small spoon scoop out the seeds. Season the cavities with salt and pepper and then fill with the rice mixture.

4 Bake for 20 minutes until the tomatoes are tender but still retaining their shape. Serve warm or cold, with salad leaves to garnish, if desired.

Vegetarian recipes are so interesting these days. Once seen as an alternative for non meat-eaters, vegetarian dishes are now enjoyed by everyone as delicious meals in their own right. The ideas in this chapter are no exception!

Where possible, buy fresh vegetables in season if you want to keep costs low. It's true that you can virtually buy any vegetable all year round, but if it's been flown in from faraway places, you can't guarantee how fresh it is.

Savoury vegetable crumble

4	Points per serving
17	Total Points per recipe

1 teaspoon vegetable oil

1 tablespoon soy sauce

2 leeks, sliced

2 carrots, diced

225 g (8 oz) button mushrooms, quartered

175 g (6 oz) baby corn, halved

100 g (3½ oz) frozen peas

275 g (9½ oz) can of Weight Watchers
   from Heinz Vegetable Soup

salt and freshly ground black pepper

For the crumble

100 g (3½ oz) plain flour

25 g (1 oz) rolled oats

50 g (1¾ oz) low-fat spread

50 g (1¾ oz) reduced-fat Red Leicester
   cheese, grated

 Serves 4. (300 Calories per serving) Preparation time 25 minutes. Cooking time 40 minutes. Freezing recommended.

1 Heat the vegetable oil and soy sauce in a pan and add the leeks, carrots, mushrooms, corn and peas. Cover and cook over a low heat for 5 minutes, stirring half-way through.

2 Stir in the soup, season to taste and heat through. Transfer to a shallow ovenproof dish.

3 Preheat the oven to Gas Mark 5/190°C/375°F.

4 Sift the flour into a mixing bowl and stir in the oats. Rub in the low-fat spread using your fingertips and then stir in the cheese. Sprinkle over the vegetable mixture and bake for 30 minutes, until the topping is golden and crunchy. Serve hot.

Variation: Try adding different flavours of soup such as tomato or mushroom. Adjust the Points as necessary.

---

menu plan

Cheap and Cheerful Vegetarian Supper

Vegetarian foods are usually reasonably inexpensive to make. This savoury crumble is an excellent example.

✳

Savoury Vegetable Crumble
page 124, (1 serving) 4 Points

✳

Fruit & Nut Baked Apples
page 162, (1 serving) 2½ Points

✳

Total Points: 6½ Points

vegetable kebabs

3	Points per serving
8	Total Points per recipe

2 red onions, cut into thick wedges

3 courgettes, cut into thick chunks

1 red pepper, de-seeded and cut into
large chunks

1 green pepper, de-seeded and cut into
large chunks

2 medium corn on the cobs, each cut into
4 rings

225 g (8 oz) cubed smoked tofu (optional)

1 tablespoon olive oil

1 tablespoon balsamic vinegar

1 tablespoon clear honey

1 teaspoon cumin seed

1 teaspoon crushed coriander seeds

1 tablespoon fresh snipped chives

½ teaspoon dried chilli flakes

salt and freshly ground black pepper

V Serves 2. (335 Calories per serving). Preparation and cooking time 20 minutes + marinating. Freezing not recommended. You can prepare the vegetables up to two days ahead of time and toss with the marinade. Keep in a covered container in the fridge until ready to grill. Serve hot on a bed of steamed couscous or herby rice, adding the extra Points.

1 Toss together the onion wedges, courgettes, peppers, corn and tofu, if desired.

2 Mix together the olive oil, balsamic vinegar, honey, cumin seeds, coriander, salt and pepper, chives and chilli flakes and drizzle this mixture over the vegetables. Marinate for at least 15 minutes in the fridge.

3 Thread alternately on to skewers and grill for 10 minutes, turning frequently.

Variation: Make a simple no-Point dressing to serve with these kebabs from 4 tablespoons of fat-free French dressing, a pinch of cayenne pepper and 1 tomato, skinned, de-seeded and very finely chopped. Season well and chill until required.

Red pepper lasagne

3½	Points per serving
13½	Total Points per recipe

4 red peppers, halved and de-seeded

1 tablespoon olive oil

1 onion, chopped

1 garlic clove, crushed

175 g (6 oz) mushrooms, sliced

400 g (14 oz) canned chopped tomatoes

2 tablespoons chopped fresh basil

25 g (1 oz) cornflour

300 ml (½ pint) skimmed milk

200 g (7 oz) low-fat soft cheese with
    garlic and herbs

6 sheets oven-ready lasagne

salt and freshly ground black pepper

(V) *Serves 4. (300 Calories per serving) Preparation time 30 minutes. Cooking time 45 minutes. Freezing recommended.*

1   Place the peppers skin-side up on to a grill rack and grill until skins are blackened. Transfer to a polythene bag and allow to cool. When cool, peel away the skins and slice thinly.

2   Heat the olive oil in a pan and fry the onion and garlic until softened. Add the mushrooms and pepper strips and cook for a further 5 minutes. Stir in the chopped tomatoes, seasoning and basil and simmer for 10 minutes.

3   Preheat the oven to Gas Mark 5/190°C/375°F. Mix the cornflour with a little of the milk to form a thin paste. Heat the remaining milk until boiling and then pour over the cornflour paste. Mix well and then return to the pan. Cook, stirring, until the sauce thickens. Reduce the heat and simmer for 5 minutes. Add the soft cheese and stir until the cheese melts into the sauce.

4   To assemble, spoon half of the pepper mixture over the base of a rectangular ovenproof dish and top with three sheets of lasagne. Drizzle with half of the sauce. Repeat the layers, finishing with a layer of sauce.

5   Bake for 30 minutes until bubbling and golden on top, serve hot.

Roasted vegetable moussaka

5	Points per serving
20½	Total Points per recipe

1 onion, sliced thickly

225 g (8 oz) courgettes, thickly sliced

2 red peppers, de-seeded and coarsely
    chopped

1 aubergine, diced

1 tablespoon balsamic vinegar

1 tablespoon sun-dried tomato purée

1 teaspoon dried oregano

400 g (14 oz) canned chopped tomatoes

400 g (14 oz) canned borlotti beans, drained

350 g (12 oz) potatoes, peeled and sliced

300 ml (½ pint) skimmed milk

2 tablespoons cornflour

100 g (3½ oz) low-fat Greek-style plain yogurt

a pinch of ground nutmeg

25 g (1 oz) fresh parmesan cheese, grated

1 beefsteak tomato, sliced

salt and freshly ground black pepper

(V) *if parmesan is vegetarian Serves 4 (325 Calories per serving). Preparation time 20 minutes. Cooking time 1¼ hours. Freezing recommended.*

1   Preheat the oven to Gas Mark 5/190°C/375°F.

2   Line a baking sheet with non-stick baking parchment. Toss together the onion, courgettes, peppers and aubergine with the balsamic vinegar, sun-dried tomato purée, seasoning and oregano. Arrange on the baking sheet. Roast for 25 minutes until the vegetables are tender. Stir in the chopped tomatoes and beans and spoon into the base of an ovenproof dish.

3   Cook the potato slices in a pan of lightly salted water until tender. Drain and arrange over the roasted vegetables.

4   Stir 3 tablespoons of the milk into the cornflour to form a paste. Heat the remaining milk until boiling and pour over the cornflour. Stir well and return to the heat, cook stirring until sauce thickens. Simmer for 2 minutes then remove from the heat and stir in the yogurt, nutmeg and parmesan.

5   Spoon the sauce over the potatoes and arrange the tomato slices over the top, return to the oven for 30 minutes until the topping is golden and bubbling.

Ratatouille

1	Point per serving
5	Total Points per recipe

2 red onions, cut into thin wedges

1 aubergine, diced

225 g (8 oz) courgettes, thickly sliced

1 red pepper, de-seeded and diced

1 green pepper, de-seeded and diced

1 yellow pepper, de-seeded and diced

1 tablespoon olive oil

1 tablespoon balsamic vinegar

1 teaspoon dried oregano

2 tablespoons sun-dried tomato purée

3 tablespoons red wine

400 g (14 oz) canned chopped tomatoes

2 tablespoons chopped fresh parsley

salt and freshly ground black pepper

Ⓥ Serves 4. (150 Calories per serving) Preparation time 15 minutes. Cooking time 40 minutes. Freezing recommended. You can serve this on its own or on a bed of cooked pasta or rice, adding the extra Points. It's even good as a topping for baked potatoes.

1 Preheat the oven to Gas Mark 6/200°C/ 400°F. Line a roasting tin with non-stick baking parchment.

2 Toss together the onion wedges, aubergine, courgettes and peppers. Mix together the oil, vinegar, oregano and seasoning and drizzle over the vegetables.

3 Toss well and then roast for 30 minutes, until tender and beginning to char at the edges.

4 Place the sun-dried tomato purée, wine and chopped tomatoes in a pan and bring to the boil. Add the roasted vegetables and simmer for 10 minutes. Sprinkle with parsley and serve.

Variation: If you want to add some protein, sprinkle some grated reduced-fat Cheddar over the top of this dish, adding the Points as necessary.

Chickpea falafel with cucumber and mint dressing

3	Points per serving
13	Total Points per recipe

1 teaspoon olive oil

1 small onion, finely chopped

1 garlic clove, crushed

1 teaspoon ground coriander

1 teaspoon ground cumin

½ teaspoon chilli flakes

425 g (15 oz) canned chickpeas, drained

1 egg

25 g (1 oz) wholemeal breadcrumbs

3 tablespoons chopped fresh coriander

salt and freshly ground black pepper

some shredded lettuce, to serve

For the dressing

150 ml (¼ pint) low-fat plain yogurt

2 tablespoons mint jelly

175 g (6 oz) cucumber, finely diced

Ⓥ Serves 4. (170 Calories per serving) Preparation time 25 minutes. Cooking time 25 minutes. Freezing recommended for the falafel only.

1 Heat the olive oil in a pan and gently cook the onion and garlic until softened but not browned. Stir in the coriander, cumin and chilli flakes. Cook for 1 minute and then remove from the heat. Place in a food processor with the chick-peas, egg, breadcrumbs, seasoning and coriander.

2 Blend until evenly combined and then, using clean hands, shape the mixture into about 20 small balls.

3 Preheat the oven to Gas Mark 5/190°C/ 375°F. Arrange the falafel on to a non-stick baking sheet and cook for 20 minutes.

4 To make the dressing, mix together the yogurt and mint jelly. Stir in the cucumber. Season to taste.

5 Serve the cooked falafel on a bed of shredded lettuce, drizzled with the mint and cucumber dressing.

Scrambled eggs with asparagus and crème fraîche

5	Points per serving
5	Total Points per recipe

50 g (1¾ oz) fine asparagus tips, halved

1 teaspoon butter

2 eggs

2 tablespoons half-fat crème fraîche

1 teaspoon snipped chives

Ⓥ *Serves 1. (285 Calories per serving) Preparation and cooking time 10 minutes. Freezing not recommended.*

1 Plunge the asparagus tips into boiling water.
2 Melt the butter in a small pan. Beat together the eggs and crème fraîche with 2 tablespoons of cold water. Add to the pan and cook, stirring, until the eggs are scrambled.
3 Drain the asparagus and toss in. Scatter with chives and serve at once.

Oriental tofu

1½	Points per serving
6½	Total Points per recipe

350 g (12 oz) firm tofu, cut into chunks

4 tablespoons hoisin sauce

1 garlic clove, crushed

1 tablespoon tomato purée

1 tablespoon sunflower oil

150 g (5½ oz) baby corn, trimmed and halved

150 g (5½ oz) mange-tout peas

150 g (5½ oz) shiitake mushrooms, sliced

150 g (5½ oz) beansprouts

6 spring onions, trimmed and sliced

1 teaspoon sesame seeds, toasted

Ⓥ *Serves 4. (180 Calories per serving). Preparation and cooking time 25 minutes. Freezing recommended.*

1 Place the tofu in a shallow dish with the hoisin sauce, crushed garlic and tomato purée. Mix well and leave to marinate for 30 minutes.
2 Heat the oil in a wok or large frying-pan. Drain the tofu from the marinade, (reserving the marinade) and stir-fry for 5 minutes. Add the baby corn, mange-tout peas and mushrooms. Stir-fry for a further 5 minutes.
3 Toss in any reserved marinade with the beansprouts and spring onions and heat through. Pile on to a serving plate and sprinkle with sesame seeds.

Cook's note: If you prefer, you could use ordinary button mushrooms but the shiitake mushrooms really are ideal since they add that Oriental touch.

Thai-style vegetables

4½	Points per serving
17½	Total Points per recipe

1 teaspoon sunflower oil

350 g (12 oz) Quorn cubes

6 shallots, halved

1 aubergine, diced

1 red pepper, de-seeded and diced

1 green pepper, de-seeded and diced

225 g (8 oz) sweet potato, chopped

175 g (6 oz) shiitake mushrooms, sliced

4 lime leaves

1 tablespoon Thai green curry paste

300 ml (½ pint) Bart 88% fat-free coconut milk

300 ml (½ pint) vegetable stock

2 tablespoons chopped fresh coriander

Ⓥ *Serves 4. (235 Calories per serving) Preparation time 15 minutes. Cooking time 35 minutes. Freezing recommended.*

1 Heat the oil in a large pan and add the Quorn, shallots, aubergine, peppers, sweet potato and mushrooms. Cook, stirring for 5 minutes, then stir in the lime leaves, curry paste, coconut milk and stock.
2 Bring to the boil and allow to bubble for 5 minutes. Reduce the heat and simmer uncovered for 25 minutes.
3 Spoon into a warmed serving dish and scatter the coriander over the top.

Welsh rarebit with roasted tomatoes

4	Points per serving
4	Total Points per recipe

3 plum tomatoes

1 teaspoon balsamic vinegar

1 thick slice of sliced bread

1 teaspoon reduced-fat spread

25 g (1 oz) half-fat Cheddar cheese, grated

1 teaspoon plain flour

½ teaspoon English mustard

4 tablespoons beer

salt and freshly ground black pepper

Ⓥ *Serves 1. (195 Calories per serving) Preparation time 10 minutes. Cooking time 20 minutes. Freezing not recommended. This cheesy toast is delicious served with oven-roast tomatoes.*

1 Preheat the oven to Gas Mark 6/200°C/400°F. Slice the tomatoes in half and season well. Drizzle each half with a little of the vinegar and arrange on to a baking sheet. Roast for 20 minutes.

2 Meanwhile, toast the bread until golden and spread with the low-fat spread.

3 Place the cheese, flour, mustard and beer in a small pan and heat gently, stirring constantly until the cheese has melted. Spoon over the toast and grill for 2 to 3 minutes, until bubbling and lightly browned.

Butternut squash and boursin risotto

4½	Points per serving
18	Total Points per recipe

1 tablespoon olive oil

4 shallots, chopped

350 g (12 oz) butternut squash, diced

225 g (8 oz) risotto rice

150 ml (¼ pint) white wine

600 ml (1 pint) vegetable stock

100 g (3½ oz) low-fat Boursin with garlic and herbs

salt and freshly ground black pepper

Ⓥ *Serves 4. (360 Calories per serving) Preparation time 15 minutes. Cooking time 25 minutes. Freezing not recommended. Risottos are at their best when served immediately, when the texture of the rice is just creamy. When left to cool, the rice becomes stodgy.*

1 Heat the olive oil in a large pan and cook the shallots until softened. Add the squash and rice and cook for a further 2 minutes.

2 Gradually add the wine and stock, a little at a time, and cook, stirring, until the rice has absorbed all the stock, the squash is tender and the risotto has a creamy texture. This should take about 20 minutes. Season to taste and then stir in the Boursin.

3 Stir until the Boursin has melted and serve at once.

Variation: Diced pumpkin or courgette could be used instead of butternut squash if preferred. A little grated orange or lemon zest is also nice. The Points will remain the same.

Grilled aubergine sandwich

6	Points per serving
12	Total Points per recipe

1 aubergine

1 tablespoon olive oil

225 g (8 oz) canned chopped tomatoes with herbs

2 tablespoons sun-dried tomato purée

1 red pepper, de-seeded and diced

100 g (3½ oz) reduced-fat mozzarella, grated

1 tablespoon dried breadcrumbs

salt and freshly ground black pepper

Ⓥ *Serves 2. (285 Calories per serving) Preparation time 15 minutes. Cooking time 15 minutes. Freezing not recommended.*

1 Thinly slice the aubergine horizontally. Season each slice and brush lightly with olive oil. Grill for 10 minutes, turning half-way through.

2 In a small pan, mix together the chopped tomatoes, tomato purée and red pepper. Heat through. Sandwich two aubergine slices together with some of the tomato mixture. Sprinkle the tops with grated mozzarella and breadcrumbs and return to the grill for 5 minutes, until the cheese melts and begins to brown.

Moroccan stew

1½	Points per serving
6	Total Points per recipe

1 tablespoon olive oil

1 onion, sliced

1 garlic clove, crushed

1 large aubergine, diced

225 g (8 oz) carrots, sliced

350 g (12 oz) butternut squash, peeled,
    de-seeded and diced

1 teaspoon ground cinnamon

1 teaspoon ground cumin

1 teaspoon ground coriander

2 tablespoons tomato purée

300 ml (½ pint) vegetable stock

200 g (7 oz) silken tofu, cubed

50 g (1¾ oz) no-soak dried apricots, chopped

2 tablespoons chopped fresh coriander

1 teaspoon chopped fresh mint

25 g (1 oz) toasted pine kernels

salt and freshly ground black pepper

Ⓥ *Serves 4. (225 Calories per serving) Preparation time 25 minutes. Cooking time 50 minutes. Freezing recommended. The aubergines soak up the flavours beautifully in this Moroccan spiced stew. The squash adds a little sweetness which is so well enhanced by the cinnamon.*

1 Heat the olive oil in a large casserole and add the onion, garlic, aubergine, carrots and squash. Cook, stirring, for 5 minutes and then add the cinnamon, cumin, coriander and seasoning. Cook for a further minute.

2 Add the tomato purée and stock. Bring to the boil, cover and simmer for 40 minutes, stirring from time to time.

3 Add the cubed tofu, apricots, fresh coriander and mint and cook for a further 5 minutes.

4 Just before serving, scatter the toasted pine kernels over the top.

Cook's note: Toasting pine kernels before adding them to dishes gives them a richer flavour so you can get away with using less. Heat a small heavy-based or non-stick pan and add the pine kernels. Cook over a gentle heat for about 2 minutes, tossing constantly until they brown a little. Take care because once they begin to brown, they will do so very quickly.

Chilli bean cakes with pineapple chutney

3	Points per serving
11½	Total Points per recipe

1 teaspoon olive oil

1 onion, chopped

1 garlic clove, crushed

350 g (12 oz) canned red kidney beans

1 teaspoon chilli powder

25 g (1 oz) wholemeal breadcrumbs

1 egg

2 tablespoons chopped fresh parsley

1 teaspoon sunflower oil

salt and freshly ground black pepper

For the chutney

225 g (8 oz) canned pineapple in natural
    juice

1 tablespoon sweet chilli sauce

1 tablespoon rice wine vinegar

1 teaspoon caster sugar

Ⓥ *Serves 4. (205 Calories per serving) Preparation time 25 minutes. Cooking time 15 minutes. Freezing recommended.*

1 Heat the olive oil in a small pan and cook the onion and garlic until softened.

2 Remove from the heat and transfer to a food processor with the kidney beans, chilli powder, breadcrumbs, egg, seasoning and parsley. Blend until well combined. Using clean hands, shape the mixture into 8 small round cakes.

3 Wipe out a frying-pan with the sunflower oil and heat. Cook the bean cakes for 2 to 3 minutes per side until piping hot.

4 To make the chutney, dice the pineapple and place in a small pan with 3 tablespoons of the juice, chilli sauce, vinegar and sugar, bring to the boil and simmer for 5 minutes. Serve warm with the cakes.

Vegetarian Christmas Lunch

Here's a delicious vegetarian alternative to the traditional Christmas lunch.

✳

Oven-Roasted Tomato Tartlets
page 24, (1 serving) 1 Point

✳

Moroccan Stew
page 132, (1 serving) 1½ Points

✳

Pears in Mulled Wine
page 159, (1 serving) 3½ Points

✳

Total Points: 6 Points

Leek and potato tortilla

3	Points per serving
12½	Total Points per recipe

225 g (8 oz) potatoes, peeled and sliced

350 g (12 oz) leeks, sliced

5 eggs

4 tablespoons skimmed milk

1 teaspoon chopped fresh dill

1 tablespoon sunflower oil

salt and freshly ground black pepper

Ⓥ *Serves 4. (220 Calories per serving) Preparation time 15 minutes. Cooking time 15 minutes. Freezing not recommended. Add other cooked vegetables such as diced peppers, sliced courgettes or mushrooms as an alternative.*

1 Cook the potato slices and leeks in a pan of lightly salted water for 5 minutes, until just tender. Drain well.

2 Beat together the eggs, milk, dill and seasoning.

3 Heat the oil in a 20.5 cm (8-inch) non-stick frying-pan and arrange the drained leeks and potato slices over the base. Pour the egg mixture over and cook over a medium heat until you see the edges of the egg setting.

4 Preheat and grill to a medium heat. Place the pan under the grill to set and finish cooking the top of the omelette.

5 Allow to stand for 5 minutes before carefully turning out on to a serving plate and cutting into wedges to serve.

Cook's note: Try to use a frying-pan with a metal handle if it is to be placed under the grill. If you don't have one, protect the handle with a double thickness of foil wrapped around it.

Brown rice with Chinese vegetables

5½	Points per serving
22	Total Points per recipe

225 g (8 oz) brown rice

1 vegetable stock cube, crumbled

1 teaspoon Chinese five-spice powder

225 g (8 oz) carrots, diced

1 red pepper, de-seeded and diced

100 g (3½ oz) mushrooms, sliced

600 ml (1 pint) boiling water

100 g (3½ oz) frozen peas

100 g (3½ oz) beansprouts

3 tablespoons soy sauce

2 tablespoons crunchy peanut butter

Ⓥ *Serves 4. (320 Calories per serving) Preparation time 15 minutes. Cooking time 45 minutes. Freezing recommended.*

1 Place the rice, stock cube and five-spice powder in a pan with 2 tablespoons water. Cook, stirring, over a low heat for 2 minutes.

2 Add the carrots, pepper and mushrooms and then pour in the water. Bring to the boil, reduce the heat. Cover and simmer for 40 minutes, until the liquid has been absorbed and the rice is tender.

3 Add the peas, beansprouts, soy sauce and peanut butter. Stir well, cover again and cook for 5 minutes. Delicious eaten hot or cold.

Cook's note: Brown rice takes a lot longer to cook than white but has a deliciously nutty flavour. If you are in a hurry however, use long grain white rice and cook it for only 20 minutes.

vegetable pie

3½	Points per serving
14	Total Points per recipe

350 g (12 oz) baby new potatoes, scrubbed and halved

175 g (6 oz) baby carrots, trimmed and scrubbed

225 g (8 oz) shelled broad beans

2 leeks, sliced

100 g (3½ oz) frozen peas

400 g (14 oz) canned chopped tomatoes

1 tablespoon mixed dried herbs

2 tablespoons vermouth

8 sheets filo pastry

25 g (1 oz) low-fat spread, melted

salt and freshly ground black pepper

V *Serves 4. (320 Calories per serving) Preparation time 25 minutes. Cooking time 35 minutes. Freezing recommended.*

1 Bring a pan of lightly salted water to the boil and cook the potatoes and carrots for 10 minutes. Add the beans, leeks and peas to the pan and cook for a further 5 minutes.

2 Drain the vegetables and toss with the chopped tomatoes, herbs, seasoning and vermouth. Spoon into an ovenproof dish.

3 Preheat the oven to Gas Mark 6/200°C /400°F.

4 Keeping the filo pastry sheets together, brush the top sheet with the low-fat spread on one side and then crumple it up. Repeat with all 8 sheets and then arrange the crumpled sheets over the vegetables. Bake for 20 minutes, until the pastry is crisp and golden. Serve hot.

Cook's note: Filo pastry is a useful standby to have in the freezer; it turns simple food into something special without adding too many calories.

vegetable noodles with ginger and soy

3½	Points per serving
15	Total Points per recipe

250 g (9 oz) medium egg noodles

1 tablespoon sunflower oil

2.5 cm (1-inch) root ginger, grated

1 garlic clove, crushed

175 g (6 oz) carrots, cut into thin sticks

2 celery stalks, trimmed and sliced

150 g (5½ oz) mushrooms, sliced

175 g (6 oz) courgettes, trimmed and cut into sticks

100 g (3½ oz) mange-tout peas, trimmed

100 g (3½ oz) baby corn, trimmed and halved

6 spring onions, trimmed and sliced

3 tablespoons soy sauce

1 tablespoon medium sherry

V *Serves 4. (340 Calories per serving) Preparation and cooking time 25 minutes. Freezing recommended.*

1 Place the noodles in a bowl and pour boiling water over. Leave to stand for 10 minutes.

2 Heat the oil in a large pan or wok and stir-fry the ginger, garlic, carrots, celery, mushrooms, courgettes, mange-tout peas and corn for 5 minutes.

3 Drain the noodles and toss into the vegetables with the spring onions, soy sauce and sherry. Cook for a further 2 to 3 minutes.

Cook's note: When you buy a piece of root ginger, keep what you don't use in the freezer so you can just grate a little as and when you need it.

French toast with mustard

Serves 1. (325 Calories per serving) Preparation and cooking time 10 minutes. Freezing not recommended.

4½	Points per serving
4½	Total Points per recipe

2 medium slices of wholemeal bread

1 egg

½ teaspoon coarse-grain mustard

150 ml (¼ pint) skimmed milk

½ teaspoon butter

salt and freshly ground black pepper

1 Cut the bread slices in half diagonally.

2 Beat together the egg, mustard and milk and season to taste. Pour into a shallow dish. Dip the bread slices in and leave to soak up the liquid.

3 Heat the butter in a non-stick frying-pan and cook the soaked bread slices for 2 to 3 minutes per side, until golden. Serve at once.

Cook's note: Try and use bread that's about 2 days old. Very fresh bread won't soak up the liquid very well.

Fresh tomato pizzas

Serves 2. (245 Calories per serving) Preparation and cooking time 20 minutes. Freezing not recommended.

4	Points per serving
7½	Total Points per recipe

2 medium English muffins, split in half

1 teaspoon olive oil

½ small onion

1 tablespoon tomato purée

1 tablespoon burger relish

1 large beef steak tomato, sliced

1 teaspoon balsamic vinegar

15 g (½ oz) parmesan, shaved

freshly ground black pepper

4 fresh basil leaves (optional)

1 Toast the muffins lightly on both sides. Heat the olive oil in a small pan and cook the onion for a few minutes, just to soften.

2 Mix together the tomato purée and burger relish and spread a little over each muffin half. Spoon over the cooked onions and then top with the tomato slices.

3 Drizzle with a little balsamic vinegar, then top with parmesan shavings and a grinding of fresh black pepper.

4 Finally top with a basil leaf, if desired.

Cook's note: Use a potato peeler to shave thin slices of the parmesan; its easier than using a knife.

Peppered Quorn stroganoff with mushroom sauce

Serves 4. (155 Calories per serving) Preparation time 25 minutes. Cooking time 35 minutes. Freezing recommended. Serve hot with freshly cooked rice or pasta, adding the extra Points as necessary.

2½	Points per serving
9½	Total Points per recipe

225 g (8 oz) Quorn pieces

1 vegetable stock cube, crumbled

1 tablespoon olive oil

1 onion, sliced

1 garlic clove, crushed

225 g (8 oz) mushrooms, sliced

300 g can of reduced-fat mushroom soup

1 tablespoon brandy

3 tablespoons half-fat crème fraîche

salt and freshly ground black pepper

1 Place the Quorn in a bowl, sprinkle the stock cube over and add 2 tablespoons boiling water. Stir well and leave to stand for 10 minutes.

2 Meanwhile, heat the olive oil in a pan and cook the onion, garlic and mushrooms until softened. Add the Quorn and cook for a further 2 minutes.

3 Stir in the soup, brandy and seasoning and simmer for 10 minutes.

4 Add the crème fraîche and heat through without boiling.

Peppered Quorn stroganoff
Fresh tomato pizzas

Meatless mince parcels

4½	Points per serving
17½	Total Points per recipe

1 tablespoon chilli oil

1 garlic clove, crushed

350 g (12 oz) frozen soy mince, thawed

225 g (8 oz) courgettes, grated

1 teaspoon ground coriander

1 teaspoon cumin seeds

1 tablespoon tomato purée

4 tablespoons boiling water

To serve

4 tablespoons sweet chilli sauce

a bowl of fresh lettuce leaves

Ⓥ Serves 4. (175 Calories per serving) Preparation and cooking time 20 minutes. Freezing recommended for the filling only. Choose large Iceberg lettuce leaves to wrap up this spicy filling.

1 Heat the chilli oil in a pan and stir-fry the garlic and soy mince for 5 minutes.

2 Stir in the courgettes, coriander, cumin, tomato purée and 4 tablespoons of boiling water. Cook for a further 5 minutes.

3 To serve, pile into a warmed serving dish, and "build" your own at the table.

4 Drizzle a little chilli sauce on to a lettuce leaf and then spoon some mince mixture into the centre. Wrap up, enclosing the filling.

Cook's note: You can flavour your own oils at home. Just place a few chillies in a screw-top jar, add enough olive oil to cover and leave to soak for at least 1 month to take up the flavour of the chillies.

Mixed bean chilli

2	Points per serving
8	Total Points per recipe

1 tablespoon olive oil

1 onion, sliced

2 garlic cloves, crushed

175 g (6 oz) carrots, diced

1 red pepper, de-seeded and diced

1 green pepper, de-seeded and diced

150 g (5½ oz) button mushrooms, quartered

1 medium cooking apple, peeled and grated

1 tablespoon mild chilli powder

225 g (8 oz) canned chopped tomatoes

400 g (14 oz) canned mixed beans in
     spicy sauce

2 tablespoons chopped fresh parsley

Ⓥ Serves 4. (200 Calories per serving) Preparation time 15 minutes. Cooking time 40 minutes. Freezing recommended.

1 Heat the olive oil in a pan and cook the onion, garlic, carrots, peppers and mushrooms for 5 minutes.

2 Stir in the grated apple and chilli powder and cook for a further 2 minutes.

3 Stir in the tomatoes and mixed beans. Cover and simmer for 30 minutes and then sprinkle in the chopped parsley and serve hot.

Cook's note: A handy dish to make up and keep in individual portions in the freezer. Try it spooned into a jacket potato or with a chunk of crusty bread. It would also be delicious with warmed pitta breads; add the extra Points as necessary.

8 chapter

pasta, rice, noodles and beans

We all eat so much more pasta than we used to; it's one of the most popular family meals. And the same goes for rice, noodles and beans too, so we thought we'd include a chapter featuring recipes using these adaptable favourites, just to give you a little more inspiration.

These days, we're all so busy doing a million and one other jobs, food and family meals often get pushed to the bottom of the list. That's where naturally fast foods come to the fore. Pasta, rice, noodles and beans all come into this category, for you can make some quick and tasty meals in minutes with any of these ingredients.

vegetable pasta bake

3	Points per serving
11½	Total Points per recipe

1 onion, chopped

1 courgette, sliced

100 g (3½ oz) fine green beans, trimmed
    and chopped

1 red pepper, de-seeded and chopped

100 g (3½ oz) mushrooms, sliced

400 g (14 oz) canned chopped tomatoes

275 g jar of tomato pasta sauce with herbs

125 g (4½ oz) no pre-cook lasagne (6 sheets)

150 g (5½ oz) low-fat plain yogurt

1 egg

50 g (1¾ oz) half-fat Cheddar-type cheese,
    grated

salt and freshly ground black pepper

Ⓥ Serves 4. (260 Calories per serving) Preparation time 15 minutes. Cooking time 45 minutes. Freezing recommended. This fresh vegetable lasagne makes a healthy and delicious meat-free meal. Serve with a leafy green salad, sprinkled with a little fat-free vinaigrette.

1 Preheat the oven to Gas Mark 5/190°C/375°F.
2 Put the onion, courgette, green beans and pepper into a large saucepan with a little lightly salted boiling water and simmer for about 5 minutes to cook them until just tender. Drain well, then add the mushrooms, canned tomatoes and pasta sauce.
3 Spoon half the vegetable mixture into an oblong ovenproof dish and top with half the lasagne sheets. Spoon the rest of the vegetable mixture on top and cover with the remaining lasagne.
4 Beat together the yogurt and egg. Season with salt and pepper and mix in half the cheese. Spread over the surface of the lasagne and sprinkle the remaining cheese over the top. Bake for 35–40 minutes until golden brown.

Roasted vegetables with pasta

5	Points per serving
20½	Total Points per recipe

1 large courgette, sliced

1 red (or ordinary) onion, sliced

1 red pepper, de-seeded and chopped

100 g (3½ oz) baby corn, halved

100 g (3½ oz) button mushrooms

2 tablespoons olive oil

a few sprigs of fresh rosemary and thyme

225 g (8 oz) pasta shapes

150 g (5½ oz) low-fat plain fromage frais

2 tablespoons finely grated parmesan cheese

salt and freshly ground black pepper

Ⓥ Serves 4. (345 Calories per serving) Preparation time 10 minutes. Cooking time 15 minutes. Freezing not recommended. Roasted vegetables taste delicious stirred through hot pasta.

1 Preheat the oven to Gas Mark 6/200°C/400°F.
2 Put all the vegetables into a roasting pan and drizzle with the olive oil. Add the herb sprigs and season with salt and pepper. Stir well, then roast for about 15 minutes, until just beginning to brown.
3 Meanwhile, cook the pasta shapes in lightly salted boiling water for about 8–10 minutes until just tender. Drain well, return to the saucepan and add the fromage frais and parmesan cheese. Heat gently for 2–3 minutes.
4 Fold the hot vegetables through the pasta. Check the seasoning, adding a little more salt and pepper, if needed. Pile on to warmed plates and serve at once.

spicy bean and vegetable supper

5½	Points per serving
21½	Total Points per recipe

1 tablespoon olive or vegetable oil

1 large red or yellow pepper, de-seeded
  and sliced

125 g (4½ oz) fine green beans, trimmed
  and sliced

1 red (or ordinary) onion, sliced

4 tomatoes, chopped

2 × 420 g cans of mixed beans in mild
  chilli sauce

225 g (8 oz) spinach leaves, thoroughly
  washed

a few drops of Tabasco pepper sauce

chopped red onion and parsley, to garnish

100 g (3½ oz) tortilla chips

salt and freshly ground black pepper

Ⓥ Serves 4. (385 Calories per serving) Preparation time 10 minutes. Cooking time 15 minutes. Freezing not recommended. Healthy, nutritious, quick and tasty. What more could you ask for when you want good food fast?

1 Heat the oil in a wok or large frying-pan. Sauté the pepper, green beans and onion until softened, about 5 minutes.

2 Add the tomatoes and canned beans. Heat until simmering, then reduce the heat and cook gently for 3–4 minutes.

3 Add the spinach and cook for 3 more minutes, stirring occasionally, until the leaves have wilted down. Check the seasoning, adding Tabasco sauce, salt and pepper according to taste.

4 Ladle the mixture onto warmed serving plates and sprinkle with chopped red onion and parsley. Serve with tortilla chips.

Cook's note: If you can't find mixed beans in a chilli or spicy sauce, used ordinary mixed pulses and add extra Tabasco sauce to the recipe, according to taste.

vegetable and haricot bean bake

4½	Points per serving
18	Total Points per recipe

450 g (1 lb) butternut squash, peeled,
  deseeded and thinly sliced

225 g (8 oz) parsnips, sliced

2 large carrots, scrubbed, unpeeled and
  thinly sliced

2 courgettes, thinly sliced

2 tablespoons olive oil

1 teaspoon cumin seeds (optional)

420 g can of haricot beans, rinsed and
  drained

400 g (14 oz) canned chopped tomatoes
  with herbs

1 vegetable stock cube, dissolved in 150 ml
  (¼ pint) hot water

2 tablespoons cornflour, blended with a little
  cold water

8 × 15 g (½ oz) slices of French bread

4 teaspoons polyunsaturated margarine

2–3 teaspoons garlic purée

salt and freshly ground black pepper

Ⓥ Serves 4. (505 Calories per serving) Preparation time 20 minutes. Cooking time 1 hour. Freezing not recommended. Roast seasonal vegetables to bring out their flavour, then mix with haricot beans and tomatoes to make a tasty, healthy casserole.

1 Preheat oven to Gas Mark 6/200°C/400°F.

2 Tip the squash, parsnips, carrots and courgettes into a large baking dish. Season, then sprinkle with the olive oil and cumin seeds (if using). Toss together, then roast for 30 minutes, turning the vegetables after 15 minutes.

3 Remove the baking dish from the oven. Reduce the temperature to Gas Mark 4/180°C/350°F.

4 Add the haricot beans, tomatoes and vegetable stock to the baking dish. Stir in the blended cornflour. Return to the oven and bake for 20 minutes.

5 Spread the slices of French bread with the margarine and garlic puree. Arrange them on top of the vegetables, then bake for another 5–6 minutes, until crispy and brown.

6 Serve the vegetable bake by topping each portion with two pieces of garlic bread.

Quick prawn and crab noodles

5	Points per serving
19½	Total Points per recipe

1 tablespoon tomato purée

1 tablespoon light soy sauce

1 tablespoon cider or light malt vinegar

1 tablespoon dark or light muscovado sugar

2 teaspoons cornflour

225 g (8 oz) thread egg noodles

2 teaspoons stir-fry oil or vegetable oil

1 red pepper, de-seeded and finely sliced

1 bunch of spring onions, trimmed and
   finely sliced

1 courgette, sliced

100 g (3½ oz) mange-tout peas, sliced

225 g (8 oz) large peeled prawns, defrosted
   if frozen

8 frozen crab sticks, chopped into chunks

salt and freshly ground black pepper

menu plan

Bank Holiday

Enjoy something quick and tasty when you've been out and about on a well-earned day off. These tasty dishes fit the bill perfectly.

Quick Prawn & Crab Noodles
page 142, (1 serving) 5 Points

Chocolate Orange Treat
page 179, (1 serving) 4½ Points

Total Points: 9½ Points

Serves 4. (440 Calories per serving) Preparation and cooking time 25 minutes. Freezing not recommended. Frozen prawns and crab sticks make a quick meal when combined with instant egg noodles and a few vegetables.

1 In a small bowl, mix together the tomato purée, soy sauce, vinegar, sugar and cornflour. Set aside.

2 Soak the noodles in boiling water for about 6 minutes, or according to the pack instructions.

3 Meanwhile, heat the oil in a wok or large frying-pan. Add the pepper, spring onions, courgette and mange-tout peas and stir-fry over a high heat for about 3 or 4 minutes.

4 Add the prawns and crab sticks and cook, stirring, for 2 minutes until hot. Stir the soy sauce mixture, add to the wok or frying-pan and cook, stirring constantly, until thickened and blended. Season to taste.

5 Drain the noodles and divide between four warmed serving plates. Pile the prawn mixture on top, then serve at once.

Cook's note: Muscovado sugar gives a lovely flavour to the sweet and sour sauce in this recipe; it doesn't really matter whether you use the dark or light variety. If you haven't got any to hand, you could use ordinary brown sugar although the flavour will not be quite as nice.

Macaroni cheese

7	Points per serving
28½	Total Points per recipe

175 g (6 oz) macaroni

2 tablespoons polyunsaturated margarine

40 g (1½ oz) plain flour

450 ml (¾ pint) skimmed milk

175 g (6 oz) half-fat Cheddar-type cheese

a good pinch of mustard powder

3 tomatoes, sliced

15 g (½ oz) fresh breadcrumbs

salt and freshly ground black pepper

Ⓥ Serves 4. (425 Calories per serving) Preparation time 10 minutes. Cooking time 20 minutes. Freezing recommended. This inexpensive and nutritious family favourite is given the Weight Watchers treatment by using reduced-fat cheese and skimmed milk.

1 Cook the macaroni in plenty of boiling, lightly salted water for about 10 minutes, or according to the pack instructions, until just tender.

2 Meanwhile, put the margarine, flour and milk into a saucepan. Heat, stirring constantly with a small whisk, until the sauce boils and thickens. Reduce the heat and cook gently for a couple of minutes. Remove from the heat.

3 Preheat the grill.

4 Stir about two-thirds of the cheese into the sauce, and allow it to melt. Season with the mustard powder, salt and pepper. Drain the macaroni thoroughly and add it to the sauce, stirring to coat. Transfer the mixture to a 1.5 litre (2¾ pint) heatproof dish.

5 Arrange the sliced tomatoes over the surface of the macaroni cheese, then sprinkle with the breadcrumbs and remaining cheese. Grill until browned and bubbling.

Variation: Use penne (pasta tubes) instead of macaroni if you prefer, or any type of pasta shape that will hold the cheese sauce.

Speedy spaghetti

7	Points per serving
27½	Total Points per recipe

225 g (8 oz) spaghetti or pasta shapes

1 tablespoon olive oil

1 bunch of spring onions, trimmed and finely chopped

100 g (3½ oz) mange-tout peas or sugar snap peas, trimmed and sliced

1 yellow or red pepper, de-seeded and chopped

3 tablespoons red or green pesto sauce

4 tablespoons finely grated parmesan cheese

fresh basil or chopped parsley, to garnish

salt and freshly ground black pepper

Ⓥ Serves 4. (330 Calories per serving) Preparation time 10 minutes. Cooking time 15 minutes. Freezing not recommended.

1 Bring a large saucepan of lightly salted water to the boil. Add the spaghetti or pasta shapes and cook for about 8–10 minutes, or according to pack instructions, until just tender.

2 Meanwhile, heat the olive oil in a large frying-pan and sauté the spring onions, mange-tout peas or sugar snap peas and pepper for about 5 minutes, until softened.

3 Drain the spaghetti or pasta well, then return it to the saucepan and add the cooked vegetables and pesto sauce. Season with salt and pepper. Heat gently for about 2 minutes, stirring, until the mixture is piping hot.

4 Divide between 4 warmed serving plates. Sprinkle with the parmesan cheese and garnish with basil or chopped parsley. Serve at once.

Cook's note: Garnishing with a few fresh herbs isn't essential but it adds a lovely finishing touch and makes your dishes look and taste fabulous.

Spinach and soft cheese cannelloni

6½	Points per serving
25½	Total Points per recipe

450 g (1 lb) fresh spinach, thoroughly
    washed
225 g (8 oz) low-fat soft cheese with
    garlic and herbs
225 g (8 oz) cannelloni tubes
1 tablespoon olive oil
1 onion, finely chopped
500 ml (18 fl oz) passata (sieved tomatoes)
1 teaspoon dried mixed Italian herbs
4 tablespoons finely grated parmesan cheese
salt and freshly ground black pepper

Ⓥ *Serves 4. (440 Calories per serving) Preparation time 25 minutes. Cooking time 40 minutes. Freezing recommended.*

1   Preheat the oven to Gas Mark 4/180°C/350°F.
2   Pack the spinach into a very large saucepan. Put the lid on and cook over a low heat for about 4 minutes, until the leaves have wilted. No water is needed, as the spinach will cook in the water that is left clinging to the leaves. Drain well, squeezing out the excess moisture with the back of a wooden spoon. Cool, then chop finely.
3   Put the soft cheese into a mixing bowl and beat with a wooden spoon to soften it. Add the spinach, mix well and season with salt and pepper.
4   Fill the cannelloni tubes with the spinach mixture. Lightly grease a shallow ovenproof dish with a little of the olive oil and then arrange the cannelloni in the baking dish.
5   Heat the remaining olive oil in a saucepan and sauté the onion for about 3 minutes, until softened. Add the passata and herbs. Cook, uncovered, for 5 minutes. Season with salt and pepper, then pour over the cannelloni.
6   Bake for 25–30 minutes, until bubbling and browned. Serve at once, sprinkled with the parmesan cheese.

Cook's note: Use frozen leaf spinach if fresh is unavailable.

Vegetable risotto

4½	Points per serving
18	Total Points per recipe

1 tablespoon olive oil
175 g (6 oz) risotto rice
1 large onion, chopped
1 garlic clove, crushed
1 red or yellow pepper, de-seeded and
    chopped
100 g (3½ oz) fine green beans, trimmed
    and sliced
1 courgette, chopped
175 g (6 oz) mushrooms, sliced
2 tomatoes, skinned and chopped
10 pitted black or green olives, halved
2 vegetable stock cubes dissolved in 900 ml
    (1½ pints) hot water
2 tablespoons chopped fresh herbs (basil,
    oregano, parsley)
4 tablespoons finely grated parmesan cheese
salt and freshly ground black pepper

Ⓥ *Serves 4. (285 Calories per serving) Preparation time 10 minutes. Cooking time 30 minutes. Freezing recommended.*

1   Heat the oil in a large frying-pan or wok. Add the rice and sauté over a medium heat for about 5 minutes, until the rice looks translucent.
2   Add the onion, garlic, pepper, green beans, courgette and mushrooms. Cook, stirring, for 5 more minutes, then add the tomatoes and olives.
3   Pour in approximately half of the hot stock and bring up to the boil. Reduce the heat and simmer gently, stirring occasionally, for about 20 minutes, adding the extra stock as needed until the rice is tender and all the liquid has been absorbed.
4   Add the herbs and half the parmesan cheese to the risotto, then season with salt and pepper. Serve at once, sprinkled with the remaining cheese.

Cook's note: Risotto rice (sometimes called arborio or carnaroli) is the best for this recipe, as it turns deliciously creamy as it cooks and absorbs the stock. Add a little extra stock or water if the rice is not fully cooked before the liquid has been absorbed.

Tex mex chicken tortillas

5	Points per serving
20½	Total Points per recipe

1 tablespoon garlic-flavoured olive oil

225 g (8 oz) skinless, boneless chicken, chopped into chunks

1 bunch spring onions, trimmed and chopped

1 red pepper, de-seeded and chopped

2 celery stalks, finely chopped

1 teaspoon chilli powder

400 g can of red kidney beans, rinsed and drained

1 tablespoon chopped fresh coriander plus extra to garnish

4 medium soft tortillas

100 g (3½ oz) low-fat plain fromage frais

2 tomatoes, finely chopped

½ small red onion, finely chopped

salt and freshly ground black pepper

Serves 4. (335 Calories per serving) Preparation time 10 minutes. Cooking time 35 minutes. Freezing not recommended. You can buy Mexican-style soft tortillas in most supermarkets. When baked, they are crisp and delicious, so do try them in this tasty recipe.

1 Preheat the oven to Gas Mark 4/180°C/350°F.

2 Heat the oil in a large frying-pan and sauté the chicken for 3–4 minutes, until sealed and browned. Add the spring onions, pepper, celery and chilli powder and cook for a few more minutes, stirring, until softened.

3 Tip the beans into the frying pan and add the coriander. Mix well and season with salt and pepper.

4 Lay the tortillas on a work surface and divide the filling equally between them. Roll up and place in a baking dish. Bake for 20–25 minutes.

5 Meanwhile, mix together the fromage frais, tomatoes and onion and season with salt and pepper. Chill until ready to serve.

6 Transfer the tortillas onto warmed serving plates. Top each one with a spoonful of the fromage frais mixture and sprinkle with chopped coriander. Serve at once.

Cook's note: If you don't want to buy garlic-flavoured oil just for this recipe, use olive or vegetable oil and add a crushed garlic clove along with the spring onions.

Peppers with Cajun rice

2½	Points per serving
11	Total Points per recipe

1 tablespoon olive or vegetable oil

100 g (3½ oz) long grain rice

1 celery stalk, finely chopped

1 small onion, finely chopped

1 garlic clove, crushed

1 small green pepper, de-seeded and chopped

1 vegetable stock cube, dissolved in 450 ml (¾ pint) hot water

2 teaspoons Cajun seasoning

6 cherry tomatoes, halved

50 g (1¾ oz) chorizo sausage, sliced

1 tablespoon chopped fresh coriander or parsley

2 red peppers, halved lengthways and de-seeded

2 yellow peppers, halved lengthways and de-seeded

salt and freshly ground black pepper

Serves 4. (225 Calories per serving) Preparation time 15 minutes. Cooking time 45 minutes. Freezing not recommended.

1 Preheat oven to Gas Mark 6/200°C/400°F.

2 Heat the oil in a large frying pan and sauté the rice, celery, onion, garlic and green pepper for 2–3 minutes.

3 Add the stock to the frying-pan, bring up to the boil, then reduce the heat and simmer for 15–20 minutes, or until the rice has absorbed all the liquid. If the rice is not tender, add a little more water and simmer until cooked.

4 Stir in the Cajun seasoning, cherry tomatoes, chorizo sausage and chopped coriander or parsley through the rice mixture. Season to taste with salt and pepper.

5 Arrange the pepper halves in a baking dish or roasting tin, fill with the rice mixture and bake for 15–20 minutes.

Cook's note 1: If you can't find Cajun seasoning, use ½ teaspoon of chilli powder mixed with 1 teaspoon of dried thyme.

Cook's note 2: Chorizo is a spicy, Spanish-style sausage, available in most supermarkets. If you can't find it, try any cooked sausage or substitute cooked ham.

Cook's note 3: You can serve this recipe as a starter in which case halve the quantities, and halve the Points per serving.

menu plan

Tasty Pasta Supper

Pasta is one of our all-time
favourites these days. Try these
easy dishes that are also suitable
for vegetarians.

✳

Pasta Pomodoro
page 147, (1 serving) 4 Points

✳

Pineapple Meringues with
Strawberry Sauce
page 169, (1 serving) 1½ Points

✳

Total Points: 5½ Points

Pasta pomodoro

4	Points per serving
16	Total Points per recipe

225 g (8 oz) pasta shapes

1 tablespoon olive oil

1 onion, finely chopped

100 g (3½ oz) mushrooms, wiped and sliced

400 g (14 oz) canned chopped tomatoes

275 g jar of tomato pasta sauce

100 g (3½ oz) roasted pepper strips in olive
    oil, rinsed and drained

salt and freshly ground black pepper

a handful of basil leaves, torn into pieces,
    to garnish

Serves 4. (330 Calories per serving) Preparation time 10 minutes. Cooking time 15 minutes. Freezing not recommended. Use some ready-made pasta sauce with a few other ingredients to make a quick and easy meal.

1 Cook the pasta in plenty of lightly salted boiling water for 8–10 minutes until tender, or follow the pack instructions.

2 Meanwhile, heat the olive oil in a large saucepan and sauté the onion for about 3 minutes, until softened.

3 Add the mushrooms, canned tomatoes and pasta sauce. Bring up to the boil, then reduce the heat and simmer without a lid for about 10 minutes.

4 Drain the pasta and add to the sauce with the pepper strips. Season to taste with salt and pepper, then serve, garnished with the torn basil leaves.

Cook's note: Instead of using pepper strips in olive oil, buy a can of red peppers and slice the amount you need. Keep the remainder in a covered container in the fridge, and use within 3 days.

Kedgeree

5½	Points per serving
21½	Total Points per recipe

225 g (8 oz) long grain rice

450 g (1 lb) smoked haddock fillet

15 g (½ oz) polyunsaturated margarine

1 onion, finely chopped

1 teaspoon cumin seeds

1 teaspoon medium curry powder

2 tablespoons chopped fresh parsley

salt and freshly ground black pepper

To serve

2 eggs, hard-boiled and quartered

a few sprigs of parsley

Serves 4. (390 Calories per serving) Preparation time 10 minutes. Cooking time 25 minutes. Freezing recommended. This smoked haddock, rice and hard-boiled egg recipe was originally served as a breakfast dish so it makes an excellent dish for a weekend brunch.

1 Cook the rice in plenty of lightly salted boiling water for about 12–15 minutes, until tender. Drain well and rinse in cold water.

2 Meanwhile, poach the fish in a large frying-pan, with just enough water to cover, until the flesh looks opaque and flakes easily. It will take about 8–10 minutes. Drain well, remove any skin and bones and flake the fish. Wipe out the pan with kitchen paper.

3 Melt the margarine in the frying-pan and sauté the onion for about 5 minutes. Stir in the cumin seeds and curry powder.

4 Add the rice and stir gently for about 3 minutes to heat thoroughly, then gently stir in the fish and chopped parsley. Season to taste with salt and pepper and cook for another minute or two, until hot.

5 Serve, garnished with the hard-boiled eggs and sprigs of parsley.

Cook's note: Use ground cumin instead of cumin seeds, if preferred. A teaspoon of ground coriander may be added too.

Variation: For a treat, use 225 g (8 oz) each of salmon and smoked haddock fillet. The Points per serving will be 6.

Lebanese rice

3½	Points per serving
14½	Total Points per recipe

15 g (½ oz) pine kernels

3 oranges

1 tablespoon walnut oil

1 tablespoon cider or white wine vinegar

2 tablespoons chopped fresh mint

50 g (1¾ oz) dates, stoned and chopped

50 g (1¾ oz) raisins or sultanas

15 g (½ oz) shelled pistachio nuts, roughly
   chopped

225 g (8 oz) cooked long grain rice

salt and freshly ground black pepper

mint leaves, to garnish

Ⓥ Serves 4. (260 Calories per serving) Preparation and cooking time 20 minutes. Freezing not recommended. A delicious dressing gives a wonderful flavour to this Middle Eastern style rice salad.

1 Heat a small frying-pan and add the pine kernels, stirring them with a wooden spoon until lightly browned. Tip them out and allow them to cool.
2 Meanwhile, mix together the finely grated zest and juice of 1 orange with the walnut oil and vinegar. Add the chopped mint, dates, raisins or sultanas, pistachio nuts, pine kernels and rice. Stir together, then season with a little salt and pepper, if needed.
3 Using a serrated knife, remove all the peel and pith from the remaining oranges, then divide into segments, removing all the membrane. Add to the salad, stir gently, then transfer to a serving dish and garnish with mint sprigs.

Cook's note: Take care when browning the pine kernels; they burn very easily.
Variation: Try using toasted sesame oil instead of walnut oil.

Mexican tacos

4½	Points per serving
18	Total Points per recipe

2 tablespoons lime or lemon juice

1 tablespoon chilli oil

1 tablespoon white wine or cider vinegar

1 small avocado, chopped

1 small red onion, finely chopped

½ green pepper, de-seeded and chopped

2 tomatoes, chopped

2 tablespoons chopped fresh coriander or
   parsley, plus extra to garnish

100 g (3½ oz) cooked long grain rice

100 g (3½ oz) canned red kidney beans,
   rinsed and drained

salt and freshly ground black pepper

8 taco shells, to serve

Ⓥ Serves 4. (265 Calories per serving) Preparation and cooking time 20 minutes. Freezing not recommended. A spicy dressing of chilli oil, lime juice and vinegar spices up this Mexican inspired salad. Serve it packed into crispy taco shells.

1 In a large bowl, whisk together the lime or lemon juice, chilli oil and vinegar.
2 Add the avocado, onion, pepper, tomatoes, chopped coriander or parsley, rice and red kidney beans. Stir well and season to taste with salt and pepper.
3 Warm the taco shells in a low oven for a few minutes, then pack with the rice mixture and serve at once, garnished with coriander or parsley.

Cook's note: Use olive oil if you don't have any chilli oil, then season the rice mixture with a dash of chilli sauce.

Chilli fried rice with prawns

5½	Points per serving
21½	Total Points per recipe

225 g (8 oz) long grain rice

2 tablespoons vegetable oil

2 garlic cloves, finely chopped

1 small red chilli, de-seeded and finely
    chopped

8 shallots, finely sliced

1 tablespoon Thai red curry paste

1 red pepper, de-seeded and chopped

100 g (3½ oz) fine green beans, chopped

225 g (8 oz) uncooked peeled prawns,
    defrosted if frozen

2 tablespoons Thai fish sauce or light
    soy sauce

salt and freshly ground black pepper

To serve

cucumber, chopped

spring onions, chopped

fresh red or green chilli, de-seeded and
    thinly sliced

Serves 4. (365 Calories per serving) Preparation time 15 minutes. Cooking time 15 minutes. Freezing recommended before adding prawns.

1 Cook the rice in plenty of lightly salted boiling water until tender, about 12 minutes. Rinse with cold water and drain thoroughly.

2 Meanwhile, heat the oil in a wok or large frying-pan and add the garlic. Cook gently for 2 minutes until golden. Add the chilli and shallots and cook, stirring, for 3–4 more minutes.

3 Stir in the Thai curry paste and cook gently for 1 minute, then add the red pepper and green beans. Stir-fry briskly for 2 minutes.

4 Tip the cooked rice into the wok or frying pan and add the prawns. Stir-fry over a medium-high heat for about 4–5 minutes, until the rice is piping hot and the prawns have turned pink.

5 Season to taste with the fish sauce or soy sauce, and season with salt and pepper, if necessary. Pile on to warmed serving plates and garnish with cucumber, spring onions and fresh chilli.

Cook's note 1: You can use cooked peeled prawns if you prefer, though they will not need to be cooked for long. Add them when the rice has been reheated, and just cook them for about 2 minutes, or else they will toughen.

Cook's note 2: You will find Thai red curry paste in the Oriental food section or with the spices at your local supermarket.

Creamy chicken pasta

6½	Points per serving
25½	Total Points per recipe

1 tablespoon plain flour

2 medium skinless, boneless chicken
     breasts, cut into chunks

2 tablespoons olive oil

225 g (8 oz) tagliatelle

100 g (3½ oz) mange-tout peas, sliced

1 courgette, chopped

300 ml (½ pint) skimmed milk

1 chicken or vegetable stock cube

1 teaspoon mixed dried Italian herbs

2 tomatoes, skinned and finely chopped

1 tablespoon finely grated parmesan cheese

salt and freshly ground black pepper

basil sprigs, to garnish

Serves 4. (420 Calories per serving) Preparation time 15 minutes. Cooking time 20 minutes. Freezing not recommended. Try this delicious pasta dish for a quick and simple supper.

1 Sprinkle the flour onto a plate and season with salt and pepper. Roll the chicken pieces in this mixture.

2 Heat the olive oil in a large frying pan and add the chicken pieces. Cook for about 6–8 minutes, turning often, until brown.

3 Meanwhile, cook the tagliatelle in a large saucepan of lightly salted boiling water for about 8 minutes, until tender. At the same time, cook the mange-tout peas with the courgette in a little lightly salted water for about 5 minutes.

4 Add the milk, stock cube and mixed herbs to the chicken and stir until just boiling. Reduce the heat and cook gently for 2–3 minutes, stirring often.

5 Drain the tagliatelle and the vegetables and toss them together with the tomatoes. Add the chicken mixture and stir together gently. Season to taste, then serve, sprinkled with parmesan cheese and garnished with basil.

Variation 1: Use your choice of pasta shapes instead of tagliatelle, and use shaves of parmesan cheese instead of grated.

Variation 2: For a vegetarian version, use 225 g (8 oz) of smoked tofu pieces instead of chicken. The Points will be 5½ per serving.

Spaghetti with green beans, peas and ham

4½	Points per serving
19	Total Points per recipe

225 g (8 oz) spaghetti

2 teaspoons polyunsaturated margarine

1 small onion, finely chopped

100 g (3½ oz) fine green beans, trimmed
     and chopped

100 g (3½ oz) lean cooked ham, chopped

75 g (2¾ oz) frozen petit pois or garden peas

225 g (8 oz) very low-fat plain fromage frais

100 g (3½ oz) low-fat soft cheese with
     garlic and herbs

a few basil leaves, torn into shreds

salt and freshly ground black pepper

basil leaves, to garnish

Serves 4. (340 Calories per serving) Preparation time 10 minutes. Cooking time 15 minutes. Freezing not recommended.

1 Cook the spaghetti in plenty of boiling, lightly salted water for about 8–10 minutes, or according to pack instructions, until just tender.

2 Meanwhile, heat the margarine in a saucepan and sauté the onion until softened, about 3 minutes. Add the green beans, ham and frozen peas. Cook, stirring, for 2–3 minutes.

3 Add the fromage frais, garlic-flavoured cheese and basil leaves to the saucepan. Heat gently, stirring from time to time, for about 4 minutes. Season with salt and pepper.

4 Drain the spaghetti well. Add the sauce and stir gently to mix. Transfer to four warmed plates and serve at once, garnished with basil leaves.

Cook's note: You don't have to use spaghetti; any pasta shapes will work well.

Red pepper and pasta tortilla

2½	Points per serving
11	Total Points per recipe

50 g (1¾ oz) pasta shapes

1 tablespoon olive oil

1 bunch spring onions, trimmed and sliced

1 garlic clove, crushed

1 red pepper, de-seeded and sliced

1 orange or yellow pepper, de-seeded
   and sliced

4 eggs

2 tablespoons milk

2 tablespoons chopped mixed fresh herbs
   (basil, chives, parsley)

salt and freshly ground black pepper

1 bag of mixed lettuce leaves, to serve

Serves 4. (210 Calories per serving) Preparation time 10 minutes. Cooking time 20 minutes. Freezing not recommended. For a quick and easy meal, make this Spanish-style omelette with cooked pasta shapes, sliced peppers, spring onions and chopped fresh herbs.

1 Cook the pasta shapes in boiling, lightly salted water for about 8–10 minutes, until just tender.

2 Meanwhile, heat the olive oil in a large omelette pan and cook the spring onions, garlic and peppers for about 5 minutes, stirring often.

3 Drain the pasta thoroughly, then add to the omelette pan. Beat the eggs and milk together, add the herbs, season with salt and pepper and pour into the pan.

4 Cook over a low heat until set on the base, then cook the surface under a medium grill until set and brown.

5 Allow the tortilla to cool for a few minutes, then cut into quarters and serve with the salad leaves.

Variation: If you're not keen on peppers, substitute sliced mushrooms instead; you'll need about 175 g (6 oz).

Salmon, mussel and noodle stew

2	Points per serving
8½	Total Points per recipe

1 large leek, trimmed and sliced

1 bunch spring onions, trimmed and
   finely sliced

1 garlic clove, finely chopped

600 ml (1 pint) vegetable stock

50 g (1¾ oz) vermicelli or thread egg
   noodles

175 g (6 oz) salmon fillet

450 g (1 lb) mussels in shells, scrubbed

150 ml (¼ pint) skimmed milk

salt and freshly ground black pepper

2 tablespoons chopped flat leaf parsley,
   to serve

Serves 4. (195 Calories per serving) Preparation time 10 minutes. Cooking time 15-20 minutes. Freezing not recommended. This easy fish dish tastes superb and you can cook it all in one pan.

1 Put the leek, spring onions, garlic and stock into a large saucepan. Bring to the boil, reduce the heat and simmer for 5 minutes.

2 Add the vermicelli or egg noodles and sit the whole salmon fillet on top. Cover and cook gently for 5 minutes. Lift the salmon from the pan and cool for a few minutes.

3 Meanwhile, check the mussels, discarding any that are damaged or remain open when tapped. Add the mussels to the saucepan. Cover and simmer for 2–3 minutes until the shells open (discard any that remain shut).

4 Flake the salmon, discarding the skin and any bones. Return to the saucepan with the milk and reheat gently. Season to taste with salt and pepper, then serve, sprinkled with parsley.

Cook's note: For extra flavour, try adding a tablespoon of Thai red or green curry paste to the stew with the mussels. Add a ½ Point per serving.

Crunchy vegetables with houmous and pitta

5½	Points per serving
23	Total Points per recipe

420 g can of chick peas, rinsed and drained

1 tablespoon lemon juice

1 or 2 garlic cloves

½ teaspoon salt

2 tablespoons tahini (sesame seed paste)

1 tablespoon chopped parsley plus extra,
     for sprinkling

2 tablespoons olive oil

450 g (1lb) fresh vegetables (carrot, celery,
     radish, red pepper)

4 medium pitta breads

lemon wedges, to serve

Ⓥ Serves 4. (400 Calories per serving) Preparation time 15 minutes. Freezing recommended for the houmous only. Home-made houmous is easy and delicious, and keeps well for several days in the fridge.

1 Put the chick peas, lemon juice, garlic, salt, tahini, chopped parsley and olive oil into a liquidiser or food processor and blend for about 20 seconds until smooth. Turn out into a serving bowl and sprinkle with extra chopped parsley.

2 Cut all the vegetables into bite-sized sticks and arrange on a serving plate around the bowl of houmous.

3 Warm the pitta bread in a toaster or warm oven. Cut into quarters and serve with the houmous and lemon wedges.

Cook's note: Serve the houmous at room temperature, but keep it covered and refrigerated until needed.

Weight Watchers note: You could omit the olive oil if you wanted to. The flavour won't be quite as good, but the Points will reduce to 4½ per serving.

Tuna and pasta salad with artichokes

2½	Points per serving
9½	Total Points per recipe

100 g (3½ oz) small pasta shapes

100 g (3½ oz) fine green beans, sliced

397 g can of artichoke hearts in brine,
     drained and halved

4 tomatoes, chopped

200 g can of tuna in brine or water, drained
     and flaked

1 tablespoon chopped fresh chives or parsley

1 garlic clove, crushed

finely grated zest of 1 lemon

2 tablespoons lemon juice

1 tablespoon olive oil

salt and freshly ground black pepper

Serves 4. (215 Calories per serving) Preparation and cooking time 20 minutes. Freezing not recommended. You just need to raid the store cupboard to make this easy, substantial salad in a matter of minutes.

1 Cook the pasta shapes in boiling, lightly salted water for about 8–10 minutes, until just tender.

2 At the same time, cook the fine green beans in lightly salted boiling water for about 3–4 minutes, until cooked yet crunchy. Drain and rinse with cold water to cool quickly.

3 Put the green beans, artichokes, tomatoes, tuna and chives or parsley into a large salad bowl and toss together. Add the drained cooked pasta and stir well.

4 Mix together the garlic, lemon zest, lemon juice and olive oil. Season with salt and pepper, and mix well to make the dressing. Spoon over the salad just before serving.

Cook's note: This salad is excellent for packed lunches and picnics so just pack up a portion and take it with you.

chapter

9

hot puddings

On the whole, there's no reason at all why puddings have to be unhealthy. In fact, most of the desserts in this chapter feature fruit, either fresh, frozen or canned, so they have firm foundations in the healthy eating camp. So if you love puddings and you don't want to do without, simply build the Points into your day.

Little Christmas puddings

3½	Points per serving
26½	Total Points per recipe

175 g (6 oz) sultanas

175 g (6 oz) currants

50 g (1¾ oz) glacé cherries, halved

90 ml (3 fl oz) rum or brandy

½ teaspoon polyunsaturated margarine

100 g (3½ oz) carrots, finely grated

75 g (2¾ oz) fresh white breadcrumbs

finely grated zest and juice of 1 small orange

1 teaspoon ground mixed spice

50 g (1¾ oz) unrefined light or dark
    muscovado sugar

1 egg, beaten

menu plan

Christmas Lunch

✳

Parsnip and Lemon Soup
page 18, (1 serving) 2 Points

Roast turkey (200 g/7 oz serving) with two
roast potatoes (your own recipe), Point-free
vegetables with gravy made with 1 teaspoon
gravy granules (1 serving) 5 Points

Little Christmas Puddings with
2 tablespoons very low-fat fromage frais
per serving
page 156, (1 serving) 4½ Points

Total Points: 11½ Points

 Makes 8 puddings (215 Calories per serving) Preparation time 30 minutes +1 day soaking. Cooking time 1 hour +1 hour to reheat (or 30 seconds to microwave). Freezing not recommended. Serve each little pudding with a spoonful of crème fraîche if you wish; just remember to count the Points.

1 Cover the sultanas, currants and cherries with boiling water. Soak for 10 minutes, then drain well. Add the rum or brandy, then cover and soak for 24 hours to swell the fruit.

2 Grease 8 individual pudding basins with the margarine. Add the remaining ingredients to the fruit mixture, and stir well. Spoon into the pudding basins, level the surfaces and cover with circles of greaseproof paper. Secure pieces of foil over each basin.

3 Steam the puddings for 1 hour, topping up the steamer with extra boiling water as required. Never allow the steamer to boil dry and always use boiling water for topping up.

4 Cool the puddings when cooked and replace the pieces of foil with fresh pieces. Store in a cool, dark place. On Christmas Day, steam the puddings for 1 hour to reheat, or microwave on High for 30 seconds per pudding, allowing them to stand for 2 minutes before serving.

Mini syrup sponge puddings

3½	Points per serving
20	Total Points per recipe

50 g (1¾ oz) polyunsaturated margarine

50 g (1¾ oz) caster sugar

2 small eggs, beaten

100g (3½ oz) self-raising flour

2 tablespoons warm water

6 heaped teaspoons golden syrup

Makes 6 puddings. (220 Calories per serving) Preparation time 20 minutes. Cooking time 40 minutes. Freezing recommended. These wonderful mini sponges are such a treat. The recipe gives a chocolate variation too, so choose your favourite! Serve with low-fat custard, remembering to add the extra Points.

1 Use 1 teaspoon of margarine to lightly grease 6 castle pudding moulds (individual pudding basins with steep sides). Cream the remainder with the caster sugar until light and fluffy, then gradually beat in the eggs.

2 Fold in the flour using a metal spoon, then add the warm water to give a soft, dropping consistency.

3 Place 1 heaped teaspoon of golden syrup in the base of each mould, and then divide the sponge mixture between them. Cover with foil or greaseproof paper.

4 Transfer the moulds to a steamer and steam for about 40 minutes, topping up with boiling water from time to time. Never allow the steamer to boil dry.

5 Turn out and serve.

Variation 1: Substitute lemon, lime or orange marmalade for the syrup, if you prefer. The Points will remain the same.

Variation 2: To make chocolate puddings, add 15 g (½ oz) of unsweetened cocoa powder, sifting it into the mixture with the flour. The Points will remain the same.

Warm peaches with amaretti and ricotta

3	Points per serving
12	Total Points per recipe

4 fresh peaches or 8 canned peach halves in natural juice

100 g (3½ oz) ricotta cheese

50 g (1¾ oz) amaretti biscuits, crushed

1 teaspoon clear honey

finely grated zest and juice of ½ lemon

Serves 4. (205 Calories per serving) Preparation time 15 minutes. Cooking time 20 minutes. Freezing not recommended. Serve warm with a spoonful of plain yogurt or scoop of Weight Watchers from Heinz vanilla ice cream, adding the extra Points.

1 Preheat the oven to Gas Mark 4/180°C/350°F. Line a baking sheet with non-stick baking parchment. If using fresh peaches, peel, then cut in half removing the centre stone. Place on the lined baking sheet. If using canned peaches, drain and arrange on to a baking sheet.

2 Place the ricotta cheese in a mixing bowl with the crushed biscuits, honey, lemon zest and juice and beat together well. Spoon equal amounts on top of each peach half and bake for 20 minutes.

Variation: Amaretti biscuits are small almond-flavoured Italian biscuits. If you prefer, you could use crushed ginger biscuits instead for the same Points.

Cook's note: To peel fresh peaches, place in a large bowl and pour boiling water over them. Leave to stand for 2 to 3 minutes and then the skins should peel away easily.

Chocolate bread pudding with luscious chocolate sauce

4½	Points per serving
19	Total Points per recipe

½ teaspoon polyunsaturated margarine

6 slices calorie-reduced white bread,
    crusts removed

1 pint (600 ml) skimmed milk

2 tablespoons unsweetened cocoa powder

2 eggs

25 g (1 oz) dark or light muscovado sugar

1 teaspoon vanilla essence

1 teaspoon icing sugar, for sprinkling

For the sauce

25 g (1 oz) plain chocolate, broken
    into pieces

1 tablespoon unsweetened cocoa powder

150 ml (¼ pint) skimmed milk

1 tablespoon cornflour

powdered sweetener, to taste

Ⓥ *Serves 4. (280 Calories per serving) Preparation time 20 minutes plus 1–2 hours soaking time. Cooking time 35–40 minutes. Freezing not recommended. Chocolate pudding doesn't have to cost a lot of Points, it just needs to be delicious!*

1   Grease a 20 cm (8-inch) square baking dish with the margarine. Cut the bread into squares and layer them in the baking dish.

2   Heat the milk and cocoa powder until lukewarm, stirring occasionally. Whisk the eggs, sugar and vanilla essence together. Add the warm milk mixture and beat well. Strain into the baking dish, making sure that all the bread is covered. Cover and chill for 1–2 hours.

3   Preheat the oven to Gas Mark 4/180°C/350°F. Bake the pudding until set, about 35–40 minutes. When cooked, allow to stand for 5 minutes whilst making the sauce.

4   To make the sauce, put the chocolate, cocoa powder, milk and cornflour into a saucepan. Heat gently, stirring until smooth and blended. Add sweetener, to taste.

5   Sprinkle the pudding with icing sugar and serve with the hot sauce.

Weight Watchers note: Instead of serving the pudding with the chocolate sauce, try it with 1 tablespoon of low-fat plain fromage frais per portion. This will reduce the Points to 4 per serving.

Fruit-full vanilla omelette

3½	Points per serving
15	Total Points per recipe

420 g can of apricots in natural juice

25 g (1 oz) raisins or sultanas

1 small banana, sliced

1 tablespoon arrowroot or cornflour, blended
    with a little cold water

a pinch of ground cinnamon

4 eggs, separated

1 tablespoon granulated sweetener

1 teaspoon vanilla essence

4 teaspoons polyunsaturated margarine

4 teaspoons icing sugar, for sprinkling

Ⓥ *Serves 4. (235 Calories per serving) Preparation and cooking time 15 minutes. Freezing not recommended. Soufflé omelettes are quick, delicious and very nutritious and they're surprisingly easy to make.*

1   Put the apricots, with their juice, into a saucepan. Add the raisins or sultanas and banana. Stir in the blended arrowroot or cornflour and heat gently, stirring until thickened. Add the cinnamon and keep warm over a low heat.

2   To make the omelettes, beat the egg yolks, adding the sweetener and vanilla essence. Using a separate, grease-free bowl and beaters, whisk the egg whites until stiff, then fold into the egg yolks.

3   Preheat the grill to medium-high.

4   Making one omelette at a time, melt 1 teaspoon of margarine in an omelette pan. Add one quarter of the egg mixture and cook for about 2 minutes until the base is set, then grill the surface until just firm.

5   Transfer the omelette to a warm plate, spoon on a quarter of the fruit mixture, fold over and serve, sprinkled with icing sugar. Repeat with the remaining mixture to make four omelettes in total.

Cook's note: Remember that egg whites will not whip if there is any trace of grease in the bowl or on the beaters and that includes the egg yolk, so be very careful when separating them.

Pears in mulled wine

3½	Points per serving
15	Total Points per recipe

4 pears (not too ripe)

300 ml (½ pint) cranberry juice drink

300 ml (½ pint) red wine

1 cinnamon stick

6 cloves

2 star anise (optional)

50 g (1¾ oz) light or dark muscovado sugar

4 tablespoons low-fat soft cheese

4 kumquats or 1 clementine, sliced

Ⓥ Serves 4. (225 Calories per serving) Preparation time 10 minutes. Cooking time 15–20 minutes. Freezing not recommended. This pretty dessert is ideal for a festive celebration and would make an excellent alternative to Christmas pudding or trifle.

1 Peel the pears but preserve the stalks. Cut a tiny slice from the base of each one to enable them to stand upright.

2 Stand the pears in a saucepan and add the cranberry juice drink, red wine, cinnamon stick, cloves, star anise (if using) and most of the sugar, reserving 4 teaspoons of sugar for later. Heat gently until simmering, then cook gently for about 15–20 minutes, or until the pears are tender.

3 Cool slightly, then slice the pears in half and remove their cores with a melon baller or sharp knife.

4 Mix together the soft cheese with 2 teaspoons of the reserved sugar. Spoon into the pears and arrange on serving plates.

5 Sprinkle the remaining sugar on top of the pears, spoon some of the red wine liquid on to the plates and decorate with the kumquats or clementine.

Variation: If you don't have the individual spices in your store cupboard, use 1 teaspoon of ground mixed spice instead.

Orchard fruit crumbles

3½	Points per serving
13½	Total Points per recipe

225 g (8 oz) plums, halved and pitted

225 g (8 oz) baking apples, peeled, cored and chopped

40 g (1½ oz) light or dark muscovado sugar

25 g (1 oz) polyunsaturated margarine

75 g (2¾ oz) Jordans Original Crunchy cereal with raisins and almonds

4 tablespoons low-fat plain yogurt

lemon balm or mint leaves (optional), to decorate

Ⓥ Serves 4 (210 Calories per serving) Preparation time 10 minutes. Cooking time 20–25 minutes. Freezing not recommended. Plums and apples taste delightful in these quick and simple crumbly fruit puddings.

1 Put the plums, apples and sugar into a saucepan with 5 tablespoons of water. Heat and simmer gently until soft and pulpy, about 10 minutes.

2 Preheat the oven to Gas Mark 4/180°C/350°F. Spoon the fruit filling into a baking dish or four ramekin dishes.

3 Melt the margarine in a saucepan and stir in the cereal. Sprinkle evenly over the surface of the fruit.

4 Bake for 10–15 minutes, until crunchy and light golden brown.

5 Serve each portion with 1 tablespoon of plain yogurt, decorated with lemon balm or mint leaves, if desired.

Variation: If you wish, just use apples or plums, instead of both.

Pancakes with lemon, lime and liqueur

3½	Points per serving
14½	Total Points per recipe

100 g (3½ oz) plain flour

a pinch of salt

1 egg

300 ml (½ pint) skimmed milk

finely grated zest and juice of 1 lime

finely grated zest and juice of 1 lemon

2 teaspoons vegetable oil

1 tablespoon caster sugar

2 tablespoons Cointreau, Grand Marnier
or brandy

Ⓥ Serves 4. (195 Calories per serving) Preparation time 10 minutes. Cooking time 15 minutes. Freezing not recommended. Whisk up this easy all-in-one batter to make pancakes. It's the perfect recipe for Shrove Tuesday, especially when flavoured with a little liqueur or brandy.

1 Sift the flour and salt into a large bowl. Add the egg, milk and grated lime and lemon zest and whisk together until smooth. Alternatively, put the ingredients into a liquidiser or food processor and blend for 15–20 seconds until smooth.

2 Heat a small, heavy-based frying-pan. Add a few drops of oil and pour in some batter, tilting the pan so that the mixture spreads over the base to make a thin pancake.

3 When the pancake has set on the surface, flip it over to cook the other side. Make 8 pancakes in this way, transferring them to kitchen paper as you cook them. When all the pancakes are cooked, fold them into triangles.

4 Wipe the frying-pan with a piece of kitchen paper, then add the lime and lemon juice and sugar. Heat gently to dissolve, then add the liqueur or brandy.

5 Return all the pancakes to the frying pan, overlapping them to fit. Cook gently for about 1 minute to re-heat. Serve 2 pancakes per person.

Grape cheesecakes

3½	Points per serving
14½	Total Points per recipe

4 light, crisp biscuits, crushed

225 g (8 oz) seedless red grapes, halved

225 g (8 oz) seedless green grapes, halved

200 g (7 oz) low-fat soft cheese

2 teaspoons lemon juice

8 teaspoons demerara sugar

Ⓥ Serves 4. (205 Calories per serving) Preparation and cooking time 15 minutes + 15 minutes chilling + cooling. Freezing not recommended. You'll love these delicious desserts. They have a fantastic flavour, ideal for rounding off any meal.

1 Sprinkle the crushed biscuits into four individual heatproof dishes, such as ramekins. Add the red and green grapes.

2 Mix the soft cheese and lemon juice together. Spoon over the fruit, levelling the surface. Chill for about 15 minutes.

3 Preheat the grill.

4 Sprinkle 2 teaspoons of demerara sugar over the surface of each dessert. Place under the grill for about 2 minutes until bubbling and golden brown. Cool slightly, then serve. Alternatively, chill before serving.

Cook's note: Be sure to keep an eye on the desserts as they are grilled to make sure that they do not burn.

Shrove Tuesday

Everyone loves pancakes, so why don't you make yours extra special with a few added ingredients. Why not make a batch for the children to begin with – without the extras!

Creamy Chicken Pasta
page 151, (1 serving) 6½ Points

Pancakes with Lemon, Lime and Liqueur
page 160, (1 serving) 3½ Points

Total Points: 10 Points

Poached boozy fruits

2	Points per serving
9	Total Points per recipe

400 g (14 oz) canned pineapple in natural
    fruit juice

2 oranges, peeled and segmented

75 g (2¾ oz) no-soak dried apricots

finely grated zest of 1 lemon

¼ teaspoon ground cinnamon

25 g (1 oz) fructose

3 tablespoons dark rum

Ⓥ *Serves 4. (160 Calories per serving) Preparation and cooking time 20 minutes. Freezing recommended. Fructose is a fruit sugar that's sweeter than sucrose. Although the calories are similar, you need to use less of it. Serve with a dollop of plain yogurt or low-fat crème fraîche if Points allow.*

1 Drain the pineapple, reserving the juice and cut into bite-sized chunks. Place in a pan with the orange segments, apricots, lemon zest and cinnamon.

2 Mix together the reserved juice, fructose and rum and pour over the fruit. Poach over a medium low heat for 5 minutes.

3 Serve warm.

Fruit and nut baked apples

2½	Points per serving
5	Total Points per recipe

2 cooking apples

25 g (1 oz) raisins

1 tablespoon flaked almonds

2 teaspoons maple syrup

a pinch of ground cinnamon

1 teaspoon low-fat spread

Ⓥ *Serves 2. (145 Calories per serving) Preparation time 10 minutes. Cooking time 25 minutes. Freezing not recommended.*

1 Preheat the oven to Gas Mark 5/190°C/375°F. Line a roasting tin with non-stick baking parchment.

2 Wash the apples well and remove the centre core. Arrange in the tin.

3 Mix together the raisins, almonds, maple syrup and cinnamon and pack equal amounts into each apple. Dot the top of each with a little low-fat spread and bake for 20 to 25 minutes, until the apples are soft and pulpy. Serve warm.

Moroccan oranges

3½	Points per serving
14	Total Points per recipe

4 oranges

25 g (1 oz) dates, stoned and thinly sliced

25 g (1 oz) sultanas or raisins

200 ml (7 fl oz) orange juice

½ teaspoon ground cinnamon

25 g (1 oz) pistachio nuts, roughly chopped

4 tablespoons low-fat plain fromage frais

4 teaspoons clear honey

Ⓥ *Serves 4. (190 Calories per serving) Preparation time 10 minutes. Cooking time 15–20 minutes. Freezing not recommended. This simple, refreshing and delicious dessert is given a North African flavour with dates, sultanas, pistachio nuts and cinnamon.*

1 Preheat the oven to Gas Mark 4/180°C/350°F.

2 Using a sharp, serrated knife, remove all the peel and pith from the oranges. Slice them crosswise and place in a heatproof bowl with the dates, sultanas or raisins, orange juice, half the cinnamon and all the pistachio nuts. Bake for 15–20 minutes.

3 Mix together the fromage frais with the remaining cinnamon. Serve with the hot fruit and drizzle a teaspoon of honey over each portion.

Variation: For a summertime version, do not bake the fruit. Simply prepare it and chill it for about 30 minutes before serving.

Marzipan baked nectarines

3	Points per serving
12½	Total Points per recipe

4 ripe nectarines or peaches, halved
    and pitted
25 g (1 oz) plain cake crumbs or crushed
    trifle sponges
25 g (1 oz) ground almonds
1 egg yolk
50 g (1¾ oz) marzipan, grated
175 g (6 oz) blueberries
1 tablespoon golden caster sugar

Serves 4. (245 Calories per serving) Preparation and cooking time 20 minutes. Freezing not recommended.

1 Preheat the oven to Gas Mark 6/200°C/400°F.
2 Put the nectarine or peach halves on to a baking sheet, cut side up. If you like, slice off a tiny piece from their bases, so that they sit still.
3 Mix together the cake crumbs, ground almonds and egg yolk. Divide between the nectarines or peaches, packing the mixture into the space where the stones were removed. Top with the grated marzipan.
4 Bake for about 6–8 minutes.
5 Meanwhile, heat the blueberries with the sugar and a tiny amount of water for about 2 minutes, until the juice just begins to run. Serve with the baked nectarines or peaches.
Variation: Frozen blackberries, raspberries or cranberries could be used to make this dessert, although cranberries will need extra sweetening with sugar or powdered sweetener. Add the extra Points if necessary.

Orange semolina puddings

2	Points per serving
8½	Total Points per recipe

25 g (1 oz) semolina
450 ml (16 fl oz) skimmed milk
powdered sweetener, to taste
finely grated zest and segments of 1
    large orange
2 eggs, separated
1 tablespoon caster sugar

Serves 4. (135 Calories per serving) Preparation and cooking time 20 minutes + cooling time. Freezing not recommended. Semolina takes on a more sophisticated slant with these lovely light puddings.

1 Preheat the oven to Gas Mark 5/190°C/375°F.
2 Put the semolina into a saucepan and stir in the milk. Bring up to the boil, stirring constantly until thickened. Reduce the heat and cook gently for 2–3 minutes.
3 Remove from the heat, cool for a few minutes, then add sweetener to taste. Stir in the orange zest and egg yolks. Divide between four individual heatproof dishes or ramekins. Top with the orange segments.
4 Beat the egg whites in a grease-free bowl until they hold their shape. Whisk in the sugar, then pile on top of the desserts. Bake for 3–4 minutes until golden brown. Serve at once.
Cook's note: Use heat-resistant glass or china teacups if you don't have individual pudding dishes. Their saucers make handy serving plates too.

Berried treasure

3	Points per serving
11½	Total Points per recipe

225 g (8 oz) strawberries, hulled and sliced

225 g (8 oz) raspberries

100 g (3½ oz) blueberries

2 tablespoons crème de cassis or low-sugar
blackcurrant cordial

1 tablespoon caster sugar

1 tablespoon polyunsaturated margarine

50 g (1¾ oz) Jordans Original Crunchy
(raisins and almonds)

25 g (1 oz) marzipan, grated

Serves 4. (190 Calories per serving) Preparation and cooking time 15 minutes. Freezing not recommended. Make the most of summer berries in this fruit-full pudding. You could substitute thawed frozen berries when fresh ones are out of season.

1 Put the strawberries, raspberries and blueberries into a saucepan. Add the crème de cassis or blackcurrant cordial and sugar, stirring to mix. Heat gently for about 2 or 3 minutes.

2 Divide the mixture between four individual heatproof dishes such as ramekins or heatproof teacups.

3 Melt the margarine and add the cereal, breaking up any large clusters. Stir to coat, then sprinkle evenly over the fruit. Top with the grated marzipan.

4 Preheat the grill. Grill the desserts until the marzipan turns golden brown, taking care as it can soon burn. Cool slightly, then serve.

Cook's note: Crème de cassis is a blackcurrant liqueur that gives these desserts a lovely flavour, though if you don't have any and don't want to buy some just for this recipe, simply substitute a low-sugar blackcurrant cordial instead.

Variation: Your could also use 25 g (1 oz) ground almonds as a topping. Add in step 3 with the cereal, and grill the topping until golden brown. The Points per serving will be 3½.

Apple and apricot cornflake bakes

3	Points per serving
12	Total Points per recipe

4 eating apples, cored

grated zest and juice of 1 lemon

4 tablespoons golden syrup

1 tablespoon polyunsaturated margarine

50 g (1¾ oz) cornflakes

25 g (1 oz) ready-to-eat dried apricots,
finely chopped

125 ml (4 fl oz) low-fat plain fromage frais

Serves 4. (230 Calories per serving) Preparation time 15 minutes. Cooking time 15–20 minutes. Freezing not recommended. Try these baked apples, stacked with toffee-tasting cornflakes for a simple, satisfying treat.

1 Preheat the oven to Gas Mark 4/180°C/350°F.

2 Slice each apple into three, horizontally. Dip the pieces into lemon juice to prevent them from going brown.

3 Warm the syrup and margarine together until melted, then add the cornflakes, stirring gently to coat. Add the apricots to the mixture.

4 On a baking sheet, or in small basins, layer the apples with the cornflake mixture. Secure with cocktail sticks. Transfer to the oven and bake for about 15–20 minutes, or until the apples are tender.

5 Mix 1 teaspoon of lemon zest into the fromage frais and serve with the apples.

Variation: Use low-fat plain yogurt instead of fromage frais, if you prefer. The Points per serving would be the same. Try substituting pears for apples next time you make the dessert. The Points per serving will be 3½.

Bread and butter pudding with raspberries

3	Points per serving
12	Total Points per recipe

6 slices of Weight Watchers from Heinz white sliced bread

25 g (1 oz) low-fat spread

150 g (5½ oz) fresh or frozen raspberries

2 eggs

300 ml (½ pint) skimmed milk

25 g (1 oz) fructose

4 tablespoons low-fat evaporated milk

Ⓥ *Serves 4. (190 Calories per serving) Preparation time 15 minutes. Cooking time 1 hour. Freezing not recommended. Raspberries give a wonderful burst of colour to this classic dish.*

1 Preheat the oven to Gas Mark 3/170°C/320°F.

2 Spread the bread slices with a low-fat spread and then cut each piece into quarters. Arrange in a shallow ovenproof dish and scatter the raspberries over.

3 Beat together the eggs, milk, fructose and evaporated milk and pour over the bread and raspberries. Allow to stand for 10 minutes and then bake for 1 hour, until set and golden. Serve warm for best results.

Cook's note: It's best to use bread that is 2 to 3 days old for this recipe since it will soak up the liquid far easier.

Slow-baked saffron rice pudding

1½	Points per serving
6	Total Points per recipe

8 saffron strands

600 ml (1 pint) skimmed milk

25 g (1 oz) caster sugar

a pinch of ground nutmeg

50 g (1¾ oz) pudding rice

Ⓥ *Serves 4. (120 Calories per serving) Preparation time 30 minutes. Cooking time 1½ hours. Freezing not recommended.*

1 Place the saffron in a measuring jug. Heat the milk until boiling and pour over the saffron. Leave to infuse for 20 minutes, stirring form time to time.

2 Mix together the caster sugar, nutmeg and pudding rice and place in a shallow oven proof dish.

3 Preheat the oven to Gas Mark 3/170°C/320°F. Pour the milk over the rice, stir well and bake for 1¼ hours, stirring half-way through cooking.

Variations: Other flavourings you can use instead of saffron include lemon zest and cinnamon or a few drops of almond or vanilla essence.

Poached pears with hot chocolate sauce

3	Points per serving
11½	Total Points per recipe

4 pears, peeled

100 ml (3½ fl oz) fresh orange juice

mint sprigs, to decorate (optional)

For the sauce

2 single-serve sachets of Options hot chocolate drink

200 g tub of low-fat plain fromage frais

1 tablespoon clear honey

Ⓥ *Serves 4. (135 Calories per serving) Preparation time 15 minutes. Cooking time 20 minutes. Freezing not recommended.*

1 Slice a thin piece from under each pear so they stand upright. Place in a small, deep saucepan and pour the orange juice and 300 ml (½ pint) water into the pan. Bring to the boil and reduce the heat. Cover and simmer for 20 minutes.

2 Turn the heat off and allow the pears to cool in the cooking liquid.

3 To make the sauce, empty the chocolate powder into a small jug and pour 50 ml (2 fl oz) boiling water over. Whisk well. Beat into the fromage frais with the honey.

4 Serve the poached pears in a pool of chocolate sauce and decorate with a mint sprig, if desired.

Variation: Low-calorie hot chocolate drinks come in a variety of flavours. Chocolate orange or chocolate and hazelnut are excellent in this recipe.

Baked lemon sponges with lemon sauce

4	Points per serving
16½	Tota Points per recipe

2 eggs

50 g (1¾ oz) caster sugar

100 g (3½ oz) plain flour

finely grated zest of 1 lemon

For the sauce

juice of 1 lemon

2 tablespoons cornflour

300 ml (½ pint) water

25 g (1 oz) fructose

3 tablespoons low-fat plain fromage frais

Ⓥ *Serves 4. (235 Calories per serving) Preparation time 20 minutes. Cooking time 25 minutes. Freezing recommended for the sponges only.*

1 Preheat the oven to Gas Mark 4/180°C/350°F. Line the base of four individual ramekin dishes with non-stick baking parchment.

2 Using electric beaters, whisk together the eggs and caster sugar until the mixture is light and foamy. Sift in the plain flour and fold in with the lemon zest.

3 Divide the sponge mixture between the ramekin dishes and bake for 20 minutes.

4 Meanwhile, to make the sauce, mix the lemon juice and cornflour together to form a thin paste. Heat the water and fructose in a small pan until boiling. Add the cornflour paste and cook, stirring, until you have a smooth thickened sauce. Reduce the heat and simmer for 5 minutes. Remove from the heat and whisk in the fromage frais.

5 To serve, run a round bladed knife around the edge of each cooked sponge and carefully remove from the ramekins on to a serving plate. Peel away the baking parchment lining and drizzle over a little of the sauce.

Variation: Use orange or lime instead of the lemon if preferred. You may however need to use 2 limes as they're not as juicy as lemons.

Peach and blueberry cobbler

5	Points per serving
21	Total Points per recipe

225 g (8 oz) self-raising flour

½ teaspoon ground cinnamon

50 g (1¾ oz) low-fat spread

25 g (1 oz) fructose

For the filling

400 g (14 oz) canned peach halves in
   natural juice

150 g (5½ oz) fresh or frozen blueberries

1 tablespoon cornflour

1 teaspoon skimmed milk

Serves 4. (345 Calories per serving) Preparation time 20 minutes. Cooking time 25 minutes. Freezing not recommended.

1 Sift the flour and cinnamon into a mixing bowl and rub in the low-fat spread with your fingertips until the mixture ressembles fine breadcrumbs. Stir in the fructose and then add enough cold water to mix to a soft dough.

2 Drain the peaches, reserving the juice and chop roughly. Toss with the blueberries. Heat the reserved juice in a small pan until it boils. Mix the cornflour with a little cold water and stir into the hot liquid. Cook, stirring, until thickened and then pour over the fruit and toss well.

3 Spoon into a shallow ovenproof dish and set aside. Preheat the oven to Gas Mark 5/ 190°C/375°F.

4 Roll out the cobbler mix on a lighty floured surface to about 1 cm (½-inch) thick. Stamp out 8 rounds using a 5 cm (2-inch) pastry cutter and arrange around the edge of the dish. Brush the cobblers with a little milk and bake for 20 to 25 minutes, until well risen and golden. Serve warm or cold.

Cook's note: Make individual portions in small ramekins. Divide the cobbler mixture into 4 large rounds and place on top of each one.

Pineapple meringues with strawberry sauce

1½	Points per serving
7	Total Points per recipe

1 small fresh pineapple

350 g (12 oz) strawberries, sliced

2 kiwi fruit, peeled and sliced

2 egg whites

25 g (1 oz) caster sugar

Serves 4. (100 Calories per serving) Preparation and cooking time 15 minutes. Freezing not recommended. This easy and impressive dessert only takes minutes to put together and it tastes fantastic.

1 Preheat the oven to Gas Mark 5/190°C/375°F.

2 Cut the pineapple into four thick slices and remove the core, using a sharp knife or a small biscuit cutter to make it easier. Place the slices on a baking sheet.

3 Reserve half the strawberries and mix the remainder with the kiwi fruit. Pile on top of the pineapple slices.

4 Whisk the egg whites in a grease-free bowl until peaks form and then add the sugar and whisk again until stiff and glossy. Pile on top of the pineapple slices.

5 Transfer to the oven at once and bake for about 4–5 minutes, until golden brown. Meanwhile, purée the reserved strawberries in a blender or food processor.

6 Serve the meringues, drizzled with the strawberry sauce.

Variation: Substitute any fresh fruit for the strawberries and kiwi fruit. You could try a combination of mango and papaya for a tropical flavour. Adjust the Points accordingly.

Baked egg custard with sultanas

2½	Points per serving
10½	Total Points per recipe

425 ml (15 floz) skimmed milk

4 cardamom pods, lightly crushed

1 vanilla pod

3 eggs

25 g (1 oz) fructose

50 g (1¾ oz) sultanas

1 tablespoon shelled pistachios, finely
   chopped

Ⓥ *Serves 4. (180 Calories per serving) Preparation time 30 minutes. Cooking time 1 hour. Freezing not recommended. Best results are achieved from long, slow cooking in a water bath to prevent the custard from separating before it sets.*

1 Place the milk in a small saucepan with the cardamom and vanilla pod. Bring to the boil, remove from the heat and allow to cool and infuse for 20 minutes.

2 Remove the vanilla pod and cardamom and whisk in the eggs. Pour through a sieve into a clean bowl or jug then stir in the fructose and sultanas.

3 Preheat the oven to Gas Mark 3/150°C/300°F. Fill a roasting tin half-full of hot water and arrange four individual ramekins in it. Spoon equal amounts of the custard into each dish and sprinkle the top of each with a little chopped pistachios.

4 Bake for 1 hour until set but just retaining a little wobble when you shake the dish. Serve warm.

Apple and cinnamon French toast

3	Points per serving
12½	Total Points per recipe

1 cooking apple

2 eggs

300 ml (½ pint) skimmed milk

1 tablespoon caster sugar

½ teaspoon ground cinnamon

4 thick slices of two-day-old white or
   wholemeal bread

low-fat cooking spray

1 teaspoon demerara sugar

Ⓥ *Serves 4. (200 Calories per serving) Preparation time 20 minutes. Cooking time 15 minutes. Freezing not recommended. Serve with a spoonful of crème fraîche if you wish, but don't forget to add the extra Points.*

1 Peel the cooking apple and core. Dice finely and place in a pan with 1 tablespoon of water. Cover and cook gently until pulpy. Allow to cool.

2 Place the eggs, milk, sugar, cinnamon and cooked apple in a food processor and blend until smooth. Transfer to a shallow dish.

3 Cut each piece of bread in half and dip in the apple and egg mixture, leaving it to soak in for 2 to 3 minutes per side.

4 Spray a non-stick frying-pan with low-fat cooking spray and heat. Cook the French toast slices for 2 to 3 minutes per side until golden. Serve 2 pieces per person, sprinkled with a little demerara sugar.

Apricot and pear crumble

3	Points per serving
12½	Total Points per recipe

125 g (4½ oz) no-soak dried apricots,
   finely chopped

450 g (1 lb) pears, peeled, cored and sliced

1 tablespoon clear honey

50 g (1¾ oz) fresh wholemeal breadcrumbs

25 g (1 oz) demerara sugar

1 tablespoon plain flour

25 g (1 oz) low-fat spread, melted

a pinch of ground nutmeg

Ⓥ *Serves 4. (200 Calories per serving) Preparation time 20 minutes. Cooking time 35 minutes. Freezing recommended. Serve with low-fat custard or yogurt, remembering to add the extra Points.*

1 Put the apricots in a saucepan with the pear slices and honey. Add 1 tablespoon of water and simmer gently, covered, for 5 minutes to soften.

2 Preheat the oven to Gas Mark 4/180°C/350°F. Spoon half the pear mixture into an ovenproof dish.

3 Mix together the breadcrumbs, sugar, flour, spread and nutmeg and scatter half over the pears. Top with the remaining pear mixture and scatter with the last of the crumbs. Bake for 25 minutes and then serve warm.

Apple and cinnamon French toast
Apricot and pear crumble

Crunchy oat-topped rhubarb with ginger

6	Points per serving
23½	Total Points per recipe

450 g (1 lb) rhubarb

3 tablespoons reduced sugar strawberry jam

50 g (1¾ oz) caster sugar

juice of 1 orange

1 tablespoon cornflour

For the topping

75 g (2¾ oz) porridge oats

50 g (1¾ oz) fresh white breadcrumbs

25 g (1 oz) demerara sugar

4 tablespoons clear honey, warmed

½ teaspoon ground cinnamon

15 sprays of sunflower low-fat cooking spray

ⓥ *Serves 4. (290 Calories per serving) Preparation time 20 minutes. Cooking time 35 minutes. Freezing recommended. Serve warm with light crème fraîche or plain yogurt, remembering to add the extra Points.*

1 Trim the rhubarb and cut into 2.5 cm (1-inch) pieces. Place in a pan with the strawberry jam, caster sugar and orange juice, cook gently until tender. Preheat the oven to Gas Mark 4/180°C/350°F.

2 Mix the cornflour with a little cold water and stir in. Cook until the juices thicken and then transfer to a shallow overproof dish.

3 Mix together the oats, breadcrumbs, sugar, honey and cinnamon.

4 Scatter over the rhubarb and spray with low-fat cooking spray. Bake for 20 to 25 minutes until topping is crunchy.

Cook's note: Sweeten the rhubarb with artificial sweetener instead of sugar if you want to save on Points. You will save a ½ Point per serving. Stir the sweetener in after you've stewed the rhubarb.

Strawberry pancakes

3	Points per serving
12	Total Points per recipe

1 egg

100 g (3½ oz) plain flour

a pinch of salt

a pinch of ground cinnamon

300 ml (½ pint) skimmed milk

low-fat cooking spray

For the filling

225 g (8 oz) fresh strawberries, hulled
    and sliced

2 tablespoons port

2 tablespoons reduced-sugar strawberry jam

1 teaspoon icing sugar

ⓥ *Serves 4. (180 Calories per serving) Preparation time 15 minutes. Cooking time 15 minutes. Freezing recommended for the pancakes only.*

1 Place the egg, flour, salt, cinnamon and milk in a liquidiser and blend until smooth.

2 Heat a heavy-based 20 cm (8-inch) frying-pan until just smoking and spray the pan with low-fat cooking spray. Drizzle a little of the batter on to the base of the pan, swirling to give a thin, even coating. Cook for 1 minute and then flip over and cook for a further minute. Continue until all the batter has been used, stacking the cooked pancakes on to a plate sitting over a pan of gently simmering water.

3 Place the sliced strawberries in a pan with the port and jam and heat gently until jam melts and coats the strawberries with a thin syrup.

4 Serve 2 pancakes each, filled with a little of the pan cooked strawberry mixture and dust lightly with a little icing sugar. Serve at once.

Cook's note: Pancakes can be frozen in single serve batches. Heat them through in a non-stick pan and fill with sliced fresh fruit for a speedy snack.

chapter 10 cold puddings

If you never feel as if you've had a proper meal unless you've finished off with a pudding, then this chapter is for you. Here, you'll find a delicious selection of truly scrumptious desserts that will leave you feeling totally satisfied.

Blackberry and apple layers

1½	Points per serving
7	Total Points per recipe

450 g (1 lb) baking apples, peeled and
    chopped
1 teaspoon finely grated lemon zest
1 tablespoon lemon juice
225 g (8 oz) fresh blackberries
powdered sweetener, to taste
25 g (1 oz) amaretti or almond macaroon
    biscuits, lightly crushed
225 g (8 oz) low-fat plain fromage frais
a few extra blackberries, edible flowers or
    mint leaves, to decorate (optional)

Ⓥ *Serves 4. (135 Calories per serving) Preparation and cooking time 20 minutes + 20 minutes chilling. Freezing not recommended. Apples and blackberries taste so good together, especially in this simple dessert. Why not pick your own blackberries from the hedgerows when they're in season?*

1 Cook the apples in about 2 tablespoons of water with the lemon zest and juice until soft and pulpy, about 5 minutes.

2 Remove from the heat and mix in the blackberries, then allow to cool. Sweeten to taste with powdered sweetener.

3 Spoon half the apple and blackberry mixture into four attractive serving glasses or ramekin dishes. Sprinkle the crushed biscuits on top, then spoon on the fromage frais and remaining fruit mixture.

4 Cover the desserts and chill them for at least 20 minutes. Serve, decorated with blackberries, edible flowers or mint leaves, if wished.

Variation 1: Use thawed, frozen blackberries when fresh ones are out of season.

Variation 2: Substitute low-fat plain yogurt for the fromage frais, if you prefer. The Points per serving will be the same.

Strawberry and mango chill with chocolate sauce

3½	Points per serving
13½	Total Points per recipe

350 g (12 oz) fresh strawberries, sliced
200 g (7 oz) low-fat plain fromage frais
powdered sweetener (optional)
1 large, ripe mango, peeled and chopped
50 g (1¾ oz) plain chocolate, broken
    into pieces
1 tablespoon clear honey or golden syrup
2 teaspoons cocoa powder
1 teaspoon cornflour

Ⓥ *Serves 4. (170 Calories per serving) Preparation and cooking time 20 minutes + 20 minutes chilling. Freezing not recommended. I love the combination of fresh strawberries and mango with a little chocolate sauce. This dessert is indulgent, yet refreshing and healthy.*

1 Use a fork to crush approximately one-third of the strawberries. Mix these into the fromage frais and add a little powdered sweetener, if you like.

2 Layer the remaining strawberries into attractive serving glasses with the mango chunks and fromage frais mixture.

3 Cover and chill the desserts in the refrigerator for about 20 minutes.

4 To make the chocolate sauce, put the chocolate, honey or syrup, cocoa powder, cornflour and 90 ml (3 fl oz) water into a small, heavy-based saucepan. Heat gently, stirring, until thickened and smooth.

5 Drizzle the hot chocolate sauce over the desserts and serve at once.

Cook's notes: A mango is ripe when it "gives" slightly when pressed at the stalk end. Slice it on either side of its large, flat stone, then peel it and chop the flesh.

Variation: Try substituting frozen summer berries when fresh strawberries are out of season or very expensive. Don't forget to thaw them first.

Raspberry orange creams

3	Points per serving
12½	Total Points per recipe

350 g (12 oz) low-fat soft cheese

4 tablespoons low-fat plain yogurt

1 tablespoon caster sugar

finely grated zest of 1 lemon

1 tablespoon lemon juice

1 large orange

350 g (12 oz) raspberries

powdered sweetener, to taste

Serves 4. (180 Calories per serving) Preparation time 10 minutes + several hours standing. Freezing not recommended. These little desserts are like mini cheesecakes. Serve them with fresh raspberries and an orange and raspberry sauce.

1 Put the soft cheese into a bowl and beat with a wooden spoon to soften it. Add the yogurt, caster sugar, lemon zest and lemon juice.

2 Put four individual heart-shaped moulds with drainage holes on to a tray or baking sheet (or use yogurt pots with a couple of holes punched in the base). Spoon the cheese mixture into them, then cover and refrigerate for several hours, or overnight.

3 Using a zester or grater, remove the zest from the orange, reserving it for decoration. Squeeze out the orange juice.

4 Reserve half the raspberries, then purée the other half in a blender or liquidiser with the orange juice. Sweeten to taste with powdered sweetener.

5 Turn out the desserts and serve with the reserved raspberries and the orange and raspberry sauce. Decorate with orange zest.

Cook's note: If you line the pots with dampened butter muslin or new J-cloths (cut to size), you will be able to turn out the desserts easily.

Variation: You can serve the desserts in their pots, if you prefer. Just top with the sauce and raspberries, then decorate with orange zest.

Fresh apricot and passion fruit fool

2½	Points per serving
10½	Total Points per recipe

500 g (1 lb 2 oz) fresh apricots, halved and pitted

powdered sweetener, to taste

350 g (12 oz) low-fat plain fromage frais

1 teaspoon vanilla essence

4 plain biscuits, such as digestives or rich tea, crushed

2 passion fruit, halved

Serves 4. (155 Calories per serving) Preparation and cooking time 25 minutes + cooling time. Freezing not recommended. Luxurious layers of puréed fresh apricots with low-fat fromage frais and passion fruit make this dessert a real treat.

1 Put the apricots into a saucepan with 100 ml (3½ fl oz) water. Heat gently, then cover and simmer for about 10 minutes, until the apricots are soft but not too mushy.

2 Allow the apricots to cool completely, then purée in a blender or food processor – or just use a potato masher. Add powdered sweetener, to taste.

3 Mix the fromage frais with the vanilla essence. Add a little powdered sweetener, if wished.

4 Layer the crushed biscuits with the apricot purée and fromage frais into four serving glasses, finishing with a layer of fromage frais. Spoon passion fruit seeds and pulp over the top of each dessert and then chill until ready to serve.

Cook's note: Use canned apricots in natural juice if fresh ones are unavailable or very expensive. Drain them well, then purée them.

Saturday sundaes

3½	Points per serving
14	Total Points per recipe

1 packet of strawberry or raspberry
   sugar-free jelly crystals

350 g (12 oz) strawberries or raspberries

powdered sweetener, to taste

1 medium banana, sliced

1 kiwi fruit, peeled and sliced

1 peach or nectarine, peeled and chopped

2 × 150 g pots of low-fat ready-to-serve
   custard

4 tablespoons aerosol cream

4 glacé cherries

menu plan

Party Food

Make favourite food for the
family when you have
something to celebrate.

✳

Mexican Tacos
page 148, (1 serving) 4½ Points

✳

Saturday Sundaes
page 176, (1 serving) 3½ Points

✳

Total Points: 8 Points

Serves 4. (155 Calories per serving) Preparation time 15 minutes + setting time. Freezing not recommended. The perfect weekend treat – fresh fruit chunks layered with fruit sauce, low-fat custard and chopped jelly – with squirty cream and a cherry on the top!

1 Make up the sugar-free jelly according to pack instructions and leave to set.
2 Purée half the strawberries or raspberries in a liquidiser or blender. Alternatively, mash them or push them through a sieve. Add a little powdered sweetener, to taste.
3 Chop the jelly and divide between four sundae glasses. Mix the remaining strawberries or raspberries with the rest of the fruit, and layer in the glasses with the custard and strawberry or raspberry purée.
4 Squirt one tablespoon of cream on to each dessert, then pop a glacé cherry on the top.
Variation: For a quick dessert that's very simple to make, substitute a 410 g can of fruit cocktail in grape or natural juice and use instead of banana, kiwi and peach or nectarine. The Points per serving will be 3.

Summer berry towers

3½	Points per serving
14	Total Points per recipe

175 g (6 oz) blueberries

175 g (6 oz) redcurrants or blackcurrants

25 g (1 oz) caster sugar

175 g (6 oz) strawberries, sliced

175 g (6 oz) raspberries

8 slices medium-cut white bread from a
    large loaf (175 g/6 oz in total)

4 tablespoons low-fat plain fromage frais

Ⓥ Serves 4. (190 Calories per serving) Preparation and cooking time 15 minutes + cooling time and overnight standing. Freezing recommended. These individual summer puddings are so delicious!

1 Put the blueberries and redcurrants or blackcurrants into a saucepan with 1 tablespoon of cold water. Add the sugar. Heat gently until the juice just begins to run. Remove from the heat and stir in the strawberries and raspberries. Leave to cool.

2 Cut the bread into 12 circles to fit into 4 individual pudding basins or teacups – you'll need 3 layers of bread in each basin or cup, so the circles need to be of different sizes to fit. Use 4 slices of bread to cut 4 large circles and the remaining 4 slices to cut out the medium and small circles.

3 Layer the bread and fruit into the basins, first the bread and then the fruit. Repeat, and finish with a layer of bread.

4 Spoon any remaining fruit juice into the basin to cover the bread, then wrap tightly with clingfilm. Place a heavy weight on top, then refrigerate for several hours, or overnight if preferred.

5 Turn out and serve with fromage frais.

Cook's note: Make the left over bread trimmings into breadcrumbs, pack in a polythene bag and refrigerate or freeze to use in another recipe.

Variation: You can use defrosted frozen summer berries in this recipe, but don't re-freeze the puddings once you have made them.

Winter fruits with mango and vanilla whip

2½	Points per serving
9½	Total Points per recipe

4 satsumas, clementines or mandarins,
    peeled and sliced

225 g (8 oz) red or green seedless grapes,
    halved

2 fresh figs, thinly sliced

1 medium banana, sliced

1 teaspoon of finely grated lime or lemon zest

2 tablespoons lime or lemon juice

1 small mango, peeled, stoned and chopped

150 g (5½ oz) low-fat plain yogurt

1 teaspoon vanilla essence

Ⓥ Serves 4. (155 Calories per serving) Preparation time 15 minutes. Freezing not recommended. Fresh fruit is so good for you, especially during the winter, when you might not eat so many salads and raw food. You need those vitamins! Remember to adjust the Points as necessary in the variations below.

1 Put the satsumas, clementines or mandarins with the grapes, figs and banana into a large serving bowl. Add the lime or lemon zest and juice and toss together to mix.

2 Put a few chunks of mango into the fruit salad, then put the remainder of the mango into a food processor or blender with the yogurt and vanilla essence. Blend together until smooth.

3 Serve the fruit salad with the mango and vanilla sauce.

Variation 1: Use 2 large oranges instead of the satsumas, clementines or mandarins. Try using a large wedge of Charentais melon instead of the mango.

Variation 2: If you're not keen on figs, use a large peach or nectarine instead.

Cherry trifles

5	Points per serving
20½	Total Points per recipe

450 g (1 lb) fresh cherries

2 tablespoons caster sugar

4 tablespoons cherry brandy or sherry

4 trifle sponges

150 ml (¼ pint) low-fat ready-to-serve custard

4 tablespoons whipping cream

2 amaretti biscuits, crushed

Ⓥ Serves 4. (295 Calories per serving) Preparation and cooking time 15 minutes + cooling time. Freezing not recommended. Make the most of fresh cherries while in season with this easy recipe.

1 Reserve four cherries with stalks. Halve and stone the remaining cherries and put them into a saucepan with the sugar and cherry brandy or sherry. Heat and simmer gently for about 2 minutes, until syrupy. Allow to cool.

2 Place the trifle sponges on to four serving plates. Spoon the cooled cherries, with their syrup, over the top. Spoon over an equal amount of custard.

3 Whip the cream in a chilled bowl until it holds its shape, then spoon a little on top of each dessert. Decorate each one with a reserved cherry and sprinkle with crushed amaretti biscuits.

Variation: Try making this dessert with fresh strawberries instead.

Weight Watchers note: You could use low-fat aerosol cream instead of fresh whipping cream to reduce the Points per serving to 4½.

Chocolate orange treat

4½	Points per serving
17½	Total Points per recipe

4 tablespoons whipping cream

125 g carton of diet orange yogurt

2 oranges, scrubbed

8 ginger thins

40 g (1½ oz) dark chocolate

mint or lemon balm leaves, to decorate

Ⓥ Serves 4. (190 Calories per serving) Preparation and cooking time 15 minutes. Freezing not recommended. This luscious layered dessert is perfect for a special occasion. It only takes a few minutes to put together and it tastes divine!

1 Whip the cream in a chilled bowl until it holds its shape. Fold in the carton of yogurt. Chill for a few minutes.

2 Meanwhile, use a zester to remove the zest from 1 orange. Reserve for decoration. Finely grate the zest from the other orange and fold through the cream mixture.

3 Using a sharp serrated knife, remove all the peel and pith from the oranges, then cut them into segments, removing all the membrane.

4 On separate serving plates, layer the biscuits with the cream mixture and orange segments.

5 Melt the chocolate in a bowl placed over a saucepan of gently simmering water, then use to drizzle over the desserts. Decorate with the reserved orange zest and mint or lemon balm leaves.

Cook's note: You should serve these desserts shortly after you've made them, or else the biscuits will go soggy.

Chocolate orange treat

Paradise pudding

4	Points per serving
16½	Total Points per recipe

4 digestive biscuits, crushed

4 tablespoons medium or sweet sherry

350 g (12 oz) seedless red and green
    grapes, halved

200 g (7 oz) low-fat soft cheese

150 g (5½ oz) low-fat plain yogurt

½ teaspoon vanilla essence

4 heaped teaspoons demerara sugar

Ⓥ *Serves 4. (300 Calories per serving) Preparation and cooking time 20 minutes + 10 minutes chilling. Freezing not recommended. This simple pudding is one of my all-time favourites. Whenever I make it, friends always ask me for the recipe!*

1   Sprinkle half the biscuit crumbs into four ramekin dishes or heatproof teacups and sprinkle with half the sherry.

2   Mix the red and green grapes together and spoon half of them into the dishes or teacups.

3   Beat the cheese with a wooden spoon to soften it, then mix in the yogurt and vanilla essence. Spoon half of it over the desserts. Repeat all the layers once more. Chill the desserts for 10 minutes.

4   Preheat a hot grill. Sprinkle 1 heaped teaspoon of sugar over each dessert. Grill until the sugar melts and bubbles, then allow to cool. Chill until ready to serve.

Variation: Instead of using demerara sugar, substitute unrefined light or dark muscovado sugar. There's no need to grill it, just leave it for about 10 minutes and it will melt.

Banana, kiwi and mango cocktail

2½	Points per serving
9½	Total Points per recipe

1 large mango, peeled and sliced

2 kiwi fruit, peeled and sliced

2 medium bananas, peeled and sliced

8 tablespoons lime and lemongrass cordial

8 tablespoons low-fat plain yogurt

lime zest and mint leaves, to decorate

Ⓥ *Serves 4. (150 Calories per serving) Preparation and cooking time 15 minutes. Freezing not recommended.*

1   Mix together all the fruits and divide them between four serving bowls or glasses.

2   Dilute the cordial with 200 ml (7 fl oz) of water. Pour over the fruit and leave for at least 15 minutes before serving.

3   Serve with 2 tablespoons of plain yogurt per portion. Decorate with lime zest and mint leaves, if you like.

Cook's note: If you can't find lime and lemongrass cordial, substitute elderflower cordial instead, adding a squeeze of lime or lemon juice.

Variation: If you're making this fruit salad for a Christmas or New Year celebration, why not add a thinly sliced star fruit to make it look really festive?

Athol brose with nectarines

2½	Points per serving
10	Total Points per recipe

50 g (1¾ oz) porridge oats

25 g (1 oz) demerara sugar

1 tablespoon clear honey

3 tablespoons whisky

200 g (7 oz) 0 %-fat Greek-style natural
    yogurt

3 nectarines, sliced

Ⓥ *Serves 4. (175 Calories per serving) Preparation time 15 minutes. Cooking time 15 minutes. Freezing not recommended. Athol Brose is a Scottish dessert traditionally made with oats, cream and whisky. Try our equally tasty but much less calorific version!*

1   Preheat the oven to Gas Mark 4/180°C/350°F. Mix together the porridge oats and demerara sugar and spread out on to a non-stick baking tray. Cook for 15 minutes and then transfer to a mixing bowl. Stir in the honey and whisky. Allow to cool.

2   When cool, beat in the yogurt, then spoon into four individual stem glasses, alternating with slices of nectarines. Chill for at least 1 hour before serving.

Early Autumn Supper

Enjoy a taste of the season with
this delicious early autumn
menu, perfect when you?re
having a few friends around
for a special meal.

✳

Sizzled Chicken with Parsley Mash
page 80, (1 serving) 5 Points

✳

Paradise Pudding
page 180, (1 serving) 4 Points

✳

Total Points: 9 Points

Raspberry sorbet

1½	Points per serving
12	Total Points per recipe

225 g (8 oz) frozen raspberries

600 ml (1 pint) cranberry and raspberry
    juice drink

100 g (3½ oz) caster sugar

4 tablespoons sweet sherry

mint leaves, to decorate (optional)

Ⓥ Serves 8. (110 Calories per serving) Preparation time 5 minutes + 2 hours freezing time. Freezing recommended. Make this fabulous sorbet to end a special meal or make it as a low-Point alternative to Christmas pudding.

1 Put the frozen raspberries, cranberry juice drink, caster sugar and sherry into a food processor or liquidiser and blend for about 15 seconds.

2 Turn the mixture out into a rigid freezer container and freeze until almost solid. Turn out and beat well to break up the ice crystals. Return to the freezer and freeze until solid.

3 Before serving, transfer the container to the fridge for about 15 minutes to soften slightly. Scoop into chilled dishes and serve at once, decorated with mint leaves.

Cook's note: If you have an ice-cream maker, use it to prepare the sorbet, following the manufacturer's instructions.

Weight Watchers note: Use this low-Point sorbet as a topping for fresh fruit salad. Just one scoop is all you need. It tastes fantastic on top of a summery combination of strawberries, raspberries and blueberries.

Rhubarb and orange fool

2	Points per serving
11	Total Points per recipe

350 g (12 oz) rhubarb, trimmed and cut
    into chunks

finely grated zest and juice of 1 orange

50 g (1¾ oz) fructose

150 ml (5 fl oz) pot of low-fat ready-to-
    serve custard

11 g sachet of gelatine

200 g (7 oz) tub of orange flavour
    fromage frais

1 egg white

Ⓥ Serves 6. (80 Calories per serving) Preparation time 20 minutes. Freezing not recommended. A fruit-flavoured fromage frais lends a lot more flavour to this easy dessert.

1 Place the rhubarb in a saucepan with the orange zest, juice and fructose. Cook over a gentle heat until the rhubarb is pulpy and then remove from the heat. Allow to cool.

2 When cool, transfer to a food processor with the custard and blend until smooth.

3 Place 3 tablespoons of water in a small heatproof dish and sprinkle the gelatine over. Allow to stand for 5 minutes, until it looks spongy. Then heat gently over a pan of simmering water until the gelatine dissolves. Add to the food processor and blend for a couple of seconds.

4 Pour the rhubarb mixture into a mixing bowl and stir in the fromage frais. Whisk the egg white until it forms soft peaks and fold into the rhubarb mixture. Transfer to six individual glasses and chill for at least 2 hours before serving.

Variation: Try using strawberry or peach flavoured fromage frais for a change.

Cook's note: You'll find the fructose in the supermarket next to the sugar.

Winter pudding

2	Points per serving
12½	Total Points per recipe

5 medium-thick slices of white bread,
crusts removed
350 g (12 oz) cooking apples, peeled
and diced
2 pears, peeled and diced
175 g (6 oz) blackberries
50 g (1¾ oz) fructose
2 tablespoons Port

Serves 6. (140 Calories per serving) Preparation and cooking time 25 minutes. Freezing recommended.

1 Use 3½ slices of bread to line the base and sides of a 450 g (1 lb) pudding basin, reserving the remainder of the bread for the top.
2 Place the apples, pears and blackberries in a saucepan with the fructose, Port and 3 tablespoons of water. Cover and simmer gently for 5 minutes, then carefully spoon into the bread-lined basin, reserving 3 tablespoons of the juice.
3 Use the reserved bread to cover the fruit, then cover the top with clingfilm. Place a saucer on top, place on a tray (to collect any drips) and then add weights to the saucer to press the level down and compress the pudding. Leave to stand overnight.
4 To serve, remove the clingfilm and carefully run a round bladed knife around the edge of the pudding and ease out on to a serving plate.
5 If any white patches of bread remain, spoon over the reserved juice before serving.
Cook's note: You'll find the fructose next to the sugar in the supermarket.
Variation: If you have trouble getting hold of blackberries, try using a pack of frozen mixed fruits which generally contain some blackberries, blackcurrants, blueberries, cherries, raspberries and strawberries.

Poached plum and port syllabub

2½	Points per serving
14½	Total Points per recipe

450 g (1 lb) ripe plums, halved and stoned
50 g (1¾ oz) caster sugar
3 tablespoons Port
150 ml (¼ pint) reduced-fat whipping cream
alternative (such as Elmlea)
2 egg whites

Serves 6. (125 Calories per serving) Preparation time 25 minutes + cooling. Freezing recommended (see Cook's note).

1 Place the plums in a small pan with the caster sugar and Port. Heat gently until the sugar dissolves and then cover and cook over a low heat for 5 minutes, until the plums have softened.
2 Push through a sieve, discarding the skins, and allow to cool.
3 Whip the cream substitute until it forms soft peaks and fold into the cooled purée.
4 Whisk the egg whites until they form soft peaks and fold in. Divide equally between six stem glasses and serve at once.
Cook's note: If you freeze the syllabub, you will end up with an ice-cream sorbet. Spoon into a freezer-proof container and freeze for 2 hours. Stir well and return to the freezer until completely frozen. To serve, remove from the freezer 15 minutes before serving and spoon scoopfuls into individual serving dishes.

Three minute trifle

4	Points per serving
16	Total Points per recipe

4 sponge fingers

225 g (8 oz) canned mandarins in
　　natural juice

400 g (14 oz) canned low-fat custard

low-fat aerosol cream

Ⓥ Serves 4. (120 Calories per serving) Preparation time 3 minutes. Freezing not recommended. A very simple dessert that's always a favourite. Use any combination of canned fruit as long as they are in natural juice.

1　Break each sponge finger into small pieces and arrange in the base of four individual glass serving dishes.

2　Divide the mandarins equally over each dish with 1 tablespoon of the juice.

3　Top each with custard and finally, just as you serve, a swirl of cream (about 1 tablespoonful each trifle).

Summer fruit whip

2	Points per serving
9	Total Points per recipe

350 g (12 oz) packet of frozen mixed
　　summer fruits or mixed fresh soft fruits

25 g (1 oz) caster sugar

350 g (12 oz) low-fat plain fromage frais

2 tablespoons reduced strawberry or
　　raspberry sugar jam

Ⓥ Serves 4. (105 Calories per serving) Preparation time 5 minutes. Freezing recommended. In the summertime when soft fruits are plentiful, this dessert can be made in batches and frozen in individual portions; it's actually delicious eaten frozen too!

1　Allow the fruit to defrost for about half an hour; they don't need to be completely defrosted.

2　Place in a food processor with the sugar, fromage frais and jam. Blend for about 30 seconds and then transfer to serving dishes and serve at once.

Tropical mango and lime fruit salad

1½	Points per serving
3	Total Points per recipe

1 ripe mango

1 lime

1 tablespoon dark rum

2 teaspoons demerara sugar

Ⓥ Serves 2. (105 Calories per serving) Preparation time 5 minutes. Freezing not recommended.

1　Peel the mango and remove the flesh from then centre stone, slice thinly and arrange in a shallow dish.

2　Finely grate the zest from the lime and scatter over the mango. Squeeze the juice and mix with the rum. Drizzle over.

3　Divide between two serving dishes and sprinkle each with a teaspoon of sugar.
Cook's note: For best results, prepare at least 2 hours ahead of time so the flavours have time to mingle.

Chocolate crème caramel

2½	Points per serving
11	Total Points per recipe

Serves 4. (195 Calories per serving) Preparation time 15 minutes. Cooking time 1 hour. Freezing not recommended. They keep well chilled for 3 days.

3 eggs

2 tablespoons cocoa powder

1 tablespoon cornflour

25 g (1 oz) caster sugar

425 ml (15 fl oz) skimmed milk

4 teaspoons chocolate syrup

1 Whisk together the eggs, cocoa powder, cornflour and caster sugar.

2 Heat the milk until almost boiling and pour over the egg mixture. Mix well. Preheat the oven to Gas Mark 2/150°C/300°F.

3 Stand four individual ramekins in a roasting tin. Pour enough hot water into the roasting tin to come half-way up the outsides of the dishes. Drizzle a teaspoon of chocolate syrup into each dish and fill with the chocolate custard.

4 Bake for 1 hour until firm to the touch, cool, and then chill for at least 2 hours.

5 To serve, carefully run the edge of a round bladed knife around the edge of each dish and turn upside down to turn out on to a serving dish.

Rhubarb and custard jellies

½	Point per serving
2	Total Points per recipe

Serves 4. (45 Calories per serving) Preparation time 10 minutes + chilling. Cooking time 20 minutes. Freezing not recommended. A very low-Point pud!

350 g (12 oz) rhubarb, trimmed and cut into chunks

1 sachet of raspberry or strawberry sugar-free jelly

2 tablespoons artificial granulated sweetener

150 g pot of low-fat ready-to-serve custard

1 Trim the rhubarb and cut into chunks. Place the rhubarb in a saucepan with 150ml (½ pint) of water. Bring to the boil, cover and simmer for 15 minutes until tender. Stir in the jelly, mixing well and simmer for a further 2 minutes.

2 Remove from the heat and whisk in the artificial sweetener and custard.

3 Divide between four individual serving dishes. Cool and then chill until set.

Individual pavlovas

2½	Points per serving
9½	Total Points per recipe

Serves 4. (150 Calories per serving) Preparation time 10 minutes. Cooking time 20 minutes. Freezing not recommended.

2 egg whites

100 g (3½ oz) caster sugar

100 g (3½ oz) fresh strawberries, hulled

1 kiwi fruit

150 g pot of low-fat plain yogurt

2 tablespoons half-fat crème fraîche

1 Preheat the oven to Gas Mark 2/150°C/ 300°F. Line a large baking sheet with non-stick baking parchment. Using a saucer as a guide, mark four circles on it with a pencil.

2 Using electric beaters, whisk the egg whites to form soft peaks. Gradually add the sugar a spoonful at a time, whisking well after each addition, until thick and glossy.

3 Spoon a little on to each marked circle and spread out, making a slight dip in the centre of each one.

4 Bake for 1½ hours, until firm to the touch, then turn the oven off and allow to cool in the oven. When cool, carefully peel off the lining paper and arrange on to serving plates.

5 Slice the strawberries, peel and slice the kiwi and divide between the meringues.

6 Mix together the yogurt and crème fraîche and drizzle over the fruit. Serve at once since if you don't, the meringues will go soggy.

Cook's note: The meringues will keep for up to two weeks in an airtight container.

Orange and lemon cheesecake

3½	Points per serving
30	Total Points per recipe

Serves 8. (190 Calories per serving) Preparation time 25 minutes + chilling. Freezing recommended if undecorated.

150 g (5½ oz) reduced-fat digestive biscuits

50 g (1¾ oz) low-fat spread

2 teaspoons golden syrup

For the filling

200 g (7 oz) low-fat soft cheese

50 g (1¾ oz) fructose

finely grated zest and juice of 1 lemon

finely grated zest and juice of 1 orange

11 g sachet of gelatine

2 × 150 g pots of low-fat orange or lemon
    flavoured yogurt

1 egg white

2 oranges, peeled and segmented, to
    decorate

1   Crush the biscuits in a food processor until you have fine crumbs. Melt together the low-fat spread and golden syrup and pour over the biscuit crumbs. Mix well and then press over the base of a 20 cm (8-inch) loose-bottomed springform tin. Chill while preparing the topping.

2   Beat together the soft cheese, fructose, lemon zest and lemon juice and orange zest.

3   Place the orange juice in a small heatproof bowl or cup, sprinkle the gelatine over and leave to stand for 5 minutes until it becomes spongy in appearance. Place over a pan of gently simmering water and heat until clear and gelatine has completely dissolved. Allow to cool for 5 minutes.

4   Beat the gelatine into the soft cheese mixture with the yogurt. Whisk the egg white until it forms soft peaks and fold in. Spoon over the biscuit base, level the top and chill for at least 3 hours.

5   To serve, carefully remove from the tin on to a serving plate and arrange the orange slices around the edge.

Cook's note 1: If we have a whole cheesecake in front of us, temptation can get the better of us. So it's a good idea to divide the cheesecake into portions and freeze some to enjoy later.

Cook's note 2: You'll find the fructose next to the sugar in the supermarket.

Lemon yogurt ice

2½	Points per serving
9½	Total Points per recipe

Serves 4. (95 Calories per serving) Preparation time 10 minutes + freezing. Freezing recommended. Freeze in single serving sized pots to avoid the temptation of eating more than you should!

finely grated zest and juice of 1 lemon

2 tablespoons granulated artificial sweetener

150 g pot of lemon-flavoured yogurt

150 g (5½ oz) low-fat ready-to-serve custard

200 g tub of 0%-fat Greek-style natural
    yogurt

4 tablespoons single cream substitute
    (such as Elmlea)

1   Mix together the lemon zest, juice and artificial sweetener.

2   Whisk together the lemon yogurt, custard, Greek-style yogurt and cream substitute. Then add the lemon juice and zest in a thin stream, whisking continuously until evenly combined.

3   Transfer to a freezerproof container and freeze for 2 hours. Remove from the freezer, whisk well and then freeze again until solid.

4   To serve, remove from the freezer 10 minutes before you are ready to serve so that it softens a little.

Variation: You can vary the flavour by using orange or mandarin yogurt together with a fresh orange or lime yogurt and a fresh lime.

11

cakes and bakes

Baking can be very therapeutic. The danger is that you're not supposed to eat everything you make, well, not all at once! So let these recipes be the ones you make for a special occasion, or when you're expecting company. And if anything is left over, freeze them and defrost to enjoy later.

Christmas cake

4	Points per serving
146	Total Points per recipe

1 kg (2 lb 4 oz) mixed dried fruit (raisins,
    sultanas and currants)
100 g (3½ oz) glacé cherries, halved
150 ml (5 fl oz) brandy or dark rum
175 g (6 oz) polyunsaturated margarine
175 g (6 oz) unrefined light or dark
    muscovado sugar
4 eggs, beaten
finely grated zest and juice of 1 small orange
300 g (10½ oz) plain flour
¼ teaspoon salt
1 heaped teaspoon ground mixed spice
For the almond paste
225 g (8 oz) ground almonds
50 g (1¾ oz) golden caster sugar
50 g (1¾ oz) golden icing sugar
1 large egg white, lightly beaten
2–3 drops lemon juice
2 teaspoons apricot jam or honey
For the Royal icing
1 egg white
225 g (8 oz) icing sugar

Ⓥ *Makes 36 slices. (240 Calories per serving) Preparation time 30 minutes + 3 days soaking. Cooking time 2½ hours. Freezing not recommended.*

1 Put the mixed dried fruit and cherries into a large bowl and cover with boiling water. Leave for 10 minutes, then drain really well. Add the brandy or rum, stir well and cover. Leave for three days, or overnight at least.

2 Grease and line a 20 cm (8-inch) square cake tin with double thickness greaseproof paper. Preheat the oven to Gas Mark 3/170°C/320°F.

3 In a very large bowl, beat together the margarine and sugar until light and fluffy. Gradually beat in the eggs, then add the orange zest and juice.

4 Sift the flour, salt and spice together. Fold into the creamed mixture using a metal spoon, then stir in the soaked dried fruit with any remaining brandy or rum, mixing thoroughly. Turn into the prepared tin and level the surface, making a slight depression in the middle.

5 Bake for approximately 2½ hours. Check after 2 hours, covering the surface with double-thickness brown paper to prevent it from getting too brown. To test if cooked, pierce with a fine skewer. If it does not come out clean, cook for a little longer. Cool in the tin. Wrap in greaseproof paper, then store in an airtight tin.

6 To make the almond paste, mix together the almonds, caster sugar and all but 2 teaspoons of the icing sugar. Bind together with egg white and lemon juice.

7 Dust a worktop with icing sugar, then roll out the paste to a 20 cm (8-inch) square. Brush the surface of the cake with jam or honey and cover with the almond paste.

8 Lightly beat the egg white, then gradually sift in the sugar using a nylon sieve, beating until the icing is smooth and glossy. Use to decorate the top of the cake.

Orange and sesame flapjacks

7	Points per serving
54½	Total Points per recipe

125 g (4½ oz) butter
125 g (4½ oz) demerara sugar
3 tablespoons golden syrup
finely grated zest of 1 orange
2 tablespoons sesame seeds
1 teaspoon ground cinnamon
225 g (8 oz) rolled oats

Ⓥ *Serves 8. (330 Calories per serving) Preparation time 15 minutes + 5 minutes cooling. Cooking time 20 minutes. Freezing not recommended.*

1 Preheat the oven to Gas Mark 5/190°C/375°F. Line an 8-inch (20 cm) square cake tin with non-stick baking parchment.

2 Place the butter, sugar and syrup in a small saucepan and heat gently until dissolved.

3 Mix together the orange zest, sesame seeds, cinnamon and oats. Pour the melted butter mixture over and stir well. Press into the lined tin.

4 Bake for 20 minutes. Allow to cool for 5 minutes. Mark into 8 squares. Allow to cool.

Easy cheesy scones

3	Points per serving
25½	Total Points per recipe

225 g (8 oz) self-raising flour

1 teaspoon baking powder

a pinch of salt

50 g (1¾ oz) polyunsaturated margarine

75 g (2¾ oz) half-fat Cheddar cheese, grated

1 large egg, beaten

150 ml (¼ pint) skimmed milk

Ⓥ *if using vegetarian cheese Makes 8. (185 Calories per serving) Preparation time 10 minutes + 10 minutes chilling. Cooking time 15 minutes. Freezing recommended. The ultimate accompaniment to afternoon tea. There's nothing like the aroma of cheese scones baking in the oven to make your mouth water. These are utterly delicious!*

1 Sift the flour, baking powder and salt into a mixing bowl. Add the margarine and rub in with your fingertips until the mixture resembles fine breadcrumbs.

2 Reserve about 2 tablespoons of the grated cheese, then stir the remainder into the scone mixture.

3 Beat the egg and milk together and add just enough to the rubbed-in mixture to make a soft, but not sticky, dough. Knead lightly for a few moments until smooth, but avoid over-handling. Wrap and chill for 10 minutes.

4 Preheat the oven to Gas Mark 7/220°C/425°F.

5 Roll out the dough on a lightly floured surface to a thickness of 2 cm (¾ inch). Cut out 8 rounds with a 5 cm (2-inch) cutter. Transfer to a baking sheet, brush with egg and milk and then sprinkle with the reserved cheese.

6 Bake for 12–15 minutes until well-risen and golden brown.

Cook's note: Avoid twisting the cutter as you stamp out the scones; this prevents the scones from rising properly.

Weight Watchers note: To reduce the Points you could make herb scones instead of cheese scones. Omit the cheese and add 2 teaspoons of mixed dried herbs with the flour. This will reduce the Points, giving you 2½ Points per scone.

Apple and rosemary cake

3	Points per serving
38	Total Points per recipe

2 sprigs of fresh rosemary

1 large cooking apple, peeled and grated

125 g (4½ oz) margarine

125 g (4½ oz) caster sugar

2 teaspoons vanilla essence

2 eggs, beaten

175 g (6 oz) self-raising flour

2 tablespoons skimmed milk

Ⓥ *Serves 12. (155 Calories per serving). Preparation time 25 minutes + 20 minutes cooling. Cooking time 50 minutes. Freezing recommended.*

1 Preheat the oven to Gas Mark 4/180°C/350°F. Line a 20cm (8-inch) square cake tin with non-stick baking parchment.

2 Remove the rosemary leaves from the stalks and chop finely. Toss with the grated apple.

3 Cream together the margarine and sugar until pale and fluffy. Add the vanilla essence and eggs with 1 tablespoon of the flour and beat well. Sift in the remaining flour and stir in thoroughly with the grated apple and rosemary mixture and milk.

4 Spoon into a prepared tin and level with the back of a spoon. Bake for 50 minutes. Allow to cool in the tin for 20 minutes, then turn out on to a wire rack to cool completely. Cut into 12 fingers.

Cook's note: We normally associate rosemary with savoury cooking, especially lamb, but you'll be surprised to see how well it works with cakes too. You should however use fresh, not dried, rosemary for best results.

Variation: If you prefer, you can use butter instead of margarine. The Points per serving will be 4.

Cranberry muffins

3	Points per serving
34	Total Points per recipe

300 g (10½ oz) plain flour

2 teaspoons baking powder

½ teaspoon ground cinnamon

150 g (5½ oz) light muscovado sugar

50 g (1¾ oz) Craisins (dried cranberries)

1 egg

225 ml (8 fl oz) skimmed milk

50 ml (2 fl oz) sunflower oil

Makes 12. (200 Calories per serving) Preparation time 15 minutes. Cooking time 20 minutes. Freezing recommended.

1 Line a 12 muffin tray with paper muffin cases. Preheat the oven to Gas Mark 6/ 200°C/400°F.
2 Sift the flour, baking powder and cinnamon in to a mixing bowl. Stir in the sugar and Craisins.
3 Beat together the egg, milk and oil and add to the dry ingredients. Mix well to a dropping consistency.
4 Spoon the mixture into muffin cases and bake for 15 to 20 minutes, until well risen and just firm. Transfer to a cooling rack to cool a little before serving.
Variation: As an alternative, use sultanas instead of Craisins and flavour with lemon or orange zest instead of cinnamon. The Points per serving will be the same.

Eccles swirls

1½	Points per serving
14½	Total Points per recipe

100 g (3½ oz) currants

25 g (1 oz) caster sugar

1 teaspoon ground nutmeg

½ teaspoon ground cinnamon

25 g (1 oz) mixed peel

1 cooking apple, peeled and grated

6 sheets filo pastry

25 g (1 oz) low-fat spread, melted

1 tablespoon demerara sugar

Serves 10. (100 Calories per serving) Preparation time 15 minutes. Cooking time 15 minutes. Freezing recommended.

1 Preheat the oven to Gas Mark 5/190°C/375°F.
2 Mix together the currants, caster sugar, nutmeg, cinnamon, mixed peel and grated apple.
3 Brush the filo pastry sheets with the melted low-fat spread. Stack two sheets together and sprinkle with a third of the currant mixture. Top with another two sheets of filo pastry and then another third of the currant mixture. Finally, top with two remaining filo pastry sheets and the last of the currant mixture. Roll up like a Swiss roll and then slice at 2.5 cm (1-inch) intervals. Lift on to a non-stick baking tray and sprinkle with demerara sugar.
4 Bake for 12 to 15 minutes, until golden and crisp.

Banana and fig loaf

3	Points per serving
29	Total Points per recipe

150 g (5½ oz) All Bran

200 ml (7 fl oz) skimmed milk

100 g (3½ oz) fructose

1 egg, beaten

100 g (3½ oz) no-soak dried figs, chopped

2 small bananas, mashed

1 teaspoon ground nutmeg

50 g (1¾ oz) sultanas

175 g (6 oz) self-raising flour

Serves 10. (200 Calories per serving) Preparation time 15 minutes + 20 minutes soaking + 20 minutes cooling. Cooking time 1 hour. Freezing not recommended.

1 Place the All Bran in a bowl and pour over the milk. Stir well and leave to stand for 20 minutes.
2 Preheat the oven to Gas Mark 4/180°C/350°F. Line a 450 g (1 lb) loaf tin with non-stick baking parchment.
3 Stir the fructose, egg, figs, bananas, nutmeg, sultanas and flour into the All Bran and milk mixture.
4 Spoon into the prepared tin, level the top with the back of a spoon and bake for 1 hour until firm to the touch. Leave to cool in the tin for 20 minutes and then transfer to a wire rack. Allow to cool completely before cutting into slices to serve.

Eccles swirls
Cranberry muffin

Decadent chocolate slice

4	Points per serving
40	Total Points per recipe

low-fat cooking spray
200 g (7 oz) light or dark muscovado sugar
50 g (1¾ oz) unsweetened cocoa powder
50 g (1¾ oz) plain flour
1 tablespoon instant coffee granules
150 ml (¼ pint) skimmed milk
100 g (3½ oz) plain chocolate drops
5 tablespoons Sunsweet Lighter Bake butter
　　and fat replacement
3 large eggs
2 teaspoons cocoa powder or icing sugar,
　　for dusting

Ⓥ *Serves 10. (225 Calories per serving) Preparation time 20 minutes + chilling. Cooking time 40 minutes. Freezing recommended. Rich, delicious and decidedly wicked, you'll love this indulgent chocolate slice. Serve for a special occasion as a dessert or for a weekend afternoon treat.*

1　Preheat the oven to Gas Mark 4/180°C/350°F. Spray a 23 cm (9-inch) springform cake tin with low-fat cooking spray.
2　In a saucepan, combine 150 g (5½ oz) of the sugar with the cocoa powder, flour, coffee and milk. Stir over a low heat until warm. Remove from the heat. Stir in the chocolate drops and Sunsweet Lighter Bake.
3　In a mixing bowl, and using a hand-held electric mixer, beat the eggs for 3 minutes, gradually adding the remaining sugar. Fold the chocolate mixture into the beaten eggs to combine, then pour the cake mixture into the prepared tin.
4　Bake for 40 minutes, or until a skewer inserted into the centre of the cake comes out with just a few crumbs; the cake will be very moist. Allow to cool, then chill for 4 hours or overnight.
5　To serve, cut the cake into 10 wedges and dust with cocoa powder or icing sugar.
Variation 1: This cake can be served with fresh fruit such as raspberries, strawberries or redcurrants; just add the extra Points.
Variation 2: Alternatively, make a fruit purée by blending in 225 g (8 oz) frozen raspberries. Strain through a nylon sieve, then sweeten with 25 g (1 oz) of golden caster sugar. Add the Points as necessary.
Weight Watchers note: Remember to add any extra Points if you serve the cake with fresh fruit or sauce.

Raspberry, ginger and lemon cake

3½	Points per serving
29	Total Points per recipe

low-fat cooking spray
200 g (7 oz) golden icing sugar
5 tablespoons Sunsweet Lighter Bake butter
　　and fat replacement
2 large eggs, beaten
1 teaspoon vanilla essence
150 g (5½ oz) plain flour
½ teaspoon baking powder
50 g (1¾ oz) stem ginger in syrup, rinsed
　　or crystallised ginger
1 tablespoon grated lemon zest
225 g (8 oz) fresh or frozen raspberries
powdered artificial sweetener (optional)
2 teaspoons golden icing sugar, for decoration

Ⓥ *Serves 8. (240 Calories per serving) Preparation time 20 minutes. Cooking time 35 minutes. Freezing recommended. Having a few friends round for coffee? Make this sensational cake for them to enjoy.*

1　Preheat the oven to Gas Mark 3/170°C/ 320°F. Spray a 23 cm (9-inch) round sandwich cake tin with low-fat cooking spray and line with greaseproof paper.
2　In a mixing bowl, beat the icing sugar with the Lighter Bake until smooth and well-blended. Mix in the eggs and vanilla essence.
3　Sift together the flour and baking powder, and stir into the cake mixture. Add the ginger and lemon zest, together with 3 tablespoons of just-boiled water. Spoon the cake batter into the prepared tin and level the surface.
4　Bake for 30–35 minutes, or until a skewer inserted into the centre of the cake comes out clean. Cool for 10 minutes, then remove from the tin and cool completely on a wire rack. Wrap and store at room temperature until ready to serve.
5　Purée most of the raspberries, adding a little powdered sweetener, if required. Cut the cake into wedges, serve with the remaining raspberries and raspberry purée and then sift with a little icing sugar.

Chocolate sponge cake

3	Points per serving
24	Total Points per recipe

3 eggs

100 g (3½ oz) caster sugar

75 g (2¾ oz) self-raising flour

25 g (1 oz) cocoa powder

150 ml (¼ pint) low-fat whipping cream
    substitute (such as Elmlea)

1 tablespoon instant coffee powder

1 tablespoon boiling water

1 teaspoon icing sugar, to serve

(V) *Serves 8. (165 Calories per serving) Preparation time 20 minutes + cooling. Cooking time 20 minutes. Freezing recommended. For a dinner party dessert, add sliced fresh strawberries or raspberries to the filling. Decorate the top with a few fruits as well as a light dusting of icing sugar, adding the Points as necessary.*

1 Preheat the oven to Gas Mark 4/180°C/350°F. Line the base of two 19 cm (7½-inch) round cake tins with a circle of non-stick baking parchment.

2 Whisk together the eggs and caster sugar with electric beaters until thick and foamy. Sift in the flour and cocoa powder and fold in with a metal spoon.

3 Divide between the two tins and bake for 20 minutes, until springy to the touch. Allow to cool on a wire rack.

4 Whip the cream substitute until it forms soft peaks. Stir together the coffee and water. Cool and then fold into the cream. Use to sandwich together the two sponges. Dust with a little icing sugar to serve.

Cook's note: This mixture can also be turned into a Swiss roll. Spoon the mixture into a lined Swiss roll tin, bake for 12 to 15 minutes until springy and then turn out on to greaseproof paper and roll up. When cool, unroll, spread with the filling and re-roll.

Lemon and orange madeleines

2	Points per serving
44	Total Points per recipe

low-fat cooking spray

125 g (4½ oz) caster sugar

4 eggs

finely grated zest of 1 orange

125 g (4½ oz) plain flour

1 teaspoon baking powder

a pinch of salt

100 g (3½ oz) butter, melted and cooled

2 teaspoons icing sugar

(V) *Makes 24. (85 Calories per serving) Preparation and cooking time 30 minutes + chilling. Freezing recommended.*

1 Lightly spray two trays of madeleine moulds with low-fat cooking spray.

2 Whisk together the caster sugar, eggs and orange zest until pale and fluffy and thick enough to leave a trail when the whisk is lifted.

3 Sift in half the flour with the baking powder and salt. Drizzle half the butter over and then carefully fold in using a metal spoon. Repeat with remaining flour and butter.

4 Cover and chill for 40 minutes. Preheat the oven to Gas Mark 7/220°C/425°F.

5 Fill the moulds two-thirds full with the mixture and bake for 10 minutes until well risen, golden and springy to the touch. Carefully transfer to a wire rack to cool and dust with icing sugar.

Cook's note 1: Make up this batch and freeze what you don't eat; they will defrost in about 30 minutes when required.

Cook's note 2: You'll find madeleine trays in all good cookshops.

Lemon and ginger roulade

2½	Points per serving
15½	Total Points per recipe

75 g (2¾ oz) caster sugar

3 eggs

75 g (2¾ oz) self-raising flour

finely grated zest of 1 lemon

100 g (3½ oz) low-fat soft cheese

4 tablespoons low-fat Greek-style natural
    yogurt

15 g (½ oz) stem ginger, finely chopped

1 teaspoon icing sugar

Ⓥ Serves 6. (175 Calories per serving) Preparation time 20 minutes. Cooking time 15 minutes. Freezing recommended.

1 Preheat the oven to Gas Mark 6/200°C/400°F. Line a Swiss roll tin with non-stick baking parchment.

2 Using electric beaters, whisk together the caster sugar and eggs until very pale and fluffy. This will take about 5 minutes.

3 Sift the flour and carefully fold in with the lemon zest using a metal spoon.

4 Pour into the tin. Bake for 12 to 15 minutes, until pale golden and springy.

5 Carefully turn out on to a clean sheet of baking parchment and peel away the lining paper. Using the clean paper as a guide, roll up the sponge and allow to cool.

6 Beat together the soft cheese, yogurt and stem ginger. Carefully unroll the cooled Swiss roll and spread with the ginger mixture. Re-roll, enclosing the filling and dust the top with icing sugar before serving in slices.

Apple drop scones

1	Point per serving
21½	Total Points per recipe

100 g (3½ oz) self-raising flour

50 g (1¾ oz) Jordans Original Crunchy
    Cereal (Raisins & Almonds)

1 apple, peeled, cored and finely chopped

a pinch of salt

25 g (1 oz) golden caster sugar

1 large egg

150 ml (¼ pint) skimmed milk

2 teaspoons vegetable oil

9 teaspoons very-low-fat spread

18 teaspoons reduced-sugar strawberry
    spread

Ⓥ Makes 18. (65 Calories per serving) Preparation and cooking time 20 minutes + 15 minutes standing time. Freezing not recommended. These scones are ideal for a tea-time treat and are best eaten when fresh and served warm.

1 Put the flour, cereal, apple, salt and sugar into a large bowl. Add the egg and milk and beat well until all the ingredients are thoroughly combined. Cover and allow to stand for 15 minutes.

2 Heat a large, heavy-based frying pan or griddle until hot. Add a little oil, then drop tablespoons of the mixture into the hot pan. Cook until bubbles appear on the surface, then flip over to cook the other side.

3 Transfer the cooked drop scones to kitchen paper to cool slightly. Continue to cook the remaining batter in the same way until it is all used.

4 Serve each scone with ½ teaspoon of very-low-fat spread and a teaspoonful of strawberry spread.

Chocolate mallow crispie cakes

1	Point per serving
19½	Total Points per recipe

150 g (5½ oz) marshmallows

25 g (1 oz) cocoa powder

15 g (½ oz) butter

125 g (4½ oz) rice crispies

Ⓥ Serves 20. (55 Calories per serving) Preparation and cooking time 15 minutes. Freezing not recommended. These simple little cakes recall happy memories from childhood.

1 Place the marshmallows in a bowl over a pan of simmering water with the cocoa powder and butter and heat gently, stirring, until the marshmallows have dissolved and you have a smooth chocolatey mixture.

2 Stir in the rice crispies and mix well. Divide the mixture between 20 individual paper cases and chill for 1 hour.

Cook's note: You can store these in an airtight container for up to 7 days.

Olive and tomato rolls with basil

3½	Points per serving
40½	Total Points per recipe

50 g (1¾ oz) sun-dried tomatoes

425 ml (¾ pint) boiling water

1 teaspoon caster sugar

1 tablespoon easy-blend dried yeast

700 g (1 lb 9 oz) strong white bread flour

2 teaspoons salt

75 g (2¾ oz) pitted black olives, diced

3 tablespoons fresh basil, torn

1 tablespoon olive oil

Ⓥ Serves 12. (220 Calories per serving) Preparation time 30 minutes + rising time + 30 minutes cooling. Cooking time 20 minutes. Freezing recommended. There's nothing like the smell of fresh bread cooking in your home, and it tastes so wonderful too.

1. Place the sun-dried tomatoes in a small bowl. Cover with the water and leave to stand for 15 minutes. Drain, reserving the liquid and then dice the tomatoes.
2. Stir the sugar into the reserved water and then place the yeast, flour and salt into a large warmed mixing bowl. Stir well. Add the hot liquid and mix to a soft dough.
3. Turn out on to a lightly floured surface and knead for 5 minutes until smooth and elastic. Place in a clean, lightly oiled bowl. Cover with a damp tea towel and leave to rise in a warm place until doubled in size.
4. Turn out on to a clean surface and knock out the air. Work in the chopped tomatoes, olives and basil by kneading them in. Divide the mixture into small rolls and lift on to a lightly oiled baking sheet. Cover with a damp tea towel and leave to rise in a warm place for 20 minutes. Brush the tops with any remaining oil and bake for 20 minutes until well risen and golden.
5. Allow to cool for at least 30 minutes before serving.

Variation 1: You may wish to make two large loaves instead of small buns. Shape the dough into two rounds and then bake for 25 to 30 minutes.

Variation 2: For extra flavour, before baking, sprinkle some chopped green olives, fresh rosemary and a little rock salt on top.

Cornbread muffins

3	Points per serving
37½	Total Points per recipe

225 g (8 oz) cornmeal

225 g (8 oz) self-raising flour

1 teaspoon salt

1 teaspoon baking powder

2 eggs

150 g (5½ oz) canned creamed sweetcorn

300 ml (½ pint) low-fat plain yogurt

50 ml (2 fl oz) vegetable oil

3 tablespoons skimmed milk

Ⓥ Serves 12. (205 Calories per serving) Preparation time 20 minutes. Cooking time 20 minutes. Freezing recommended. These are delicious with soup and a lovely alternative to bread rolls.

1. Place the cornmeal in a bowl and sift in the flour, salt and baking powder.
2. Preheat the oven to Gas Mark 5/190°C/375°F. Line a 12 muffin tin with paper muffin cases.
3. Beat together the eggs, sweetcorn, yogurt, oil and milk and add to the dry ingredients. Mix well and then divide between the muffin cases. Bake for 20 to 25 minutes, until well risen and springy to the touch.

Cook's note: A spoonful of chilli flakes livens up these little muffins. If you don't have a muffin tin, pipe the mixture through a large plain nozzle on to a baking sheet and cook as above.

Focaccia with roasted peppers

20	Points per loaf
40½	Total Points per recipe

700 g (1 lb 9 oz) strong white flour

½ teaspoon salt

1 tablespoon easy-blend dried yeast

425 ml (¾ pint) warm water

2 tablespoons olive oil

½ teaspoon salt flakes

1 red pepper, de-seeded and sliced

1 green pepper, de-seeded and sliced

1 yellow pepper, de-seeded and sliced

1 tablespoon balsamic vinegar

1 garlic clove, crushed

low-fat cooking spray

Ⓥ Makes 2 loaves. (1390 Calories per loaf) Preparation time 20 minutes + 1½ hours rising. Cooking time 20-25 minutes. Freezing recommended.

1 Sift the flour and salt into a mixing bowl and stir in the yeast. Make a well in the centre and add the warm water. Mix to a soft dough and then turn out on to a lightly floured surface and knead for 5 minutes.

2 Place in a lightly oiled bowl. Cover with a damp tea towel and leave to rise for about 1½ hours until doubled in size.

3 Turn out on to a clean surface, knock the air out, divide the dough in half and shape into two long, rough oval-shaped loaves. Lift on to non-stick baking trays. Use the end of a wooden spoon to mark holes in the dough randomly and drizzle with the olive oil.

4 Sprinkle with salt flakes, cover with a damp tea towel and leave to rise for about 30 minutes.

5 Preheat the oven to Gas Mark 6/200°C/400°F. Toss the peppers with the balsamic vinegar and garlic, arrange in a roasting tin, spray with the low-fat cooking spray and cook for 20 minutes (the same time that you cook the bread for).

6 Cook the focaccia for 20 to 25 minutes until well risen and golden brown.

7 Arrange the pepper slices over the bread and leave to cool.

Variation: You can also top them with cooked mushrooms and sage, red onion and rosemary or slow-roasted oven tomatoes and basil.

Spiced currant buns

3	Points per serving
35	Total Points per recipe

150 ml (¼ pint) skimmed milk

2 tablespoons caster sugar

1 tablespoon easy-blend dried yeast

450 g (1 lb) strong white flour

1 teaspoon salt

1 teaspoon mixed spice

grated zest of 1 lemon

125 g (4½ oz) currants

25 g (1 oz) margarine, melted

1 egg, beaten

Ⓥ Serves 12. (190 Calories per serving) Preparation time 20 minutes + rising. Cooking time 20 minutes. Freezing recommended.

1 Warm a mixing bowl in the oven on a very low heat. Warm together the milk and 4 tablespoons of water until hand hot. Stir in 1 tablespoon of sugar.

2 Mix together the remaining sugar, yeast, flour, salt and spice in the warmed mixing bowl. Stir in the lemon zest and currants. Add the warm milk, melted margarine and beaten egg. Mix well to form a soft dough.

3 Turn out on to a lightly floured surface and knead for 5 minutes, until smooth and elastic.

4 Place the dough in a clean, lightly oiled, bowl. Cover with a damp tea towel and leave to rise until doubled in size (this will take about 1 hour).

5 Turn the dough out onto a clean lightly floured surface and knock out the air, kneading for a further 2 minutes.

6 Divide the dough into 12 balls and place well apart on non-stick baking sheets. Cover with a damp tea towel and leave to rise for 30 minutes.

7 Preheat the oven to Gas Mark 6/200°C/400°F.

8 Bake the buns for 20 minutes until risen and golden. Allow to cool on a wire rack.

Cook's note: If you want to glaze the buns, heat 1 tablespoon of golden syrup or honey with 1 tablespoon of water and brush over the tops of each bun while still warm. The Points per serving will be the same.

Variation: You can use butter instead of margarine if you prefer. The Points per serving will be the same.

Banana squares

| 1½ | Points per serving |
| 27 | Total Points per recipe |

low-fat cooking spray

100 g (3½ oz) light muscovado sugar

50 g (1¾ oz) polyunsaturated margarine

2 eggs, beaten

1 medium banana

5 level tablespoons Sunsweet Lighter Bake
    butter and fat replacement

1 teaspoon vanilla essence

175 g (6 oz) self-raising flour

a pinch of salt

200 g packet of low-fat soft cheese

50 g (1¾ oz) ready-to-eat dried apricots,
    chopped

25 g (1 oz) dried banana chips

Bonfire Night

Warming food is the order of the day on Bonfire night. Be prepared with these tasty little numbers which can be served indoors or out.

✳

Spanish Bean Soup
page 12, (1 serving) 3½ Points

✳

Tandoori Turkey Bites
page 95, (1 serving) 2½ Points

✳

Banana Cake Squares
page 200, (1 serving) 1½ Points

✳

Total Points: 7½ Points

Menu plan

V *Makes 16. (145 Calories per serving) Preparation time 15 minutes. Cooking time 45 minutes. Freezing recommended before decorating. A delicious treat mid-morning or mid-afternoon with some tea. Children will love them anytime! By using a butter and fat replacement made from pure fruit purée, you can reduce the fat and calorie content of this scrumptious cake.*

1 Preheat the oven to Gas Mark 4/180°C/350°F. Lightly spray a 20 cm (8-inch) square cake tin with low-fat cooking spray and then line it with greaseproof paper.

2 Beat the sugar and margarine together until thoroughly blended, then gradually beat in the eggs. Mash the banana and stir it into the cake mixture with the Lighter Bake and vanilla essence.

3 Sift the flour and salt together, then fold into the mixture, using a metal spoon. Transfer to the prepared tin and level the surface.

4 Bake the cake for about 45 minutes, until risen, golden brown and springy to the touch. Cool in the tin for a few minutes, then transfer the cake to a wire rack to cool completely.

5 To decorate the cake, spread the soft cheese over the surface of the cake, then sprinkle with the apricots and banana chips.

Cook's note: Dried banana chips are available in most supermarkets and health food stores.

Fruit loaf

1½	Points per serving
20	Total Points per recipe

2 fruit tea bags (eg. mandarin or mixed fruit)

250 ml (9 fl oz) boiling water

50 g (1¾ oz) ready-to-eat dried apricots,
    chopped

50 g (1¾ oz) sultanas or raisins

50 g (1¾ oz) dried papaya or mango

25 g (1 oz) glacé cherries, halved and rinsed

low-fat cooking spray

2 eggs, beaten

50 g (1¾ oz) bran flakes

175 g (6 oz) self-raising flour

a pinch of salt

1 teaspoon ground mixed spice

Ⓥ Serves 12. (115 Calories per serving) Preparation time 20 minutes + 1 hour soaking + 15 minutes cooling. Cooking time 1 hour. Freezing recommended. It's perfect for packed lunches and picnics, and for a tea-time treat.

1   Put the fruit tea bags into a measuring jug and add the boiling water. Allow to infuse for 10 minutes and then remove the tea bags.

2   Put the apricots, sultanas or raisins, papaya or mango and cherries into a bowl and pour over the fruit tea, stirring to mix. Cover and allow to soak overnight, or for a minimum of 1 hour, to plump up the fruit.

3   Preheat the oven to Gas Mark 4/180°C/ 350°F. Spray a 900 g (2 lb) loaf tin with low-fat cooking spray and then line with greaseproof paper.

4   Drain the fruit mixture, reserving any liquid. Add the eggs and bran flakes. Allow to soak for a few minutes, then sift in the flour, salt and spice. Mix together, stirring in enough reserved liquid to give a soft, dropping consistency.

5   Spoon the mixture into the prepared tin and then bake for about 1 hour. Test that the cake is cooked by inserting a fine skewer into the centre; it should come out clean. If not, bake the cake for another few minutes.

6   Cool in the tin for about 15 minutes, then transfer to a wire rack to cool completely.

Cook's note: The cake keeps well for up to a week in an airtight container.

Weight Watchers note: Why not cut the cake into portions, then wrap and freeze separately to use for your packed lunches and picnics? That way you're not tempted to eat too much all at once.

Carrot and orange Easter cake

3½	Points per serving
42	Total Points per recipe

low-fat cooking spray

100 g (3½ oz) polyunsaturated margarine

100 g (3½ oz) light muscovado sugar

3 eggs, beaten

175 g (6 oz) carrots, finely grated

225 g (8 oz) self-raising flour

a pinch of salt

1 teaspoon baking powder

1 teaspoon ground mixed spice

2 teaspoons finely grated orange zest

40 g (1½ oz) sultanas or raisins

For the topping

175 g (6 oz) low-fat soft cheese

1 tablespoon icing sugar

To decorate

orange zest

lemon zest

Ⓥ Serves 12. (220 Calories per serving) Preparation time 20 minutes. Cooking time 1½ hours. Freezing recommended. This delicious carrot cake is perfect for Easter! To decorate, choose some pretty spring flowers, such as primroses, violets or tiny rosebuds and brush their petals with lightly beaten egg white. Dip into caster sugar, then leave to dry on sheets of greaseproof paper.

1   Preheat the oven to Gas Mark 4/180°C/350°F. Spray a 20 cm (8-inch) round cake tin with low-fat cooking spray and line with greaseproof paper.

2   Warm the margarine and sugar together over a low heat, until the sugar has dissolved. Cool slightly.

3   In a large bowl, combine the eggs, carrots and melted mixture. Sift in the flour, salt, baking powder and mixed spice. Add the orange zest and sultanas or raisins and mix well.

4   Transfer to the prepared tin, level the surface and bake for about 1 hour 10 minutes, until firm to the touch. Check with a fine skewer; it should come out clean. Cool for 10 minutes, then turn out and cool completely on a wire rack.

5   To decorate, beat the soft cheese and icing sugar together. Spread over the cake and sprinkle with orange and lemon zest.

Cook's note: This cake can be kept in the refrigerator for 2–3 days.

Petal cakes

3	Points per serving
38½	Total Points per recipe

125 g (4½ oz) caster sugar

125 g (4½ oz) polyunsaturated margarine

125 g (4½ oz) self-raising flour

2 large eggs, beaten

a pinch of salt

1 teaspoon vanilla essence

For the decoration

1 egg white

25 g (1 oz) caster sugar

12 tiny edible flowers, such as primroses,
    violets or rosebuds

25 g (1 oz) icing sugar

Ⓥ *Makes 12. (190 Calories per serving) Preparation time 20 minutes. Cooking time 20 minutes. Freezing recommended before decorating.*

1 Line a 12-hole patty tin with paper bun cases. Preheat the oven to Gas Mark 5/ 190°C/375°F.

2 Put the sugar, margarine, flour, eggs, salt and vanilla essence into a large mixing bowl. Beat together vigorously with a wooden spoon for 1 minute.

3 Divide the mixture between the bun cases and bake for 18–20 minutes until risen and firm. Remove from the tin and allow to cool completely.

4 Meanwhile, make the crystallised flowers. Beat the egg white lightly and sprinkle the caster sugar on to a saucer. Paint the flower petals with the egg white and dip into the sugar. Allow to dry.

5 Mix the icing sugar with a little water to make a smooth glacé icing and spread on to the buns. Decorate with the crystallised flowers (but do not eat the flowers unless you are sure they are edible).

Cook's note: If you prefer, buy some crystallised violets or rose petals to save time decorating the buns. Add Points if necessary.

Tiny cheesecake tarts

2	Points per serving
21½	Total Points per recipe

150 g (5½ oz) sweet shortcrust pastry,
    thawed if frozen

100 g (3½ oz) cottage cheese

1 small egg, beaten

25 g (1 oz) currants

25 g (1 oz) golden caster sugar

finely grated zest of 1 lemon

pinch of ground nutmeg

Ⓥ *Makes 12. (85 Calories per serving) Preparation time 20 minutes. Cooking time 20–25 minutes. Freezing recommended. Good for an Easter treat.*

1 Preheat the oven to Gas Mark 4/180°C/350°F.

2 Roll out the pastry on a lightly floured surface. Use to line 12 small tartlet tins or a 12-hole patty tin, using a fork to prick the base of each one. Place the tins on a baking sheet.

3 Mix together the cottage cheese, egg, currants and sugar. Spoon the mixture into the pastry-lined patty tins. Sprinkle each one with lemon zest and ground nutmeg.

4 Bake for 20–25 minutes, until set and golden brown. Serve warm or cold.

Chocolate nests

6	Points per serving
47½	Total Points per recipe

125 g (4½ oz) dark chocolate

40 g (1½ oz) polyunsaturated margarine

3 Shredded Wheat biscuits

24 mini chocolate eggs

Ⓥ *Makes 8. (190 Calories per serving). Preparation and cooking time 15 minutes + 20 minutes chilling. Freezing recommended. The perfect recipe for Easter.*

1 Melt the chocolate and margarine together by putting them into a large heatproof bowl placed over a saucepan of gently simmering water. When smooth and melted, remove from the heat.

2 Break up the Shredded Wheat biscuits and stir into the chocolate mixture.

3 Spoon the mixture into paper bun cases, making slight depressions in the centre of each one to form a nest. Chill in the refrigerator until firm, about 20 minutes.

4 Serve with 3 tiny chocolate eggs in each nest.

Weight Watchers note: You can reduce the Points by having just 1 mini chocolate egg.

Easter Treats

Why not create a special spread
of delicious cakes for friends?

✳

Spiced Currant Buns
page 199, (1 serving) 3 Points

✳

Carrot and Orange Easter Cake
page 201, (1 serving) 3 Points

✳

Tiny Cheesecake Tarts
page 202, (1 serving) 2 Points

✳

Chocolate Nests
page 202, (1 serving) 6 Points

Carrot and raisin tea bread

3½	Points per slice
44	Total Points per recipe

350 g (12 oz) carrots, peeled and
    coarsely grated

100 g (3½ oz) butter

75 g (2¾ oz) demerara sugar

4 tablespoons golden syrup

225 g (8 oz) self-raising flour

½ teaspoon baking powder

1 tablespoon mixed spice

50 g (1¾ oz) raisins

1 egg, beaten

Serves 12. (200 Calories per serving) Preparation time 20 minutes + cooling Cooking time 1 hour. Freezing not recommended.

1 Preheat the oven to Gas Mark 3/170°C/320°F. Lightly oil and line a 700 g (1 lb 9 oz) loaf tin with non-stick baking parchment. Place the carrots in a bowl.

2 Place the butter, sugar and syrup into a small saucepan and heat gently until the sugar dissolves. Remove from the heat and allow to cool a little.

3 Sift the flour, baking powder and mixed spice into a mixing bowl. Stir in the raisins and grated carrot. Beat the egg into the butter mixture, then pour over the dry ingredients and mix well.

4 Spoon into the prepared tin and bake for about 1 hour, or until a skewer inserted into the centre comes out clean. Allow to cool on a wire rack before slicing thinly to serve.
Cook's note: Keep well wrapped in an airtight tin for up to 6 days.

Almond and cherry scones

2	Points per scone
20½	Total Points per recipe

225 g (8 oz) wholemeal flour

2½ teaspoons baking powder

½ teaspoon salt

50 g (1¾ oz) low-fat spread

25 g (1 oz) caster sugar

50 g (1¾ oz) glacé cherries, roughly
    chopped

3 drops of almond essence

150 ml (¼ pint) skimmed milk

25 g (1 oz) flaked almonds

Serves 10. (130 Calories per serving) Preparation time 15 minutes. Cooking time 20 minutes. Freezing recommended. The almond essence adds a stronger flavour to these tasty scones.

1 Preheat the oven to Gas Mark 6/200°C/400°F. Line a baking sheet with non-stick baking parchment.

2 Sift the flour, baking powder and salt into a mixing bowl. Return the bran, which will have been left behind in the sieve, to the mixture and stir well. Rub in the low-fat spread using your fingertips until the mixture resembles fine breadcrumbs. Stir in the sugar and cherries and make a well in the centre.

3 Add the almond essence to the milk and pour into the dry ingredients. Mix well to form a soft dough and then roll out on a lightly floured surface and stamp out 10 scones using a 5 cm (2-inch) round cutter. Brush the tops with a little milk and sprinkle over the flaked almonds.

4 Bake for 20 minutes, until well risen and golden.
Cook's note: Scones are at their best when just warm so give them each a 10 second blast in the microwave just before serving.
Variation: If you wish, you can replace the almond essence with the grated zest of 1 orange.